THE KEY IN THE WINDOW

The Key in the Window

Marginal Notes in
Bunyan's Narratives

Maxine Hancock

REGENT COLLEGE PUBLISHING
— Vancouver, Canada —

The Key in the Window
Copyright © 2000 by Maxine Hancock

Published 2000 by Regent College Publishing,
an imprint of the Regent College Bookstore,
5800 University Boulevard, Vancouver, B.C. Canada V6T 2E4

E-mail: orders@regentpublishing.com
Website: www.regentpublishing.com

The views expressed in works published by
Regent College Publishing
are those of the author and may not necessarily
represent the official position of Regent College.

Printed in the United States of America

Canadian Cataloguing and Publication Data

Hancock, Maxine.
The key in the window

Includes bibliographical references.

ISBN 0-88865-418-9 (Canada)
ISBN 1-57383-115-8 (U.S.)

1. Bunyan, John, 1628-1688. Pilgrim's progress. 2. Bunyan, John,
1628-1688--Technique. I. Title.

PR3330.A9H36 2000   838'.407   C98-910313-7

For Cam,
With Love

Nor do thou go to work without my Key,
(In mysteries men soon do lose their way)
And also turn it right if thou wouldst know
My riddle, and wouldst with my heifer plow,
The margent   *It lies there in the window, fare thee well,*
My next may be to ring thy Passing-Bell.

John Bunyan, "To the Reader,"
The Holy War

Contents

Acknowledgements

Debts grow as a work grows, and I am indebted to many for help and encouragement in bringing this book to publication.

The initial research and writing of this manuscript was undertaken while completing doctoral studies at the University of Alberta under the mentorship of Professor James F. Forrest, distinguished Bunyan scholar and editor. His knowledge of the entire field of Renaissance literature, and his special expertise in Bunyan studies, was of inestimable value to me; his interest in my investigation and his constant encouragement to bring my work to publication kept this project alive. Other members of the Department of English at the University of Alberta, especially Professors Patricia Demers and Greg Hollingshead, were generous with their time and helpful in their reading and response to my work. When, on completion, my doctoral dissertation was awarded the Governor-General's Gold Medal by the University of Alberta, I was encouraged to see the work through revision and rewriting to publication.

The extensive seventeenth-century holdings of the Bruce Peel Special Collections Library at the University of Alberta, which includes a particularly strong Bunyan collection, made it possible for me to do most of the research for this book in Canada. My thanks to Dr. John Charles, Curator and to all of the staff who helped me with my research there. Social Sciences and Humanities Research Council of Canada Doctoral Fellowships supported my research and writing; an Alberta Heritage Trust Fund Scholarship paid the expenses of the earlier years of my graduate studies. Professors Juliet McMaster and Patricia Demers, successive Chairs of Graduate Study at the University of Alberta, encouraged and supported my desire to return to study, recognizing as valid my womanly career path in which the opportunity for academic inquiry came after I had raised a family and established myself as a freelance writer.

The trust in my work expressed by their support and the financial support I received throughout my studies will, I hope, be fully repaid in the years ahead, with the publication of this work a first payment.

My friends were present in this enterprise as well. Fellow doctoral students Arlette Zinck, Greg Randall, and Carole Everest, were part of a company who encouraged each other to excellence throughout our years of research. Glorie Tebbutt, another companion of the journey, typed in manuscript revisions. Margaret Avison, friend and mentor, was fierce in her insistence that I complete the work. And now a new community of help and support has worked with me to bring this work to publication. Rob Clements of Regent College Publishing and an impressive small army of people have worked on final copy editing and quotation verification to bring this work to publication. Thank you to David Stewart of the Regent Carey Theological Library for verifying quotations and to copy-editors and proofreaders, Sara Letcher, Keith Hyde, and Sharon Jebb.

Undergirding my reading and study is an early acquaintance with Bunyan and a knowledge of the Bible begun in my childhood. For the transmission to me of this heritage, literary and spiritual, I am grateful to my parents, Max and Ruth Runions.

And what can I say about the support of my husband, Campbell? Simply that his steadfast love and encouragement have sustained me, and I am blessed among women.

MAXINE HANCOCK
Regent College, Vancouver
Fall 1999

Introduction

This work began, as all inquiry must, with a guess. I had a hunch, based partly on memories of the charm and nuance the marginal notes added to my own encounters as a young reader with *The Pilgrim's Progress*, that Bunyan's marginal notes might interact with his narrative texts in ways more complex and more significant than had yet been adequately explored. During the time I was testing this hypothesis by a close re-reading of Bunyan's major narratives and related seventeenth-century works, German young people danced on the Berlin Wall; the Soviet Union disintegrated and the Cold War thawed; a short, deadly war was fought in the Middle East and a long, vengeful war tore apart what had been Yugoslavia. My own small country, Canada, lurched from constitutional to economic to national unity crises. At news time each evening, my enquiry often seemed very marginal indeed. I pressed on with my work, reminding myself that, at the very least, I was not hurting anyone.

But, of course, I intend that this study should be more than innocuous. This work argues that the marginal notes to John Bunyan's narratives add an important dimension to the reading of those narratives; that as literary elements, they interact with the main narrative texts in ways that are significant and worthy of being added to the critical discussion of Bunyan's works. It is my hope that this study will enrich the conversation about Bunyan's narratives with new understanding of the complex demands the marginal notes make on the reader, and the rewards they offer those who attend.

Until quite recently, Bunyan's marginal notes were seen as irrelevant distractions to twentieth-century readers. U. Milo Kaufmann, for instance, identifies the marginal notes to the *The Pilgrim's Progress* as presenting a problem to "many modern readers ... [who are] troubled by suspicions about the originality and wholeness of a work that so persistently points beyond itself."[1] Practical editions of *The Pilgrim's Progress* were produced by reputable publishers and editors without the marginal biblical references.[2]

But a number of developments in literary criticism have set the stage for reconsideration of the importance of the marginal notes in early modern texts. Attention has been paid to marginal notes as literary elements; to the way in which they link central texts to intertexts; and to the process by which dual texts were created and read. Recent thinking about visual and physical aspects of textual presentation, about the conditions which surround the production and consumption of literary texts, and about the way in which any piece of literature relates to other texts has contributed to this general reevaluation of marginal literary elements.

All who pay attention to the forms which printed texts take and the social and economic conditions in which they are produced owe a debt to Leona Rostenberg and Elizabeth Eisenstein for their work on the process of book production in the seventeenth and eighteenth century.[3] Physical and visual aspects of the layout of print text have been regarded with a new attentiveness since Jacques Derrida's *Margins of Philosophy* which highlighted marginal, peripheral, and paratextual elements in discourse.[4] Indeed, anything "marginal" has come to merit special attention, perhaps at least in part to make up for historical oversight. Clearly, this attention to visual aspects of text creates a climate which suggests a serious re-reading of Bunyan's narratives as commented upon and expanded by his marginal notes.

The new attention given to marginal literary elements may also be seen as an extension (if only on the grounds of semantic association) of a growing preoccupation on the part of social historians with marginalized groups in society, and with the communication processes by which such elements emerge from invisibility to claim power in society or in history. An interest in the politics and economics of literary production, and, in particular, in the literature of economically and socially marginalized groups within society has brought intense interest to bear on texts produced by the persecuted Nonconformists in England during the Restoration. Christopher Hill's absorbed attention to the period of the Puritan Revolution and the Restoration has resulted in a corpus of new readings of the period.[5] Literary historians and critics including Richard Greaves, Neil H. Keeble, Nigel Smith, and John R. Knott, Jr. have produced recent significant studies of the literature and thought of the period,[6] following on the publication, under the general editorship of Roger Sharrock, of definitive editions of Bunyan's complete works by Oxford at the Clarendon Press.

The deliberate cross-referencing of Bunyan's narratives to the Bible, however distracting or offensive to the kind of reader Kaufmann describes, is now of particular interest to critics who attempt to take into account the matter of literary intertextuality. Michael Riffaterre who, along with Julia Kristeva has been the major proponent of theoretical attention to intertext, defines "intertext" as "a corpus of texts, textual fragments, or textlike segments of the sociolect that shares a lexicon and, to a lesser extent, a syntax with the text we are reading."[7] Kristeva's idea of intertext has to do with "semiotic polyvalence; the transposition of one or more sign system(s) into another ... the mosaic of quotations of which any text is constructed."[8] Bunyan's works have everything to gain from this interest in the literary repertoire on which writers and readers draw, and the way in which "textual fragments" interact within the text. His narratives consciously and continuously point to and incorporate into themselves as intertext the vast interior mental landscape of the King James Version of the Bible, which serves as backdrop to the narrative action and which is in continuous interplay with the textual events. His confident uptake of scriptural elements into his work both acknowledges the authority the Bible holds for him, and appropriates a measure of that authority for his own work.

In the past two decades, under the influence of theory, all critical reading has become intensely self-conscious. "If the various roads down which literary theory has gone in the past thirty years converge, it is on having made the specific nature of literature more explicit, by analysis of its complex means and speculation about its sources and purposes."[9] We do not merely read, or even read critically; we now ask questions about the possibility and the meaning of meaning and of how and to what degree it can be exchanged through literary texts. We examine ourselves and others in the process of coming to meaning from text. This interest in the process of reading and interpreting literature has also brought new attention to Bunyan's narratives. In opening up much of the current critical discussion of the role of the reader *vis à vis* the literary text, Stanley Fish and Wolfgang Iser each devote a chapter in seminal works to the experience of reading *The Pilgrim's Progress*.[10] Although taking quite different approaches, each finds *The Pilgrim's Progress* a rich and interesting site in which to test his theories.

Fish describes what he claims to be his own experience as a reader of *The Pilgrim's Progress*, arriving, apparently inductively, at the generalization that "[t]he illusory nature of the pilgrim's progress is a large part of Bunyan's point.... His intention ... is nothing less than the disqualification of his work as a vehicle of the insight it pretends to convey."[11] Iser, on the other hand, attempts to reconstruct "the implied reader" of *The Pilgrim's Progress* as an analogue to Wayne C. Booth's construction, "the implied author."[12] Iser describes this reader as motivated by a high level of anxiety regarding predestination, and very engaged with a text that offers assurances of election. Fish's account of a reading experience in *The Pilgrim's Progress* is open to criticism as idiosyncratic and fictionalized,[13] and Iser's anxiety-driven "implied reader" is surely too monolithic a figure. But the readings offered by both Fish and Iser serve to re-establish Bunyan's narratives on the critical agenda within reader-response and phenomenological criticism.

At the same time that interest has been shown in the process by which a particular text is received by particular readers or groups of readers, a fresh interest in attempting to reconstruct the mode of reading as a whole in various time periods has resulted in fresh work by literary historians like Robert Darnton and historians of literacy Eugene R. Kintgen, David Cressy, and Margaret Spufford.[14] The interest in contemporary modes and materials of reading has potential benefit for the re-reading of Bunyan with a new sensitivity to the ways in which meaning may have been experienced by his original readers.

Reflecting many of the critical currents already discussed, narratology has become an area in which increased precision has been introduced into the language of criticism, distinguishing between "story" and "discourse;" between "ideal," "real," "inscribed" and "authorial" audiences; between author and narrator; and between reader and "narratees."[15] There has been a good deal of important investigation of temporality both as inscribed within the structures of narrative and as part of the process of reading, from explorations like Gerard Genette's to definitive works like Paul Ricoeur's.[16] As literary theory has moved rapidly through formalism, structuralism, post-structuralism and post-deconstructionism, discussions about the language structures within narrative continue to absorb the attention of important critics.

All of these currents in criticism have promoted a new interest in close reading, in the process of reading, and in paratextual elements such as margins. One could not begin to read Bunyan today without attending to the format of the dual text which Bunyan adopts and adapts, and to the way in which this dual text extends the dialogue of reader and text to include an intra-textual dialogue between marginal and narrative text as well as a dialogue between narrative text and intertext. To the long-neglected seventeenth-century marginal notes as to Arthur Miller's marginalized Willy Loman, "attention must be paid."[17] That attention is being paid in works which give particular attention to the prominence of marginal notes and their effect on the text.

Lawrence Lipking in, "The Marginal Gloss" and Valentine Cunningham in "Glossing and Glozing: Bunyan and Allegory," argue that marginal notes reveal authorial anxiety about the potential instability of narrative texts—and therefore serve to reveal, or even help to create, that instability. William Slights' seminal articles, "The Edifying Margins of English Renaissance Books," and "'Marginall Notes that spoile the Text': Scriptural Annotation in the English Renaissance," move the discussion of Renaissance marginal notations into the mainstream of literary criticism of sixteenth- and seventeenth-century texts.[18] Slights' article on "Edifying Margins" reviews the convention of marginal notes and offers both a rough classification according to function and some models of critical discussion by way of readings in Spenser and Erasmus which take into account the marginal notes. I am indebted to his work on both fronts, although I will be modifying both the taxonomy he offers and the method of investigation to suit my particular interest in Bunyan's narratives.

Some of my observations parallel those of Evelyn B. Tribble, whose important work, *Margins and Marginality: The Printed Page in Early Modern England*, was published too late to be foundational to this work.[19] Although Tribble's central thesis—that the gradual displacement of annotations from the margins to the bottom of the page reveals a contest for authorial control of the entire page—is somewhat different from my argument that changes in print text reflect a change in attitude as to the nature of reality, Tribble's work bears out my conviction that the marginal notes are significant literary elements worthy of close examination.

This study will argue that, for Bunyan and for the readers for whom he wrote, the references in the margins were highly important elements in constant interplay with the narrative. This work goes ahead, as all such works must, on the basis of a number of presuppositions and assumptions, some of which we can state at this point;

none of which we can fully explore. The authorial integrity of Bunyan's margins as coming from his hand and belonging with his narratives, and the artistic integrity of his marginal notes with his narrative text is defended in Chapter 2, and for the rest of this study, assumed.

Although not specifically aligned with any one literary theory, and quite willingly accepting illuminating insights from a number of theorists, this study proceeds on the basis of a relational and communicative model of literature. Any experience of literature is the result of two intentional processes: the intentional project of the author in writing and the intentional project of the reader in reading. Rather than the text merely being a site for the projection or introjection of the reader, I see the text as a place of genuine "I-Thou" human encounter in which writer and reader engage: one self, the reader, encounters another self, the writer as manifest in his or her creation, across distances of time and space. I opt for the "I-Thou" stance which respects the virtually present author in engagement with the engaged reader rather than an "I-It" approach to text which develops when either the text or the reader is seen as quite autonomous of the author. Obviously, I adopt and adapt the language of dialogue from Martin Buber's *I and Thou*. I aspire, as a reader and critic, to be what Buber calls "the receptive beholder."[20]

With Paul Ricoeur, I choose an approach which "deals lovingly with the symbol in an effort to recover a meaning hidden in it" rather than one which "seeks to destroy the symbols as the representation of a false reality."[21] Ricoeurian terminology fits quite well my view of the reader engaging with the author's thought as manifest in the structures of the text, the authorial "configuration" of the text being met by the reader's "refiguration" of it: "The dialectic between the prefiguration of human understanding of the world of action and the work of composition or configuration is played out by the reader, the operator, whose act of reading is a refiguration of the configured work."[22]

Nor is Bunyan himself silent on the reading process. As we shall see, he is a highly self-conscious reader; as an author, he is acutely conscious of the process of reading by which his works will be appropriated. He demonstrates his awareness of the reading process not only in his apologies and prefaces but also within the text of his narratives. The episode in *The Pilgrim's Progress* in which the two pilgrims, Hopeful and Christian, attempt to decipher the meaning of "*a strange monument*" describes a reading event through which we can learn a good deal about the way in which reading and the construction of

18

meaning proceeded for the newly literate readers for whom Bunyan originally wrote.

> *They see a*
> *strange monument*
>
> Now I saw, that just on the other side of this Plain, the Pilgrims came to a place where stood an old *Monument*, hard by the High-way-side, at the sight of which they were both concerned, because of the strangeness of the form therof; for it seemed to them as if it had been a *Woman* transformed into the shape of a Pillar: here therefore they stood looking, and looking upon it, but could not for a time tell what they should make thereof. At last *Hopeful* espied written above upon the head thereof, a Writing in an unusual hand; but he being no Scholar, called to *Christian* (for he was learned) to see if he could pick out the meaning: so he came, and after a little laying of Letters together, he found the same to be this, *Remember Lot's Wife*. So he read it to his fellow; after which, they both concluded, that that was the *Pillar of Salt into which *Lot's Wife* was turned for her looking back with a *covetous heart*, when she was going from
>
> *Gen.19.26.
>
> *Sodom* for safety. Which sudden and amazing sight gave them occasion of this discourse. (*TPP*, 108-09) [23]

From the reading activity described here, we can infer a good deal about the way in which Bunyan expected his readers to arrive at (or to use Ricoeur's term, to "achieve") meaning.[24] The reading act described here is a shared, communal activity, the more able reader helping the one who is "no Scholar." Introductory material added by one Jo[hn] Geree to the fourth edition of Nicholas Byfield's popular *Directions for the Private Reading of the Scriptures* (1648) instructs those who cannot read to "seek a supply of this defect ... either the husband may use the help of the wife, or the wife of the husband, or both of a childe, or at least of a servant to read to them." Servants, those least likely to know how to read, are encouraged to attach themselves to households in which there is daily reading of the Scriptures.[25]

Hopeful and Christian's reading is not only communal but oral. The transformation of graphic text into spoken language is the first step, with the more competent reader being the one who can phonetically sound and blend the sounds to create spoken words by "laying of Letters together." Only after turning the printed word into speech do the two readers "pick out the meaning."[26] At last, they are able to draw conclusions concerning the significance of the words. First, they name and identify the monument on which the words occur as epitaph as being "the Pillar of Salt into which *Lot's Wife* was turned." With the help of a marginal reference to the Bible story in Genesis 19, the pilgrims can also place the words in their narrative context. Although the text referred to by the marginal note states only, "But his wife looked backe from behind him, and she became a pillar of salt," the pilgrims supply a midrash: Lot's Wife had "look[ed] back with a *covetous heart.*" In the ensuing discourse, the words are given application as a specific warning against covetousness. "[T]his example ... ministreth occasion to us to thank God, to fear before him, and always to remember *Lot's* Wife" (110).

The process by which the pilgrims achieve meaning through reading is triadic, a hermeneutic process of understanding, interpretation, and application, rooted in seventeenth century sermonic structure. The seventeenth-century sermon was triadic, the sections variously titled: explication, confirmation, application,[27] or "right interpretation, true exposition of doctrine, and sound application to life and judgment."[28] Like the Jauss-Gadamer hermeneutic,[29] Ricoeur's triadic description of the reading process as consisting of explanation, understanding, and application bears acknowledged affinities to this sermonic model.[30]

The scene of Hopeful and Christian "picking out the meaning" illustrates the interaction of elements of textual presentation with the process of making meaning. The writing they read occurs in a particular relationship to the *"Monument"*: "above upon the head thereof." The script is problematic, being "a Writing in an unusual hand" (108).[31] The position and graphic form in which the words are presented affects the deciphering of the meaning, drawing attention to and emphasizing the "strangeness of the form" of the monument. Analogously, we will argue, marginal notes to a text affect the way in which that text is read; the use, for example, of a different type size and of italic and roman letters creates a "strangeness"; the position of marginal notes is "alongside," providing the continuous companionable presence of an interpreter.

The authorially-inscribed margin at once quite consciously restricts the range of meanings which may legitimately be "picked out" and vastly enlarges the literary resonances of the story. Continuous insistence on interpretive action on the part of the reader by means of the marginal notes conditions the act of reading at every point, both by teasing the mind of the reader out into related associations and by intensifying attention to specific aspects of the central text. What Shari Benstock says of footnotes is equally true of marginal notes: they are "innately referential ... reflecting on the text, engaged in dialogue with it, and often performing an interpretive and critical act on it, while also addressing a larger, extratextual world in an effort to relate this text to other texts."[32] *The Pilgrim's Progress* is a work in which the reader must become deeply involved in a reading experience, and yet one which, the reading being conditioned by the marginal notes, can never absorb him or her imaginatively without the countervailing claim of intellectual processes of association, interpretation, and application.

In Bunyan's fictional texts, the author's presence in the marginal notes is a continual reminder that this fiction is not to be read as mere entertainment but as commentary and teaching. The summoning of the biblical intertext creates a sense in the reader that the material is not only weighty but also amply buttressed and supported by scriptural authority. The visual layout of the page, with its core text and marginal notations, forces the reader to continuously read in two places and two modes virtually simultaneously. The significance of this to an allegorical presentation is great. Allegory is more than merely story, even than very great story. It is story and meaning, the two never entirely absorbed into each other. Bunyan's dual texts make effective visual representation of the nature of allegory which, according to Michael Murrin, "is the essential human speech because it alone expresses human nature. Man mirrors the cosmos, and allegory automatically reveals cosmic relationships, particularly in its combination of the ... invisible and visible words which imitate that combination of appearance and invisible power which make up the cosmos and the human being."[33] Bunyan's textual layout is mimetic of the act of reading and responding to allegory as both story and commentary.

Fish is astute in his observation that, "the marginal note is not offered as a key to the episode; rather the episode points the reader to an understanding of the marginal note."[34] He is, however, too restrictive. The marginal note *is* offered as a key to the episode, but the traffic of meaning-making between margin and narrative runs both ways: the episode also points the reader to an understanding of the marginal note. And the traffic of meaning-making runs beyond the text, as well. Bunyan's narratives and their marginal notes reflect what

Barbara K. Lewalski sees to be a central Protestant concern to connect the biblical text and the Christian's own experience. "The Christian's experience is to comment upon the biblical text, and the text upon his experience."[35] Bunyan is quite clear in his intention that the reading of his narratives should explain and expand the reader's own life, that the reader's life is, itself, a narrative text glossed and commented upon by the allegory.

The primary intended readership—what Peter Rabinowitz terms the "authorial audience"[36]—of Bunyan's narratives is comprised of fellow-believers with Bunyan, Nonconformists like himself who share a set of assumptions about the nature of human life in relationship to the divine. "[T]he … unregenerate … were not commonly intended as the sole readers," says Keeble of the readership of Nonconformist literature.[37] And yet Bunyan intended that his works would be read not only by the elect, but also by those less certain of their salvation, including a secondary audience to his work, the unregenerate reader. *"This Book will make a Traveller of thee, / If by its Counsel thou wilt ruled be,"* Bunyan advises the reader of *The Pilgrim's Progress* (6, lines 33-4) and invites the reader to discover *"whether thou art blest or not,/By reading the same lines"* (7, line 24). When the voice in the margin warns "Mark this, you that are churles to your godly Relations," (*TPP* 2, 177) the reader addressed is antagonistic to the faith. In the aside to the devil in *The Holy War*—"That's false, Satan" (39)[38]—Bunyan may even be seen to address cosmic powers from his margins. The implied audience of the margins is thus as broad as Bunyan's sense of his "real" audience: running the range from those who were biblically literate enough to "hear" each scripture reference and understand its significance, to those outsiders to whom an occasional aside could be cast.

Yet, paradoxically, there is an exclusionary role played by the marginal notes: the reader who does not inform himself of an intertext which may no longer speak as it did to the original audience will be without the keys to Bunyan's narratives. Cryptic scripture references play a role not unlike that of the riddling Shepherds of the Delectable Mountains who both reveal and conceal meaning. The discovery by the reader of whether "[he] be blest or not" is at least partly the discovery of whether or not the references in the margins "speak" to him. The reader I postulate is not so monolithic a construct as Iser's anxiety-driven reader, but rather a reader who remembers, recognizes, and responds to numerous cues. The intended reader is "gamesome," involved with the play of text and intertext, delighted to find himself an insider to allusions and cross-references which might well elude others, from the King's censor down to conforming neighbours. The pleasure of reading and of recognizing a rich intertext must surely have motivated many readers.

This study concerns itself with a number of relationships which are reflected in the marginal notes. Bunyan's own relationship to reading, especially to reading the Bible, serves as a model by which to examine the readers whom he addresses and the readings he expects his texts to engender. I hope my work in this area will be part of carrying out what Roger Sharrock stated as the "[t]he new task for criticism ... to establish how Bunyan read the Bible."[39] The relationship of the various types of marginal notes to the narratives which they not only embellish but at every point enrich is also explored, as is the relationship between the text of the narratives and the intertext of the Bible.

In Chapter 1, *Grace Abounding* is read as a record of Bunyan's development as a reader. I will propose that Bunyan wrote his books for readers like himself: newly-literate, self-taught to a large degree, and highly motivated. Bunyan received the convention of the authorial marginal note from the format of the books he read. These books are reviewed in Chapter 2. I propose that authorial marginal notes were, for Bunyan, an intrinsic part of both reading and writing. Thus, as he writes, his marginal notes convey and reflect ideas and attitudes towards the act of written communication in general as well as towards the particular text at hand. In Chapter 3, an examination of how the marginal notes function in Bunyan's narratives leads to a taxonomy illustrated by examples from his four fiction narratives, *The Pilgrim's Progress, First Part* (1678); *The Life and Death of Mr. Badman* (1680); *The Holy War* (1682); and *The Pilgrim's Progress, Second Part* (1684). The artistic and playful effects created by the marginal notes will be examined in Chapter 4. Chapter 5 offers an exegesis of the opening paragraph of *The Pilgrim's Progress*, demonstrating that a reading of the text which includes both the central narrative text and the marginal comments opens out the primary themes and motifs of the work.

The power and wonder of approaching any great text is that it somehow transcends the gap that separates the reader from the writer; that while our "horizon of reception" cannot fuse with the original, it can put us into a position from which meaning can be glimpsed, sometimes even grasped; that Bunyan can say to us, his readers distant from him in history, geography, and underlying assumptions, "*I being taken from you in presence ... do look yet after you all, greatly longing to see your safe arrival into THE desired haven.*"[40] The "desired haven" to which this study intends to direct its readers is a fuller experience and appreciation of Bunyan's powerful narratives.

CHAPTER 1

Bunyan As Reader:
The Record of Grace Abounding

In his four major narratives, John Bunyan produced interactive dual texts in which marginal notes interact with the main narrative. Of course, he was making use of the conventions of textual presentation available to him, but his own attitudes towards reading, interpreting, applying, and producing text illumine our consideration of these dual texts. Bunyan's decision to embellish and amplify his stories by means of marginal notes reflects not only the conventions of print which he shares with his readers, but also his seriousness about the act of reading. From the nature of the marginal notes in Bunyan's narrative texts we can infer a good deal about his expectations concerning his intended reader's attitudes, reading abilities, and knowledge.[1]

It seems reasonable to assume that Bunyan wrote for readers much like himself. He describes his own emergence from semi-literacy by means of reading popular literature, first secular and then religious, and above all through encountering the richly varied literary texts of the Bible. Historians of literacy concur that "literacy rates were higher amongst nonconformists than in other sections of society.... [T]hey were heirs to the educational drive of Puritanism and ... [were] enthusiastic advocates of the benefits of literacy."[2] How the economically disadvantaged lower classes became readers despite their often brief periods of schooling is a very interesting aspect of the new literacy of the English working class in the second half of the seventeenth century. Understanding what we can of the Bunyan-as-reader whom we encounter in his earliest narrative, *Grace Abounding*, is of central importance to our understanding Bunyan-as-writer, and the readers for whom he wrote.

In this chapter, we will first examine Bunyan's development as a reader from his own record of that development in *Grace Abounding*; we will then consider his hermeneutic methods and his attitude towards the Bible. Finally, we will examine Bunyan's response to the physical aspects of books and reading. Our attention to Bunyan as a developing reader will lead us to evaluate the seriousness with which he wrote even when choosing the less didactic and more playful forms of his narratives. It will become evident that the references and other notations which Bunyan places in the margins of his narratives are placed there very consciously, amd are intended to be responded to by readers who would have considered them as important and integral to the narrative text.

I

Robert Darnton suggests that in order to recover information about the reading process in previous periods of history, "[w]e might begin by searching the record for readers."[3] He feels that "historians should be able to capture something of what reading meant for the few persons who left a record of it."[4] Using several other of Darnton's suggested sources to reconstruct reading in Tudor times, Eugene Kintgen examines manuals about reading and explicit instructions in "To the Reader" prefaces. Kintgen admits that, having made such an examination, "we still won't have an individual reader to examine."[5]

Fortunately for those whose interest lies in the manner and method of reading in the widening population of the relatively newly literate in England after the middle of the seventeenth century, Bunyan's spiritual autobiography offers us such an individual reader to examine. An examination of the record left by this individual reader will supply a good deal of information about how readers like Bunyan read; about how books like those Bunyan wrote were read. This study may also contribute to a better understanding of "how unlearned people developed the skills and audacity to challenge learned clerics."[6] For readers such as those for whom Bunyan wrote, marginal notations were not mere ornaments or accidentals, but were integrally related to the interpretation of the central narrative text, and to the linking of the narrative to the intertext of Scripture.[7]

Throughout *Grace Abounding*, Bunyan is overwhelmingly conscious of his own reading experience and of the impact on him of written text. In almost every paragraph, he discusses an interaction with text: through reading, remembering, and reflecting, he is in continual dialogue with words which he first encounters in the written text. (Interestingly, the brief biographical sketch which prefaces "Doe's Folio" speaks of Bunyan's reading and study in terms of this dialogue: "His business was to converse much with the Word of God, and to pray over it"[8] [*Works* A-1].) While *Grace Abounding* is first and primarily a spiritual autobiography, it is also an intellectual history. It supplies for students of Bunyan's works a self-conscious representative reader of the type Margaret Spufford classifies as the "non-gentle reader before 1700."[9]

Bunyan recalls having learned to read and write at school "the which I also attained, according to the rate of other poor mens children" (*GA*, para. 3). His sensitivity as a writer to the struggles of young readers may suggest retained memories of his own struggles at school. In his address "To the Reader" of *A Book For Boys and Girls*, he encourages his young readers:

> *Nor let them fall under Discouragement,*
> *Who at their Horn-book stick, and time hath spent*
> *Upon that A, B, C, while others do*
> *Into their Primer, or their Psalter go.*
> *Some Boys with difficulty do begin,*
> *Who in the end, the Bays, and Lawrel win.*[10]
> (*MW*, 6, 193, lines 105-110)

Spufford's attempts to discover what might have been what Bunyan termed "the rate of ... poor men's children" lead her to conclude that "[i]n the seventeenth century, the opportunity to receive any schooling was socially restricted. Once a child could earn wages which made a difference to the family economy, it would be removed from school unless these wages could be dispensed with."[11]

From evidence gleaned from autobiographies from the period, Spufford offers as a working hypothesis that children who did go to school would have learned to read by seven years of age, and to write by eight. According to her account, many of those who were allowed to go to school stayed only long enough to learn how to read before joining the work-force, the number of readers therefore being considerably greater than the number of writers.[12]

Bunyan is conscious of being privileged above his class in having had the opportunity afforded him by his parents "to learn both to Read and Write" (*GA*, para. 2). It was a struggle for poor people to send their children to school, and entailed some degree of sacrifice. Since biblical literacy is foundational to faith, Christian parents were encouraged by their pastors to send their children to school. Benjamin Keach, a Nonconformist writer contemporary with Bunyan, depicts a spiritual struggle underlying the financial struggle of poor people in sending their children to school. In *The Progress of Sin* (1684), the temptation of Peccatum to poor parents is satirically presented:

> He presenteth to many Parents the great Charge of putting their *Off-spring* to School; perswading them (they being poor, and low in the *world*) they could not be at this cost ... lest by their attaining to the knowledge of Letters, they should take to read the *Holy Bible*, which he dreads exceedingly; because when understood, it vanquisheth (at once) his *Darling Ignorance*.[13]

Despite having had the opportunity to go to school, however, Bunyan confesses, "I did soon lose that little I learned, and that even almost utterly" (*GA*, para. 3). Spufford points out that writing began in Latin.[14] Since Bunyan did continue to read popular vernacular literature, perhaps it is the loss of Latin which he laments. When he uses a Latin phrase in *The Pilgrim's Progress, Part 2*, he adds—might it be a bit ruefully?—the marginal aside, "*The Lattine I borrow*" (*TPP 2*, 229).

Bunyan claims that when he was a young person, he was not only without interest in spiritual reading matter, but actually felt a kind of claustrophobia while watching others read religious materials: "[W]hen I have but seen some read in those books that concerned Christian piety, it would be as it were a prison to me" (*GA*, para. 10). This physicality of response to print is an aspect of Bunyan's reading which is frequently encountered throughout *Grace Abounding*, and will be examined more fully later in this chapter. Although manuals of Christian behaviour were not appealing to him, we know from his comments about romances and ballads that he did read the normal chap-book fare of his class. "[G]ive me a Ballad, a Newsbook, *George* on Horseback, or *Bevis of Southampton*, give me some book that teaches curious arts, that tells of old fables; but for the holy Scriptures I cared not," he writes elsewhere (*A Few Sighs*, *MW 1*, 333).

His official introduction to spiritually-oriented reading material came through his wife's dowry: two popular "godly books," Arthur Dent's *A Plaine Mans Pathway to Heaven* and Lewis Bayly's *The Practice of Pietie*. He credits these books with engendering a spiritual interest (*GA*, para. 16) which he began to satisfy by reading narrative material in the Bible: "I betook me to my Bible, and began to take great pleasure in reading, but especially with the historical part thereof: for, as for *Pauls* Epistles, and Scriptures of that nature, I could not away with them ..." (*GA*, para. 29). At this stage in his development as a reader, Bunyan introduces himself with delight to the stories of the Bible, no doubt already familiar to him in oral form through readings or pulpit retellings and elaborations. He seems to have made a quite natural transfer of reading skills from reading chap-book adventure stories to the more challenging reading of biblical narrative.

Bunyan describes his sequential reading in the Bible in terms of physical motion: "And as I went on and read, I lighted on that passage ... ," (*GA*, para. 47) a tellingly physical phrase which is echoed memorably in the opening first sentence of *The Pilgrim's Progress*: "As I walk'd through the wilderness of this world, I lighted on a certain place" (*TPP*, 8). This sense of reading being a physical pilgrimage through print is reiterated elsewhere in *Grace Abounding* and suggests something of the slow and persistent toiling towards meaning that reading would have been for beginning readers of Bunyan's social class and educational background.

Later, Bunyan turns with a hungry mind and "new eyes" to more complex biblical materials. "And now, me thought, I began to look into the Bible with new eyes, and read as I never did before; and especially the Epistles of the Apostle S. Paul were sweet and pleasant to me" (*GA*, para. 46). The development of Bunyan's reading skills is apparent here. Narratives are rare in the epistles; Bunyan's developing repertoire of reading strategies had now expanded to include means of dealing with argumentation, exhortation, and propositional declarations. The intense attention Bunyan gives to the Epistle to the Galatians in an early stage of his pilgrimage into literacy (*GA*, para. 129) is of interest in this regard, since that epistle contains a more extensive passage of narrative than is usual in the epistolary literature of the New Testament. The narration tells of Paul's immediate post-conversion experiences and encounters with church leaders, including a dramatic confrontation with Peter (Gal. 1:11-2:14). This epistle, containing as it does both narrative and hortatory material, may have created a bridge by which Bunyan could both apply and extend his reading skills, aided in his comprehension of the more complex materials by Luther's commentary. Making meaning at this challenging new level of reading brought Bunyan pleasure: the meanings arrived at "were sweet and pleasant" to him as a developing reader. The enthusiasm of the newly literate for the experience of understanding text is apparent here.

Having learned reading strategies for dealing with narrative and epistolary material, Bunyan now goes on to create a broader framework of understanding. A remembered text from the Apocrypha pops into his mind, *"Look at the generations of old, and see, did ever any trust in God and were confounded?"* (*GA*, para. 62), and Bunyan acts upon the text as a directive to a motivated reading of the entire Bible. His plan is to *"Begin at the beginning of Genesis, and read to the end of the Revelations, and see if ... there was any that ever trusted in the Lord, and was Confounded"* (paras. 62, 63). Such a task would daunt most modern readers; we need to consider what an accomplishment it was for a reader like Bunyan.

We also need to consider how rich a literary resource the English Bible was to newly-literate readers like Bunyan, a great which provided a wide range of types of genres and various levels of reading material all woven together into a single great pattern of meaning. According to Northrop Frye, "Those who do succeed in reading the Bible from beginning to end will discover that at least it has a beginning and an end, and some traces of a total structure. It begins where time begins, with the creation of the world; it ends where time ends, with the Apocalypse, and it surveys human history in between."[15]

The questing reading of the entire biblical text which Bunyan now undertook established for him a whole-book approach to the Scripture. This "big picture" underlies all of his wide-ranging biblical references. It is within this broad context that Bunyan conducts his free movement from Old Testament to New Testament and back again.[16] For Bunyan and his readers, the Old Testament and the New Testament formed one book, the Old Testament linked to the New Testament by an intricate pattern of types and antitypes, of prophecy and perceived fulfillment, all thematically unified in the person and redemptive work of Jesus Christ, read as the fulfillment of the Messianic hopes expressed by writers in the Old Testament. Bunyan and his readers were the heirs of the Reformation attitude that "the canon is one because the meaning of all of it is salvation in Jesus Christ."[17] Bunyan was, therefore, perfectly comfortable in using Old Testament characters to exemplify Christian truth: Manasseh, a king in the Old Testament, is set side by side with Mary Magdalene as a "great sinner" saved by God's grace (*Saved by Grace, MW 8*, 196). Examples can be drawn with ease from both testaments to prove a point: "[T]he greatness of Sense of Sin, the hideous Roarings of the Devil, yea, and abundance of Revelations, will not prove that God is bringing the

Soul to Jesus Christ: As *Balaam, Cain, Judas* and others can witness"
(*Come and Welcome, MW* 8, line 355). Landscape descriptions draw on
biblical imagery from throughout the Bible. John R. Knott, Jr. notes
Bunyan's increasing dependence on Scripture for landscape imagery
as Christian nears the end of his journey in *The Pilgrim's Progress*,
Bunyan "skillfully fusing the Old Testament and the New" in the vi-
sion of the Delectable Mountains, the River of Life which "is David's
River of God as well as the river of Revelation," and the fusing of Old
and New Testament "visions of blessedness ... in the juxtaposition of
Beulah and the New Jerusalem."[18]

When we go on to consider Bunyan's use of marginal notes, we
must bear in mind that whenever Bunyan cites a text, he is expecting
his reader to be aware of — or to become acquainted with — a complete
biblical context: both an immediate context in a particular chapter,
psalm, or story, and a general context created by placing the particular passage into the sweep of Bible history from the beginning to the
end of all things temporal.

II

For Bunyan, his whole-book reading of the Bible gives way, under the
duress of his quest for assurance of salvation, to repeated searching
for particular remembered texts (see, for example, *GA*, para. 147).
Having gained an overview of Scripture and having experienced it
subjectively through at least some moments when he feels a sense of
being among the elect, Bunyan is ready for a careful study of texts
within their contexts to "weigh their scope and tendence" (*GA*, para.
222); to ascertain "the New Testament stile and sence" of Old Testament passages — that is, to interpret them in the light of typology and
fulfillment; or to determine the meaning of a text "without restraining
the natural force of one syllable thereof" (*GA*, para. 249).

Three basic hermeneutic approaches can be seen to operate as
Bunyan struggles to understand specific texts as they occur to his
mind, placing them in the context of his own life, and within the unity
of the entire text of the Bible. While much has been written about Puritan hermeneutics, the discussion which follows is based on the actual hermeneutic methods which Bunyan discusses or applies in the
process of his formation as a reader as he describes it in *Grace Abounding*.[19]

The first hermeneutic approach which Bunyan applies is that of reading to find the plain sense of a passage (e.g., *GA*, para. 249). This was in line with Reformation hermeneutic principle which accepted typology and figural readings, but rejected the more elaborate allegorical readings of biblical texts, seeking first to be instructed by the plain, grammatical meaning of the passage.[20]

The second hermeneutic principle which guides Bunyan is to read for an understanding of the passage "in a New Testament stile and sence" (*GA*, para. 226) — which he elsewhere calls the "Evangelical ... or Gospel" sense in contrast with the "Legal" sense of the passage as it occurs in the Old Testament (*Doctrine of the Law & Grace*, *MW* 2, 72). The "New Testament stile or sence" seems to refer to the assimilation of the Old Testament passages to New Testament applications, either by seeing stories as *exempla* or by reading passages typologically or figurally. Bunyan's use of the Old Testament to illustrate New Testament truth is frequent and unapologetic; he follows not only the Protestant reformers, but the New Testament writers themselves in absorbing Old Testament into the New, or in reinterpreting the Hebrew scriptures in the light of the Christian understanding of a new covenant of grace.

The third hermeneutic principle is that of harmonization. "When I had thus considered these Scriptures, and found that thus to understand was not against but according to other Scriptures," (*GA*, 228) Bunyan finds himself confirmed in his interpretation. In line with the Reformation conviction of the unity of Scripture, Bunyan seeks to read a passage in such a way as to fit it into an overall harmony of Scripture. He was, we know, aware of a methodology of reading laid down by the unnamed translators of Martin Luther's *Commentary on Galatians*. The "Christian Reader" of the English version is admonished "firste to read it wholy together, and not by peeces and parts here and there, but take it in order as it lieth, conferring one place with another, whereby to understand the better the right meaning of the author."[21] If the courtesy of this kind of reading was expected to be extended to Luther, one can be sure that it was also expected to be extended to the writers of Holy Scripture.

We need some understanding of this constant and conscientious placing of texts in contexts, and of juxtaposing texts and harmonizing them in relationship to each other and to the entire text of the Bible if we are to recover something of the intended and probable impact of Bunyan's marginal notations on his seventeenth-century readers.

While Bunyan's hermeneutics may have been more often implicit than explicit, they are anything but simple or simplistic. Every reference he places in a marginal note represents a text which can only be understood in the light of its context in the Bible, and in the network of images, allusions and interlocked meanings to which it provides access. Each reference is a synecdoche for the whole of the sacred text and summons the whole late-Reformation attitude concerning it. Biblical references in the margin are serious signals to his audience to recall and reflect the biblical text to which Bunyan at every point refers.

Against this background of progressively developing reading competence, Bunyan goes on to create a synthesis that is, in effect, a systematic theology. This synthesis he discovers in a restrospective analysis of the themes of his sermons. He preaches first on the sinfulness of man, "crying out against mens sins, and their fearful state because of them" (*GA*, para. 278); then on the person of Christ, "in all his Offices, Relations, and Benefits unto the World" (*GA*, para. 278); and finally "on the mystery of union with Christ" (*GA*, para. 279). Again using the image of physical travel, Bunyan comments: "And when I had travelled thorow these three chief points of the Word of God, about the space of five years or more; I was caught in my present practice and cast into Prison" (*GA*, para. 279). For Bunyan, both reading and preaching are journeys into and "thorow" truth.

Thus, the young man who claims to have lost what little he had learned about reading at school becomes capable of a systematic theological approach to the Bible together with a deeply subjective, personalized reading.[22] That is to say, he is fully biblically literate, with the Scriptures readily available to his mind as words, as pictures, or as doctrinal principles, all within the framework of a grand scheme of meaning which includes within its scope the nature of man as revealed by creation and the fall; the means of redemption through the person and work of Jesus; and the mystical union of the soul with Christ.

For Bunyan, reading is always closely linked to the mental activity of both understanding and making judgments about text. He is at his best a critical thinker — even when the text is sacred text. He first mentions the importance of being able to form a judgment in relation to Ranter writings. These troubled him because he was "not able to make a Judgement about them" (*GA*, para. 44). He examines both Ranter and Quaker teachings critically, and goes on to apply critical reading skills to the Bible as well. U. Milo Kaufmann goes so far as to claim that in Bunyan's "use of Scripture ... lay the seeds of historical criticism, evident also in the work of Richard Baxter, that came to bloom only after the lapse of a century."[23] To the degree that both Bunyan and Baxter believed the Bible to be able to stand up to the most rigourous and thoughtful scrutiny, this claim may be true.

After a painful mental struggle caused by apparently contradictory scriptural messages concerning the state of his soul, Bunyan settles the matter once for all by setting himself the task of understanding "those most fearful and terrible Scriptures, ... to come close to them, to read them, and consider them, and to weigh their scope and tendence" (*GA*, para. 222). While convinced that the Bible is the Word of God and is wholly true and trustworthy, once envisioning the writers of Scripture saying to him, "All our words are truth, one of as much force as another" (*GA*, para. 209), Bunyan remains critical of his own interpretations and those of others. He goes back to revise his own earlier, more naïve readings of biblical texts. "[C]onsidering the place more fully" (*GA*, para. 147), he sometimes confirms an earlier reading and sometimes replaces it with a more satisfactory reading, always pressing towards interpretations which harmonize one scripture with another, and which are true to his own experience.

Bunyan's critical readings have a double intent: he attempts to understand scriptural texts in their contexts, and he attempts to understand how to apply the text to his personal spiritual life. Given that guides to Scripture interpretation were bound into many editions of the Bible and that manuals of direction for new readers were available,[24] Bunyan may have been helped in this complex process of learning how to read Scripture judiciously by some note of "how to Take Profite" or "Guide to Reading of Scripture." Such a guide had been bound, for example, in the front-matter to the Geneva Bible published by Robert Barker in 1610. In order to understand "the scope and thrust of Scripture," readers were instructed to:

> Mark and consider:
> 1. Coherence of the text and how it hangeth together.
> 2. Course of times and ages, with such things as belong
> unto them.
> 3. Maner of speach proper to the Scriptures.
> 4. Agreement that one place of Scripture hath with an
> other, whereby that which seemeth darke in one is made
> easie in another.

Such an approach to reading Scripture is quite different from the religious enthusiasm of personal inspiration of which Dryden accuses Nonconformist sectarians: "Study and pains were now no more their care;/Texts were explain'd by fasting and by prayer."[25] Bunyan's kind of reading involves an awareness of the effect of grammatical structures on meaning; a knowledge of the general historical context of a passage and of its place in the pattern of a developing revelation; an ability to respond appropriately to figures of speech, modes of address, and matters of form; and finally, an understanding of a system of internal harmony within Scripture and an ability to conduct interpretation within this system by cross-referencing a text or passage to other biblical passages.

While all of these interpretive strategies might be engaged in by the individual alone, the "Guide" recommends that an individual's interpretations be compared with those of other readers who comprise the "interpretive community" of which the reader is part.[26] The seventeenth-century reader is encouraged to:

> *Take opportunities to*
> 1. *Reade interpreters, if he is able.*
> 2. *Conferre with such as can open the Scriptures.*
> 3. *Heare preaching, and to prove by the Scriptures that which is taught.*

There is a clear social and educational scale implied in this listing. The first instruction, to "reade interpreters," is qualified by an ambiguous "if he is able," suggesting that many readers would be unable to read commentaries in either the sense of having insufficient literary or language competency or of lacking economic access to such commentaries. During the persecution after the Restoration, another meaning of being "able" to consult commentaries comes into play: imprisoned and away from the resources of their libraries, writers had to rely on their memories for their annotations.[27]

The second instruction, to "conferre," would be possible for a greater number of people. Conferring would include the kind of discussions which Bunyan had with John Gifford: "*Mr. Gifford* ... himself also took occasion to talke with me ... he invited me to his house, where I should hear him confer with others about the dealings of God with the Soul" (*GA*, para. 77). The entire general public was able to "heare preaching" and then to engage in the process of "prov[ing] by the Scriptures that which is taught" — the after-sermon exercise of dili-

diligently looking up Scriptures cited and considering the teaching that had been offered. And when persecution made that kind of conferring impossible, the Nonconformist conferred by reading sermons: "Read much writings of our old solid Divines," Richard Baxter instructs his congregation when separated from them by imprisonment. "You may read an able Divine when you cannot hear one...."[28]

Bunyan was not "able," in any of the senses we have discussed, to "reade interpreters," lacking both classical languages and the economic means to procure commentaries. His opportune encounter with Luther's *Commentary on Galatians* represents the exception rather than the rule in his studies. But he was able to "conferre" in the more democratic sense of meeting frequently for discussion with John Gifford, minister of the Bedford church; there is no doubt that he joined other Nonconformists of his day in frequent attendance at sermons, followed by attentive study of the passage of Scripture on which the teaching had been based. While he lacked access to commentaries that would have linked him to an interpretive community reaching back to the first century, Bunyan was initiated by sermon-hearing and intense discussion into the Calvinistic community of nonconforming English Puritanism.

As reader and interpreter, Bunyan has an intensely personal and ego-involved relationship to text. As he begins to read the gospels, he visualizes and places himself in the scenes of which he reads. "[M]e thought I was as if I had seen him born, as if I had seen him grow up, as if I had seen him walk thorow this world from the Cradle to his Cross; ... I saw how gently he gave himself to be hanged ... " (*GA*, para. 120-21). Bunyan is capable of visualizing not only the events of which he read, but also the authors of the biblical accounts. In the midst of his spiritual depression, it seems to Bunyan "as if both *Peter*, and *Paul*, and *John*, and all the Writers did look with scorn upon me, and hold me in derision" (para. 209).

Related to visualization, yet distinct from it, is Bunyan's habit of identification with characters and events in printed text. He reads the words of Jesus, "*And yet there is roome*" as a personal invitation, "[W]hen the Lord Jesus did speak these words, he then did think of me ... and [did] leave it upon record, that I might find help thereby..." (*GA*, para. 68). Of Luther's spiritual experiences described in his *Commentary on Galatians*, Bunyan states, "I found my condition in his experience" (*GA*, para. 129). He also makes a terrifying identification of himself with the apostate Spira (*GA*, para. 163). He attempts to judge the seriousness of his sin of "selling Christ" by measuring it against the sins of Bible characters. He compares his sin with David's sin of adultery covered up by murder and finds his to be worse:

> Then again, being loath and unwilling to perish, I began to compare my sin with others, to see if I could find that any of those that are saved had done as I had done. So I considered *David's* Adultery and Murder, and found them most hainous crimes, and those too committed after light and grace received: but yet by considering, I perceived that his transgressions were onely such as were against the Law of *Moses* ... but mine was against the *Gospel*, yea, against the Mediator thereof; I had sold my Saviour. (*GA*, para. 151)

He goes on to measure his sin against the denial of Peter and the betrayal of Judas:

> After this I came to consider of *Peters* sin which he committed in denying his Master; and indeed this came nighest to mine, of any that I could find; for he had denied his Saviour as I, and that after Light and Mercy received; yes, and that too, after warning given him: I also considered that he did it both once and twice; and that, after time to consider betwixt. But though I put all these circumstances together, that if possible I might find help, yet I considered again, that his was but *a denial of his Master*, but mine was *a selling of my Saviour*. Wherefore I thought with my self, that I came nearer to *Judas*, than either to *David* or *Peter*. (*GA*, para. 154)

Bunyan's intensely personalized reading of text is an expression of the Protestant demand that a reader experience subjectively what he reads about in the Scripture. One needed to have God "convince [him] of the reality thereof, ... and set [him] down therein, by his own Spirit in the holy Word" (*GA*, para. 117). In all of his reading, from following narratives to the "more narrow search of the Scriptures" (*GA*, para. 125), Bunyan is certain that there is a difference between the natural reading engaged in by the unregenerate man and the spiritual reading done by a man who has experienced spiritual enlightenment. After his initial spiritual illumination, Bunyan records that he "read as [he] never did before ..." (*GA*, para. 46). In his vision of the sunlit mountain, he sees the Word as "the wall ... that did make separation between the Christians and the world" (*GA*, para. 55), the wall he has to pass through by faith in Jesus Christ. There is, he says, "an exceeding difference betwixt the notions of flesh and blood, and the Revelations of God in Heaven" (*GA*,118). This need for a personal and subjective experience of the truth, both of the Bible as the Word of God in general and of the personal assurance of salvation derived from it, is distinctively Calvinistic. Calvin writes:

> [O]ur conviction of the truth of Scripture must be derived from a higher source than human conjectures, judgments, or reasons; namely, the secret testimony of the Spirit.... For as God alone can properly bear witness to his own words, so these words will not obtain full credit in the hearts of men, until they are sealed by the inward testimony of the Spirit. The same Spirit, therefore, who spoke by the mouth of the prophets must penetrate our heart.... The Spirit is called an earnest and seal to confirm the faith of the godly.... Enlightened by him ... we feel a divine energy living and breathing in it.... This singular privilege God bestows on his elect only.... [N]one comprehend the mysteries of God save those to whom it is given. (*Institutes* I.vii. 4, 5)[29]

More directly than from Calvin, however, Bunyan could have learned the principle of personally validated reception of texts from Lewis Bayly who, in *The Practice of Pietie*, instructs his reader regarding Bible reading, "Read not these chapters as matters of historical discourse; but as if they were so many letters, or epistles sent down from God out of heaven unto thee ...."[30]

Personal apprehension of biblical texts was clearly and necessarily an evidence of election to salvation. So, too, was a sense of hearing the Word of God spoken directly to one's own mind and spirit. While Bunyan everywhere affords special privilege to the canonical text of the Bible, keeping clear the Protestant distinction between the inspired and authoritative canon and the Apocrypha, he finds that God speaks to him through both. He is surprised—and a bit disconcerted—to discover that the directive he received to "*Look at the generations of old,*" (*GA*, para. 62) comes not from "those Texts that we call holy and Canonical" (*GA*, para. 65). Nonetheless, he acknowledges that "this sentence was the sum and substance of many of the promises" and therefore, "it was of God to me" (*GA*, para. 65).

In making this statement, Bunyan is making clear that, however important the specific words and their canonical source may be, the ultimate authority of a "sentence" lies, firstly, in the truth (or "sum and substance") of its content, a truth to be established by the norm of canonical Scripture; and, secondly, in the force and effectiveness with which such a word is received by the individual. Dayton Haskin convincingly places the tension which Bunyan experiences between the authority of the scriptural text and the authority of the subjectively experienced revelation within the context of Bunyan's dialogue with the radical sects, seeing Bunyan as at once repudiating and attracted to the radical sectarian emphasis on immediate, subjective revelation.[31]

There are two other instances described in *Grace Abounding* in which sentences not strictly from Scripture have the force of authoritative word for Bunyan. One is described in a paragraph first added in the fifth edition of 1680, in which Bunyan describes an event so singular that he is reluctant to make a judgment on it. Bunyan calls it a "strange dispensation," describing how,

> Suddenly there was as if there had rushed in at the Window, the noise of Wind upon me, but very pleasant, and as if I heard a Voice speaking, *Didst ever refuse to be justified by the blood of Christ?* ... [M]y heart answered groaningly *No.* Then fell with power that Word of God upon me, *See that ye refuse not him that speaketh,* Heb. 12:25. (*GA*, para. 174)

This combination of sensory experience, private dialogue and voiced scriptural text creates an event which Bunyan does not know how to judge: "I have not yet in twenty years been able to make a Judgment of it.... I know not yet what to say of it" (*GA*, para. 174). He makes it clear that he does not claim the experience to be definitive nor normative: "I lay not the stress of my Salvation thereupon, but upon the Lord Jesus, in the Promise" (*GA*, para. 174). Nonetheless, Bunyan acknowledges that, with or without scriptural authority, the words he heard spoke to him in a definitive way.

The other story of an extra-canonical sentence having the force of an authoritative word occurs as Bunyan ends the narrative of his conversion:

> I suddenly felt this word to sound in my heart, *I must go to Jesus*; at this my former darkness and atheism fled away,

and the blessed things of heaven were set within my view;
while I was on this sudden thus overtaken with surprise,
Wife, said I, is there ever such a scripture, *I must go to Jesus?*
She said she could not tell; therefore I sat musing still to see
if I could remember such a place; I had not sat about two or
three minutes, but that came bolting in upon me, *And to an
innumerable company of angels,* and withal, Hebrews the
twelfth about the mount Zion was set before mine eyes.
(*GA*, para. 262)

The concept of the authority of Scripture is so central to Bunyan's
faith and experience of God that he is deeply disturbed by a storm of
doubt as to "whether the holy Scriptures were not rather a Fable and
cunning Story, than the holy and pure Word of God" (*GA*, para. 96).
"Everyone doth think his own religion rightest," he says, reliving the
grip of such doubts, "... and how if all our faith, and Christ, and
Scriptures, should be but a think-so too?" (*GA*, para. 97). Bunyan acknowledges that an argument for scriptural authority from scriptural
sources is circular and thus unconvincing (para. 98). For Bunyan, the
external or objective authority of the canon of Scripture must be re-
authorized within his own mind and soul by the Holy Spirit in order
to be valid. It was under the teaching of John Gifford that Bunyan
learned "to cry mightily to God, that he would convince us of the reality thereof, and set us down therein by his own Spirit in the holy
Word" (*GA*, para. 117). Bunyan is then, by the Spirit of God, "orderly
led into" a personal experience of the truth and reality of the gospel,
(*GA*, para. 120) and this personal experience moves him past intellectual obstacles into a full, personally authorized apprehension of the
truth of the Scripture.

Bunyan would always hold the canonical text, however delivered
to his mind, in the highest regard. But he would grow in his ability to
respond to the whole word rather than to a particular text received
with particular force. He says of this new level of maturity,
"[F]ormerly I thought I might not meddle with the Promise unless I
felt its comfort; .... Now ... I was glad to catch at that word ... ; and
even to leap into the Bosom of that Promise" (*GA*, paras. 248-9). His
conclusion concerning the Word of God is that "God had a bigger
mouth to speak with, than I had heart to conceive with; ... he spake
not his words in haste, ... but with infinite wisdom and judgement,
and in very truth and faithfulness" (*GA*, para. 249). Here, at last, was

a concept of God's Word that was big enough, evoking a faith strong enough, "to lean a weary Soul upon" (*GA*, para. 250).

It seems safe to say that Bunyan's use of texts within, or adjacent to, his narratives is a highly conscious and personal act, not a mere acquiescence to convention. Scriptural references are not cited lightly in the margins of Bunyan's narratives: each text has come to have a personally appropriated subjective meaning as well as objective authority. Wherever texts are cited, they are meant to be "heard" as the very Word of God, and to be responded to.

III

While the realm in which Bunyan operates with respect to Scripture is a suprarational domain, it is not an irrational one. Precisely because he believes in revealed, authoritative truth, he seeks a reasonable assurance of his salvation. Precisely because he believes the entire Bible to be the Word of God, he must reconcile the conflicting textual evidence which is brought to his mind.

Bunyan's intense mental involvement with the printed text is related to the development of pictorial imagery in his active imagination. This process is evident in his visualization of texts, of scenes represented by them, and even of the authors of those texts. When Bunyan remembers a text, the letters which make up the text have a physical quality, including size and shape—and sometimes even lustre. When a scripture comes to him with unusual force and apparent significance, he sometimes not only hears the words spoken but also sees them written in different sizes: he speaks of "such a *great* word ... writ in *great* letters" (*GA*, paras. 203, 206). Scriptures "glister," (*GA*, para. 122) "shine before," (*GA*, para. 126) and "spangle in my eyes" (*GA*, para. 235).

We have already noted the language of physical motion with which Bunyan describes his reading of scripture as a "progress." There are other aspects of the physicality of Bunyan's experience with words and meanings. He is frequently conscious of the physical form of books such as the book of "M. Luther" which, Bunyan says, was, "so old that it was ready to fall piece from piece, if I did but turn it over." Bunyan expresses a true booklover's delight in the book-as-thing: "Now I was pleased much that such an old book had fallen into my hand" (*GA*, para. 129). He describes his new close reading of Scripture as a determination "with careful heart and watchful eye, with great seriousness, to turn over every leaf," (*GA*, para. 247) a phrase which connects his own physicality with the material reality and physical quality of the book. Bunyan recounts that once, upon failing to find comfort in a text, "I ... threw down my Book in a pet" (para. 204). In this event, his wrestling with Scripture becomes an actual, physical experience. Interestingly enough, this acting out of anger in a way which seems to disrespect the Bible as a book does not seem to cause Bunyan any particular anxiety. Despite his obvious appreciation of books as objects, he values the Bible most as means to the end of "see[ing] what might be the mind of God," (*GA*, para. 226) not as a sacred or magical object in itself.

Bunyan is particularly intrigued by the way in which the physical book is able to communicate meaning across time and distance; amazed, for instance, that Luther could speak so directly to his condition, "for thus thought I, this man [Luther] could not know anything of the state of Christians now, but must needs write and speak of the Experience of former days" (*GA*, para. 129). As Luther's work transcends time, Bunyan is able to see his own writing from prison as transcending distance; he invokes that possibility in the opening lines of *Grace Abounding*. For Bunyan as reader and as writer, the book represents its author and his ideas, recreating the virtual reality of his presence for the reader.

Individual words, too, have a physical existence for Bunyan, or at least Bunyan describes his interaction with them in physical metaphors. They have weight and form, as when a sentence "fell with weight upon my spirit" (*GA*, para. 62). Promises and encouragements of Scripture are "stayes and props," (*GA*, para. 197) or like spars to "a man asinking" (*GA*, para. 248). The sentence, *"This sin is not unto death,"* supports Bunyan in the midst of his doubts "like a Mill-post at my back" (*GA*, para. 188-9).

This sense of the physicality of words is extended into the attribution of physical action to texts, a form of personification. Bunyan describes texts as having the ability "to seize," (*GA*, paras. 64, 174, 182) to "tear and rend," (*GA*, para. 104) to "pinch me very sore," (*GA*, para. 178) or to "hold me down" (para. 145). Sometimes this personification of words is rendered in a military metaphor, as when "this word faith put me to it," (*GA*, para. 47) or "this scripture would strike me down, as dead" (*GA*, para. 185). In other kinds of personification of word or text, Bunyan sees words as having the power to "beget ... desires," (*GA*, para. 16) to induce terror even while "kindl[ing] fire in my Soul," (*GA*, para. 75) or to awaken the soul (*GA*, para. 288). His scriptural texts "glance" at him (*GA*, 113) even as he gazes at them. The physicality of texts finds its strongest expression in Bunyan's description of the crucial final encounter of his battling texts, Hebrews 12:17 taking on 2 Cor.12:9. The two texts, one condemning him and one assuring him,

> boulted both upon me at a time, and did work and struggle strongly in me for a while; at last, that about *Esau's* birthright began to wax weak, and withdraw, and vanish; and this about the sufficiency of Grace prevailed, with peace and joy. (*GA*, para. 213)

After this decisive encounter, Bunyan studies the Scriptures which so afflicted him and found "their visage changed, for they looked not so grimly on me as before I thought they did" (*GA*, para. 223). Later, Bunyan fears that the promise which had brought him such joy "did shut its heart against me," but decides that he must risk all and "leap into the bosom of that promise" (*GA*, para. 249).

A mind which as readily personifies texts as does Bunyan's is clearly unusually well-equipped to personalize abstract qualities into personalities, such concrete realization through personification being the stuff of his allegories. The vitality with which he effects this personalization is what makes his allegories great; that vitality seems to spring from his energetic, concrete, and deeply physical imagination, equalled in English literature perhaps only by Wordsworth's.[33]

While personification is the most frequent of Bunyan's figures of speech for explaining his experience of words, he uses metaphors as well. He describes the Scriptures as food, finding them to be "sweet," (*GA*, para. 68, 202, 322) being "refreshed," (*GA*, para. 194) and "sustained" (*GA*, para. 204) by words. Bunyan also sees words as having the physical qualities of light or darkness, as when a newly-gained truth would "shine like the Sun before me," (*GA*, para. 157) or "all would be clouded and darkened ... by [a] sentence," (*GA*, para. 173) or a sentence would "flie in my face, like to lightning" (*GA*, para. 191). Texts even grow "stronger and warmer" (*GA*, para. 91) or weaker and more remote (*GA*, para. 189). Of course such attribution to Scripture of physical qualities is characteristic of seventeenth-century poetics rather than unique to Bunyan. One could, for comparative example, place Bunyan's physical descriptions of Scripture alongside those in George Herbert's "The H. Scriptures. I" and "The H. Scriptures. II."[34]

Another physical characteristic of words to which Bunyan is everywhere responsive is their oral quality. Of the mode of reading among common people in early modern Europe, Darnton states:

> [I]t was usually a *social* activity — not the private communion of reader and author that we associate with reading today.... While children played, women sewed, and men repaired tools, one of the company who could decipher a text would regale them with ... adventures ... from the standard repertory of cheap, popular chap-books.... [B]ooks had audiences rather than readers.[35]

For Bunyan, much of the Bible may well have been clothed with sound before he read it: through his having heard the Scriptures read aloud by a parent or teacher; through sermons; through godly discourse such as that of the "three or four poor women sitting at a door in the Sun, and talking about the things of God" (*GA*, para. 37). Bunyan's sensitivity to sound is evident in the significance he gives to the discourse of these women, and the details he notes in recounting the incident. What he notices particularly is tone and diction: "they spake as if joy did make them speak; they spake with ... pleasantness of Scripture language" (*GA*, para. 38). It is, of course, entirely possible that Bunyan's reading was habitually oral rather than silent; that in his reading of text he actually constructed and reproduced the sounds of the words. At any rate, he *hears* rather than merely *sees* the words he reads, and they echo in his mind. Clearly, he is attuned to the sounds of words as a part of their texture.

The "Word" creates "over and over ... this joyful sound within my Soul" (*GA,* para. 92) that makes one think of a round of bells; but scriptures can also sound like a mortar, "so often and so loud ... sounding and ratling in mine ears" (*GA*, para. 95). He hears a text "as an ecco or sounding again" (*GA*, para. 190); one scripture answers another "as an eccho doth answer a voice" (*GA*, para. 188). More than once Bunyan describes a scripture coming to his mind with such aural force that he thought he heard someone calling it out to him (e.g., *GA,* para. 93, 173).

The absolute sureness with which Bunyan reproduces idiom, incorporates scriptural phrases, and personalizes speech patterns in his narratives tells us about his sure ability to hear and reproduce the sounds of language. This aural facility is something he recognizes and celebrates, writing in "The Apology" to *The Pilgrim's Progress*:

> *This Book is writ in such a Dialect*
> *As may the minds of listless men affect:*
> *It seems a Novelty, and yet contains*
> *Nothing but sound and honest Gospel-strains*
> (*TPP*, 7, lines 8-11)[36]

One must, of course, be careful not to oversimplify this review of Bunyan's intensely physical interaction with language, and of his application of physical characteristics to language. Frequently, in the personification or materialization of texts, Bunyan is speaking metaphorically, in a language familiar to the sermon-goers and Bible-readers whom he addresses. But the fact that the kinds of metaphors he uses are so consistently physical, granting weight and form and personality and colour and taste and sound and shape to words, indicates something of the intensity with which words affect Bunyan's mind, and something of the sensory impact which he intends they should have on his readers. For Bunyan, reading is not merely a pastime, but an intense mental and spiritual activity, so real that it can be described only in physical terms.

Throughout *Grace Abounding*, Bunyan finds himself everything from comforted to assaulted by "texts" or "sentences" which come to him from biblical or extra-biblical sources. Bunyan describes several reflective post-reading experiences, and makes a clear distinction between his own musing or remembering, by which he apparently means consciously thinking about texts or passages, and the sudden irruption into his mind of scriptures. Such irrupting words seem to him to come from outside his own mind: from God, or from the devil. The modern reader might more likely explain the texts as coming from Bunyan's "long-term" or "deep" memory, or perhaps from his "unconscious." But there is no reason why his experience of having a word or words "bolt in upon him" should seem particularly bizarre, given the intensity and physicality of Bunyan's response to language.

There have, of course, been a range of judgments made on the phenomenon. William James sees these irrupting phrases as "automatisms," symptomatic of Bunyan's pathologies.[37] Peter Carlton places Bunyan's claims "of falling and bolting Scriptures" within a Puritan convention of "disclaiming locutions" which "Puritans used ... to

45

transform their thoughts into authoritative utterances proceeding from God."[38] Graham Ward, who also offers an analysis of *Grace Abounding* as a journal of reader development, suggests that Bunyan only gradually comes to recognize his own consciousness as separate from text.[39] While no doubt each of these readings reflects some aspect of the whole reality of Bunyan's engagement with text, when we give full acknowledgement to the vividness and concreteness of Bunyan's imagination and the excellence of his memory, the "problem" of the voiced scriptures seems less acute. Of the many critics who have re-marked upon the vividness and vocal quality of the scriptures which Bunyan recalls, Brainerd P. Stranahan is most perceptive. He suggests that Bunyan "developed the power to recall applicable Scriptures spontaneously in response to a particular requirement; he could also combine these passages into new imaginative wholes."[40]

What is impressive about Bunyan's relationship to the great text which dominates and ultimately shapes his mind is that although sentences from the Bible come to him, apparently unbidden, Bunyan is insistent upon "looking up" the text. He is profoundly disturbed when he cannot place texts into larger contexts. Despite, or perhaps because of, his intense attention to specific words or texts, it is the whole Word of God — over and above and through specific words — which he is most eager to hear.

While it is necessary to note the seriousness of Bunyan's approach to reading, we should not forget that pleasure is nonetheless an important motivator. Since he had, at first, been a reluctant reader, Bunyan is conscious of the need to motivate the reader. He never forgets the great pleasure of encountering biblical narrative for himself, and he makes every effort to create pleasure for the reader — even though he feels a need to apologize for doing so. He rests his difficult decision as to whether or not to publish *The Pilgrim's Progress* on the considera-tion that not to do so would be to rob people "[o]f that which would to them be great delight" ("Apology," *TPP* 2, line 22). By the time he is ready to "send forth" *The Pilgrim's Progress, Part 2*, he is more con-fident both of his ability and of his right to entertain his readers: "*Yea, they can't refrain / From smiling, if my* Pilgrim *be but by*" (*TPP* 2, 169, lines 24-28).

When one turns to Bunyan's sprightly writing after an encounter with the dry didacticism of other writers of the day, including even those who, like Arthur Dent or Richard Bernard, attempted to shape teaching as story, one meets at every turn the pleasure of Bunyan's distinctive narrative style. Even within his sermonic treatises, he brings life and colour to the didactic text with illustrative anecdotes or dialogues like the vigourous dialogue between God and the "fruitless professor" in *The Barren Fig-Tree* (*MW 5*, 50-55), or tightly written autobiographical passages like those in *The Doctrine of the Law and Grace* (*MW 2*, lines 156-60).

If pleasure is one motivator recognizable in Bunyan's reading and writing experience, mental or intellectual hunger is another. Bunyan's early reading in the Bible was driven, according to his account, by such a hunger: "[M]y mind ... lay like a Horseleach at the vein still crying out, *Give, give*" (*GA*, para. 42). Many, if not most, of Bunyan's first readers would have experienced just such an intellectual and spiritual hunger. It was intellectual as well as spiritual hunger that brought people flocking to hear the great preachers of the day. And it was this intellectual hunger they finally were able to satisfy through access to inexpensive print material like Bunyan's own works.

Fear or anxiety is yet another motivator which drove Bunyan to read, and which he, in turn, uses to motivate his readers, as both Iser and Haskin point out.[41] Bunyan's apologies address themselves implicitly to the readers' fears of failing to be among the elect, linking the reader's ability to respond to the stories with the assurance of effectual calling. In "To the Reader" of *Holy War*, Bunyan offers to deal with "things of greatest moment," (*HW*, 5, line 22) again alluding to the need of the reader to be sure of salvation. Even less subtly, he reminds the reader of potentially imminent death: "[F]are thee well / My next may be to ring thy Passing-Bell" (*HW*, 5, line 28). In prefacing his work with this dire warning in the best of the *memento mori* tradition, he follows seventeenth-century practice. Lewis Bayly's "To the Reader" in *The Practice of Pietie*, for example, enjoins holy speed-reading: "Yet reade it, and that speedily, lest before thou hast read it over, God (by some unexpected death) cut thee off...."[42] With death seen to be imminent and eternal destiny seen to be at stake in the understanding or misunderstanding of the words, reading would have been done with a kind of intensity and energy which late twentieth-century readers can scarcely imagine. If rightly to read *The Pilgrim's Progress* is to read it experientially and anxiously, knowing—or having known—the burden of conviction of sin and the reality of doing combat for eternal stakes with the enemy of one's soul, then the level of intensity with which Bunyan's "implied reader" approached his narratives may be greater than any modern reading for pleasure, curiosity, or scholarly analysis can fully recover.

In Bunyan's account of himself as a reader, he is candid about periods of time when he experiences severe reading disturbances or difficulties. Plagued by doubts and distracting thoughts, he confesses that sometimes, "I have neither known, nor regarded, nor remembred so much as the sentence that but now I have read" (*GA*, para. 106). Even after his period of faith-testing and his entry into more fruitful reading and study, Bunyan is honest about the variability of his subjective enjoyment of Scripture:

> I have sometimes seen more in a line of the Bible then I
> could well tell how to stand under, and yet at another time
> the whole Bible hath been to me as drie as a stick, or rather
> my heart hath been so dead and drie unto it, that I could
> not conceive the least dram of refreshment though I have
> lookt it all over!   (*GA*, Conclusion, 4)

His own awareness of the difficulties which may be encountered in reading keeps Bunyan sharply aware of the need of the reader to be prompted, reminded, and encouraged; now drawn forward by the story and now compelled to examine its meanings. For this kind of writer-to-reader guidance, the standard Renaissance dual text offered him a ready-made instrument: the margins allowing him to awaken, warn, nudge, encourage, and direct his readers; the narrative allowing him to draw the reader forward through the book to its conclusion.

All of this discussion of Bunyan as reader has far more than marginal significance for our discussion of Bunyan's use of margins to buttress, intensify, and amplify the narrative text of his great stories. It does not seem unreasonable to assume that Bunyan's intended reader would be one much like himself: highly motivated, deeply involved, seeing marginal notes offering biblical references to texts alluded to or embedded within the narrative as much more than dry, scholarly footnotes. Many of Bunyan's readers would have been able to see a reference in the margins and hear the corresponding scripture in memory, a text complete with context. What to the modern reader may appear to be only a tedious list of biblical references could well be, to such a reader, a "spangling" collection of truths, as, for example, the references to scriptures describing the eternal joy of the believer, (*TPP*, 13) truths to be remembered and ruminated over as a feast of good things like the feast enjoyed by the pilgrims in their stopover at Gaius' house (*TPP 2*, 259-65). Furthermore, the marginal notes were a continual reminder of an authorial presence. The reader is not alone in the act of interpretation. There is a guide coaching from the margins, a sort of analogue to the Holy Spirit on whose teaching the Protestant reader relied in reading Scripture.

Sacred words, even when merely alluded to, have extra weight and force and significance when reproduced in the reader's mind. By means of the biblical phrases embedded in the narrative text and marginal notes, Bunyan again and again summons all the resources of the Scripture-laden minds of his original readers to bear on the interpretation of his narratives.

CHAPTER 2

Bunyan's Margins:
The Received Convention

In order to discuss Bunyan's use of the margins, we must pay some attention to what can be known about the production of marginal notes in early modern texts and about the conventions which governed both the writing and reading of these annotations. I use "convention" in what Steven Mailloux typifies as the "widest application," referring to "shared practices" in the production and reception of literature.[1]

In this chapter, I will first seek to consider evidence for the authorial integrity of Bunyan's marginal notes, and then to look at antecedents for his use of notes within the genres and specific works of literature with which he was familiar. We will then look more particularly at a cluster of works which most certainly influenced his work, and finally draw some conclusions concerning the authorial choices which Bunyan exercised in creating the dual texts of his narratives.

I

The use of the margins for commentary additional to the main text was a fully established convention of printed books during Bunyan's time, a convention to which a number of recent studies have drawn attention, with Evelyn B. Tribble's *Margins and Marginality: The Printed Page in Early Modern England* providing the most comprehensive discussion. In spite of the attention suddenly being paid to marginal notes, the precise relationship between an author's manuscript and the printed version is difficult to reconstruct. Was the book design a result of a collaboration between author and printer? Or did the author have the primary voice in how his book would appear? Roger Sharrock, in his introduction to the definitive version of *The Pilgrim's Progress*, states: "Whether Bunyan was responsible for all the marginal glosses or only some of them seems impossible of determination"

(*TPP*, xxxiii). William Slights points out that marginal notes in Renaissance texts can be attributed to "commentators, scholarly annotators, translators, editors, printers, and authors."[2]

Lacking, as we do, any manuscript copies of Bunyan's works, we have to draw inferences from other evidence as to whether Bunyan was responsible for the notes to his works. While such inferential evidence can never be wholly conclusive, there are a number of valid reasons why it is reasonable to attribute the marginal notes in Bunyan's works to his pen, and to consider them a "significant ... aspect of Bunyan's semiotic art."[3]

There is considerable evidence to suggest that it may have been, in general, an author's decision rather than a printer's to present a central text accompanied by marginal notes in some cases and without marginal notes in others. A comparison of similar materials published by the same printer shows distinctions of style which must be attributed to the authors rather than to the printer. John Owen's and John Bunyan's works make a good case in point, since they were frequently published by the same printer, Nathaniel Ponder.

In Owen's works, as produced by Ponder, there is either an absence of marginal notes or an extremely sparing use of the margins. Owen's *Exercitations on the Book of Hebrews* (1668), which was Ponder's first entry in the Term Catalogues, is produced in folio with very wide margins which are quite remarkably empty. Despite Owen's erudition, for which the margins create a ready-made showcase, there are only a few citations from the ancients, an occasional Greek word, and some scriptural cross-references. The only consistent use made of the margins is to index the discussion by paragraph numbers. *A Brief Vindication of the Doctrine of the Trinity* (1669) is printed in a duodecimo format; here also, although perhaps more explicably in view of the small size of the pages, there are no marginal notes. Likewise, there are no marginal notes in *A Brief Vindication of the Nonconformists* (1680), although this book is in quarto and has large enough pages to have made marginal notes easy to add. This standard unannotated presentation of Owen's texts in a variety of page sizes suggests that the presence or absence of marginal notes were neither a function of page size nor of Ponder's printing style.

When Ponder, as the original publisher of *The Pilgrim's Progress*, *The Pilgrim's Progress, The Second Part*, and *The Life and Death of Mr. Badman*, presents Bunyan's narratives, marginal notes are always a part of the presentation of text, even though, after the first edition in small octavo, the format of the books is the pocket-size duodecimo.

Another example of a printer publishing similar materials in different formats is William Marshall, who publishes "at the Bible in Newgate Street." He also publishes works by both Owen and Bunyan, in 1692 bringing out Bunyan's *Works* as compiled by Charles Doe; in 1693, publishing Owen's *Two Discourses Concerning the Holy Spirit and His Work*. While both books are of a didactic religious nature, Owen's octavo has no marginal notes whatsoever; Bunyan's texts, in double-columned folio format, are accompanied with the marginal notes which had been a part of them in the earlier small-format editions.

Other indirect evidence that Bunyan himself, rather than a printer, is responsible for the marginal notes to his narratives can be derived from the similarity in presentation of his annotated narratives even when he changes publishers. Although *The Holy War* was published not by Ponder but by other London printers, Dorman Newman and Benjamin Alsop, the abundant use of marginal notes in *The Holy War* is similar to that in the works produced by Ponder.

Given that works by the same author produced by different printers take on the same form; given that, as we have noted, Ponder clearly did not feel obligated to produce marginal notes alongside religious texts; and given that page size is quite obviously not a deciding factor as to whether or not marginal notes are used, we can argue that marginal notes were printed if the author supplied them; that is, that they originated in the author's manuscript as received by the printer. A comparison of the first edition of *Some Gospel Truths Opened* (1656) with the reprint of it in Doe's *Works* (1692) shows that the marginal notes have been faithfully reprinted along with the central text, suggesting that the notes were seen as part of the work and not as extrinsic to it.

There are, of course, a number of Bunyan's works which are without marginal notes, works which Bunyan either felt did not need marginal notes or for which he did not take time to prepare marginal notes. *Grace Abounding*, printed for George Larkin, 1666, does not have marginal notes; neither do such didactic works as *Seasonable Counsel* (for Benjamin Alsop 1684), or *The Acceptable Sacrifice* (posthumously published by George Larkin, 1689). This last is particularly interesting because of a note by George Cokayn in "The Preface to the Reader," dated 21 September 1688, just a few weeks after Bunyan's death: "[T]his whole Book was not only *prepared* for, but also *put on the Press* by the Author himself, whom the Lord was pleased to Re-move ... before the sheets could be all *wrought off.*" This note suggests how closely involved Bunyan usually was in the production of his text.

Other comments made in printers' advertisements in a number of Bunyan's books would also support authorial responsibility for the marginal notes. In the printer's "advertisement" to the fourth edition of *The Pilgrim's Progress*, Nathaniel Ponder decries the tampering with notes in spurious editions of *The Pilgrim's Progress*: "*Thomas Bradyl* a Printer ... hath ... abominably and basely falcified the true Copie, and changed the Notes." Ponder, by implication, argues for the authorial integrity of the marginal notes in his editions.

A similar claim, by implication, for authorial responsibility for text can be seen in Ponder's request in *A Treatise of the Fear of God* (1679) that the reader should correct errors "occasioned by the Printer, by reason of the absence of the Author." This implicit assignment to the author of final responsibility also occurs in a note before the Printer's Errata in Bunyan's earlier work, *A Defence of the Doctrine of Justification by Faith* (1672), where the printer (in this case, Francis Smith) says, "Reader, thou art desired to mend these Errataes with thy Pen, and to bear with some mis-pointings that have hapned by reason of the Authors absence from the Press" (118). If even the correctness of the "pointings" were seen as the responsibility of the author, it seems reasonable to assume that marginal notes would certainly have been an author's responsibility as well.[4]

A parallel example from another Nonconformist writer of the period also suggests that it was usual for authors to write their own marginal notes. Richard Baxter explains his additions to the second edition of *The Saints Everlasting Rest* (1651), noting that the book had originally been written while he was sick, "distant from home, where I had no Book but my Bible and therefore could not add the concent of authors." This lack Baxter makes up in the second edition, explaining: " ... I have added many Marginal quotations, especially of the Ancients: which though some may conceive to be useless, and others to be meerly for vain ostentation; yet I conceived useful."[5]

In the light of available evidence, it seems reasonable that the privilege of the margin which Baxter claims was any author's privilege; that the responsibility for the work, down to the "pointings," was the author's responsibility; and that the text of Bunyan's narratives, complete with marginal notes and additions and corrections to the notes in at least the first several editions, can be attributed to Bunyan himself.

Although our evidence from production methods of the day is impressionistic and incomplete, the cumulative effect is quite convincing for placing with Bunyan, rather than with his printers or booksellers, the responsibility for the marginal notes to his texts. This impression is corroborated by contemporary testimony in Joseph Moxon's *Mechanick Exercises Applied to the Art of Printing* (1683).

Moxon states it as a "law" of the printing trade that "a Compositer is strictly to follow his Copy, viz. to observe and do just so much and no more than his Copy is to be his Rule and Authority." Although he goes on to allow for the compositor "to discern and amend the bad Spelling and Pointing of his Copy," creation of marginal notes would go far beyond the printer's responsibility. In fact, Moxon describes the compositor "looking a little over his *Copy*, to see how it pleases him ... viz. well or ill writ, if it be a *Written Copy*, or much *Italick, Latin*, or *Greek* or Marginal Notes ... for this he likes not in his *Copy*." It is not hard to imagine the mutterings of a compositor over a manuscript like one of Bunyan's.

In a closing "Advertisement to Authors," Moxon advises, "It behoves an Author to examine his *Copy* very well e're he deliver it to the *Printer*, and to Point it, and mark it so as the Compositer may know what word to *set* in Italick, English, Capitals, &c." Clearly, the primary responsibility for the text, including any accompanying marginal notes, lies with the author of the work. [6]

As convincing as external evidence for Bunyan's authorship of his marginal notes may be, internal evidence is even more compelling. Stylistic evidence points in the direction of Bunyan's authorship for many of the notes, certainly the most interesting ones. We can apply a stylistic test of Bunyan's own devising to the marginal notes. In the "Author's Way of Sending forth His Second Part of the Pilgrim," Bunyan instructs his book to define itself as his authentic work as distinct from any counterfeits by "*say[ing] out thy say / In thine own native Language, which no man / Now useth, nor with ease dissemble can*" (TPP 2, 168, lines 26-7). Many of the marginal notes in his narratives demonstrate the same sure command of idiom and proverb, of dramatic tension and preacherly admonition, that Bunyan demonstrates in the narrative text. Sharrock comments: "Some of these glosses are so colourless that they might very easily have been added by another hand;

others are very distinctly tinged with the Bunyan flavour" (*TPP*, lxxxiii).

Of course, the biblical references which form the great majority of the marginal notations could arguably have come from a hand other than Bunyan's. But given Bunyan's vast knowledge of the Bible and his reliance on "my Bible and Concordance" as "my only library in my writings," (*Solomon's Temple, MW* 7, 9) the greatest number of the multitudinous biblical references are best seen as Bunyan's own.[7] Even some of the errors which occur in the biblical references may serve to authenticate the marginal references as having come from a busy author's pen, Bunyan seeming frequently to rely on his memory rather than turning up the passage in his Bible or consulting his concordance. James F. Forrest comments, "Although his range of citation is astonishing, Bunyan not infrequently mistakes biblical chapter and verse," adding that it is one of the tasks of the modern editor to correct these erroneous references.[8]

Most telling of all in validating the claim that the marginal notes are Bunyan's are his own comments about the references in the margins of his works, and on marginal readings in other texts. These demonstrate that the margins were, for Bunyan, part of the communication, whether he was reading or writing. In *The Life and Death of Mr.Badman*, Bunyan has Mr. Wiseman comment on *"the breaking of Mr. Badmans legg"* as "an open stroak" of judgment: "And it looks much like to that in *Job; … He striketh them as wicked men in the open sight of others:* Or as the Margent reads it, *in the place of beholders"* (*Mr. B*, 134).[9] In offering an alternative marginal reading as part of the scriptural quotation, Bunyan grants an insight into the significance of marginal readings to readers of the sacred text, and, by extension, to writers and readers of religious texts. Not only does he read the marginal note as a significant addition to the meaning of the primary text; but also, "the Margent reads [the text]," that is, the marginal note engages the primary text in an interpretive exchange.

In *A Holy Life* (1684), Bunyan indicates the importance he gives to the marginal biblical references adjacent to his own texts, telling the reader to, "See these Scriptures in the Margent, and take heed" (*MW* 9, 304). This direct command to the reader suggests the conscious deliberation with which Bunyan penned the references in the margins; it is also clear that, in this case, Bunyan wrote the marginal references at the same time as the central text, with the clear intention that his

reader should either recognize or take the trouble to become acquainted with the texts noted.

Finally, in the prologues to several of his narratives, we find direct
statements by Bunyan which describe the marginal notes and the relationship he intends them to bear to the reading of the story. In "The
Author to the Reader" of *The Life and Death of Mr.Badman*, Bunyan defines his terms of reference for a particular marginal device, the "fist"
or "sign manual":

> All which are things either fully known by
> me, as being eye and ear witness thereto, or
> that I have received from such hands, whose
> relation as to this, I am bound to believe.
> And that the Reader may know them from
> other things and passages herein contained,
> I have pointed at them in the Margent, as
> ☞ with a finger thus. (*Mr. B*, 4)

Bunyan makes reference to the marginal notes as answers to riddles, and hence as explanations of the allegory, in "The Apology"
prefacing *The Pilgrim's Progress*: "*Would'st thou read Riddles, and their
Explanation … ?*" (*TPP*, 7, line 14); and in "The Sending Forth" of *The
Pilgrim's Progress, The Second Part*: "*Those Riddles that lie couch't within
thy breast/ Freely propound, expound*" (*TPP 2*, 173, lines 24-25). The invitation to make use of the marginal notes becomes a command in "The
Conclusion" to *The Pilgrim's Progress* where the reader is instructed,
"*Put by the Curtains, look within my Vail;/Turn up my Metaphors and do
not fail*" (*TPP*, 164, lines 13-14). It is in his preface to the *The Holy War*,
however, that Bunyan expresses most clearly his intention that the
marginal notes should guide the interpretation of the allegory: "*Nor
do thou go to work without my Key / It lies there in the window, fare thee
well*" (*HW*, lines 33-37).

In order to preclude any debate over where the key to Bunyan's
riddles might lie, "window" is glossed with a marginal note of its
own: "The margent." There can be little doubt therefore that Bunyan
wrote his own marginal notes and intended them to be an integral
part of his narratives.

We might even, at this point, hazard a conjectural reconstruction
of Bunyan at work on his stories. He describes the sudden creative
flow of words that became *The Pilgrim's Progress*:

> *Thus I set Pen to Paper with delight,*
> *And quickly had my thoughts in black and white.*
> *For having now my Method by the end;*
> *Still as I pull'd, it came; and so I penn'd*
> *It down, until it came at last to be*
> *For length and breadth the bigness which you see.*
>
> *(TPP, 1-2, lines 29 ff.)*

Bunyan may possibly have interrupted this wonderful outflow of the story long enough to jot an occasional biblical reference, probably drawn from memory, in a margin. Then would come the rewriting process to which Bunyan refers in *The Holy City*, where he reflects on method: "(first with doing and then with undoing, and after that with doing again) I thus did finish it" (*MW 3*, line 70). This would probably have included making revisions on his first draft ("undoing") and then the preparation of copy for the printer by a complete rewriting on fresh sheets ("doing again"). During this revising and rewriting process, the explanatory marginal notes and the majority of Bible references would likely have been written in. Gaining an increasing distance from the text, Bunyan would probably have finally sat down and read the text as its first reader, now serving as an intermediary between the text and the reader, adding asides and clarifying notes as well as indexing his story by means of headings and summaries.[10] Further minor corrections may have been made during the reading of the "proofs" pulled from the press, although Moxon warns that the compositor "cannot reasonably be expected ... [to] be so good natured to take much pains to mend such Alterations as the second Dictates of an Author may make."[11] Before the work went back to press for each new edition, the author had opportunity to revise his text and, as is evident from succeeding editions of *The Pilgrim's Progress*, to continue to add to the marginalia.[12] An author's additions and corrections were often proudly proclaimed by the publisher on title pages of editions after the first.

II

In supplying marginal notes, Bunyan is choosing to use, and adapting to his artistic and didactic purposes, an established convention of books of his time. Recent studies by social and cultural historians have greatly increased our understanding of Bunyan's literary milieu. Bunyan writes within an established tradition of the production and reception of religious texts. This awareness does not, however, force us to accept the accusation that Bunyan purposely conceals the breadth of his reading in order to claim a greater degree of spiritual authority for his writing. William York Tindall's tone is characteristically sarcastic when he says:

> To maintain his professional repute and the legend of his gift, John Bunyan wisely announced the literary aid of the Holy Ghost and concealed by silence and the boast of illiteracy the carnal sources of his work.... Reason and history compel us to ascribe the literary pretensions of John Bunyan to prudence and policy.[13]

But Bunyan's works reveal quite clearly all of his seminal sources. What he scants or does not mention he considers to be either irrelevant to, or clearly understood by, his readers. For example, he says little about the romances and ballads he read before his conversion, apparently considering them to be irrelevant to the serious business of salvation. Nor does he list the titles of Nonconformist sermons or pamphlets which he is certain to have read. He takes for granted such religious reading when it runs parallel to his own thinking, and takes up his pen in vigorous polemic when it does not. He is neither more nor less meticulous than most late Renaissance writers about acknowledging literary borrowings.

As to his stated dependence upon his Bible and concordance, Bunyan is saying little more than that he studied the Bible at first hand. He makes such statements with a Nonconformist's self-consciousness about lacking formal education, something about which people outside of the academy felt keenly. Even that "man of letters," Richard Baxter, is very sensitive about lacking a university degree, writing, "In the Youth of my Ministry Pride made me often blush with shame for want of academical degrees."[14] In claiming only his Bible and his concordance as his sources, Bunyan is also sensitive about the less-than-scholarly contents of his marginal notes. He does not, as do many other seventeenth-century writers, place citations from the early church fathers or from the classical writers in the margins. Nor are his margins adorned with Latin and Greek sentences, as are those of many learned writers of his day. Perhaps his gloss,"The Lattine I borrowe," (*TPP* 2, 229) is a good-humoured parody of the prodigious Latin quotations in the marginal notes of many of his contemporaries, as well as a self-deprecating comment on his own lack of classical languages.

Bunyan's use of the convention of marginal notes evokes a particular reading attitude in his readers. Marginal notes call for attitudes towards reading usually associated with the reading of religious treatises and the Bible. These conventional attitudes would include the expectation of edification, the intention of application of what is learned to one's own life, and the mental attitude of seriousness and attentiveness, not only to the central text but also to the intertext summoned by the marginal notes.

III

With Bunyan one can look rather precisely at the works he had read to see how he takes up the convention of marginal notes from sources available to him, and transforms them for the purposes of his highly interactive narrative texts. In the study which follows, an attempt has been made to look at the specific works Bunyan names as having read, as well as other works representative of the kinds of materials he must have encountered. My concern, somewhat different from most studies of sources which tend to seek for links between ideas, themes, or modes of expression, is to understand the convention of marginal notes as represented in these works. For, however unconsciously Bunyan may have assimilated them, the works he read gave him the format and style he chose to use in his narrative works. In *The Holy War* Bunyan describes Diabolus' attack on Mansoul by means of Mr. Filth who orders "an odious, nasty, lascivious piece of beastliness to be drawn up in writing" (*HW*, 31). This piece of beastliness Bunyan glosses in the margin as:

> Odious
> Atheistical
> Pamphlets and
> filthy Ballads
> & Romances full of baldry.

This marginal note could be taken as a summary statement of Bunyan's pre-conversion reading habits viewed from the point of view of his post-conversion attitude toward such reading matter. There is no doubt that in naming such specific works as "George on Horseback" or "Bevis of Southampton," (*MW 1*, line 333) Bunyan is merely gesturing towards the entire genre which each represents as it was available to "the unlettered reader of the seventeenth century, who had 2d or 3d to spend."[15] As Spufford shows, a newly literate reading public in the seventeenth century had access to a wide range of inexpensive reading materials—some of it scurrilous—in the form of broadsheets and chap-books.[16]

Whatever Bunyan may have taken from these works in terms of lions or giants or dragons or merely the pleasure of ongoing adventure tales, it is not from these "penny merries" that he learned how to create the dual text of narrative plus margins. In them there are no margins to spare, with the print running out to the edges of the pages (probably as a matter of thrift), the stories told without marginal commentary.

Bunyan's conversion is both through and to religious reading. Indeed, in Spufford's terms of reference, Bunyan's conversion can be seen to have been one from "penny merries" to "penny godlies."[17] He himself marks the beginning of his personal conversion with the reading of the religious books which were his wife's dowry. But, of course, there are some kinds of popular religious literature that were familiar to Bunyan, perhaps from as far back as his childhood. From echoes in his work it is apparent that Bunyan knew hymn-books, the metrical Psalms of Sternhold and Hopkins, the Geneva Bible, and the Book of Common Prayer. But apart from the richly annotated Bible, these would not have affected his chosen format of text plus marginal notes.

There is also no doubt that Bunyan was fully familiar with the emblem genre. Francis Quarles' *Emblemes, Divine and Moral* (1643) was published while Bunyan was a youth. As has long been recognized within Bunyan criticism, Bunyan assimilated the emblem form into his narratives, particularly in scenes like the House of the Interpreter and House Beautiful (*TPP*) and Gaius' Inn (*TPP 2*).[18] The emblem form did influence Bunyan's marginalia, not because emblems were themselves annotated, but because elements of the form were readily adaptable to marginalia. Marginal notes could "emblematize" an item in the narrative, drawing attention to its specifically emblematic character, as does the note to the *"Golden Anchor"* (*TPP 2*, 233). They could function as emblem titles, as does a note which titles a speech by Incredulity as "The true picture of unbelief" (*HW*, 48). Or they could function in a way similar to the epigrams of the emblem books, as do many didactic generalizations; a typical example would be, "There is no perswasion will do, if God openeth not the eyes" (*TPP*, 39). In Chapter 4 we will give fuller discussion to the relationship of marginal notes and emblematic passages of narrative.

Bunyan's early religious reading also included the very popular *A Plaine and Familiar Exposition of the Ten Commandements* by John Dod and Robert Cleaver (1604), to which he makes an approving marginal reference in his own *The Doctrine of the Law and Grace Unfolded* (1659): *If thou would-est have a more full discourse hereof, read Dod upon the Commandments* (*MW* 2, 35).

Dod's work went through nineteen editions up to 1635, most of which seem to have followed the original presentation in quarto with extensive marginal notes including doctrinal statements, appropriately headed, "*Doctrine*"; adages such as, "Men must bee just, before they can bee mercifull"; directives such as, "Lust should be slaine in the conception"; and rubrics such as, "Markes to know whether we love God or no."[19] These are just the kind of marginal notes that come readily to Bunyan's hand when he writes.

Bunyan also read "judgement books" of various kinds, probably both before and after his conversion. He tells of the depressing effect of "that dreadful story of that miserable mortal, Francis Spira" (*GA*, para. 163). This cautionary tale he would have encountered in Nathaniel Bacon's *A Relation of the Fearful Estate of Francis Spira, in the Year 1548*. The 1665 edition of this book is not marginally annotated. Later, Bunyan draws on Samuel Clarke's *A Looking Glass for Saints and Sinners* (1671), dutifully citing his source by chapter and number in the margins of *The Life and Death of Mr. Badman*. Precise citation was made easy by Clarke's use of narrow-ruled margins in which his case-studies were numbered sequentially within each chapter.

Like all Puritan readers of his time, Bunyan must have read sermons, quite possibly including *The Workes of Thomas Adams* (1629).[20] Thomas Adams' *Workes* will, at any rate, serve as an example of sermons in print. Printed with ruled margins, Adams' sermons have marginal notes which index main headings in the sermon, supply scriptural references for quotations or allusions, and add quotations in the classical languages. In the famous sermon, "The White Devill," a marginal note offers a rubric, "Three theeves well met," which could as well title a play or a fairy tale as index to a sermonic text. In this text, the personification turns a small sketch into vivid allegory:

Three theeves well met   Thus the pot robs him of his wit, he robs himselfe of grace, and the Victualler robs him of his money. This theft might yet be borne: but the Common- wealth is here robbed too. Drunkenesse makes so quicke riddance of the Ale, that this raiseth the price of Mault; and the good sale of Mault, raiseth the price of Barley: thus is the Land distressed, the poores bread is dissolved into the drunkards cup....[21]

Similar active, dramatic rubrics occur frequently in Bunyan's mar- ginal notes.

Seventeenth-century sermons are not, by and large, accompanied by luxuriant marginal notes. In her study of English printers in the seventeenth century, Leona Rostenberg credits Puritan printer Mi- chael Sparke (fl. 1616-53) with the popularization of the printed ser- mon. "Through Sparke the oral sermon became the printed word. His bleak and unadorned quartos circulated among the people, awaken[ing] them to political and social issues."[22] However the style was set, there is no doubt that the sermon was a highly popular form of reading, and that its print format was therefore very familiar. For Bunyan, it was also a writing form which came easily to hand. When he writes his expanded sermons as treatises, he observes the decorum set by preachers and printers before him, with few marginal notes ex- cept for headings which index the work and, of course, references for biblical quotations.

Tindall and others who have followed his lead in researching Bunyan's sources are quite right in assuming that Bunyan had a wide reading knowledge of the literature of religious debate and polemic to which he adds his own titles.[23] In general, much of the literature of re- ligious controversy seems to be somewhat sparing in the use of mar- ginal notes, relying on notes mostly for indexing the contents of a work or for cross-referencing to another work, for annotating (and thus claiming spiritual authority), and occasionally for adding an afterthought.

The haste in which most of the diatribes were written may have something to do with the paucity of margination. Fowler's octavo volume *The Design of Christianity* (1671) produced a vehement re- sponse in the form of Bunyan's *A Defence of the Doctrine of Justification by Faith* (1672). Bunyan's response was a hasty work. The "Premoni- tion to the Reader" is dated "From Prison, the 27th of the 12th month, 1671." In his further preface, an open letter to Edward Fowler, he writes, "Sir — Having heard of your Book ... I was desirous of a view thereof.... But I could not obtain it till the 13th of this 11th month" (B-2). Bunyan apparently read and responded to Fowler's book within approximately six weeks; the text of his hurried response is nearly devoid of marginal notes. There are some scriptural references and occasional page references to Fowler's book, but there are no comments or additional comments made in the margins. This lack of margination in a work so swiftly written may bear out my conjecture that most marginal notes were added as a manuscript was being revised. A manuscript such as *Defence* would not have received the re-reading and re-writing that went into major endeavours such as Bunyan's narratives, and therefore shows only the kind of marginal notes which Bunyan might have written alongside a first writing.

In another religious controversy, Bunyan tangled with fellow-Baptists. With the publication of *Confession of Faith, and a Reason for my Practice* (1672), he fell out of favour with the stricter Baptists. His further statement of openness on the matter, *Difference in Judgment about Water-Baptism no Bar to Communion* (1673), provoked a sharp response from Henry D'Anvers in *A Treatise of Baptism And A Brief Answer to Mr. Bunyan* (1673). Bunyan responded to this and other retorts from former friends and associates among the strict Baptists by affirming *Peaceable Principles and True* (1674). Using D'Anvers work as representative of this exchange, we find his margins used almost exclusively for identifying sources, ranging from early church fathers to contemporaries like "Drs. Hammond and Taylor," "Dr. Usher," and "Mr. Bax." The margin as a place of claiming authority is evident; in this use Bunyan becomes proficient, his biblical references serving not only to annotate but also to grant authority to his text.

Bunyan is known to have read some works by the Ranters (*GA*, para. 44) — and to have found them nearly as puzzling as might a modern reader. Some Ranter writings have bare margins or very few marginal notes.[24] Others make extravagant and dramatic use of marginal notes. Abiezer Coppe, in *Some Sweet Sips, of some Spirituall Wine* (1649), adds an appendix titled "An Additional and Preambular Hint, — As a general Epistle written by ABC" with a double column of marginal notes, one giving general biblical references keyed to the main text with alphabetical index letters, the other providing a detailed and graphically illustrated commentary which reads very much like mystical poetry. In *A Fiery Flying Roll* (1649), Abiezer Coppe uses the margins as a place of ironic humour and enigma. His account of having received divine instruction to go to London to utter his prophecies is accompanied by this marginal notation:

> *It not being shewen to me, what I should do, more than preach and print something, &c. very little expecting I should be so strangely acted, as to (my exceeding joy and delight) I have been, though to the utter cracking of my credit, and to the rotting of my old name which is damned, and cast out (as a toad to the dunghill) that I might have a new name, with me, upon me, within me, which is, I am—
> — _.[25]

The ending of this marginal note with the enigmatic "I am" might be read as Ranter blasphemy, the author assuming the most holy of all God's names, or merely as an unfinished sentence, a sort of fill-in-the-blank game for the reader. At any rate, the gamesomeness of such a marginal note demonstrates in an extreme form the play potential of the margins, a potential which Bunyan discovers and puts to good use, if in a more chaste style.

Bunyan's mention of "the errors of the Quakers" (*GA*, para. 123-4) tells us that he read pamphlets by this sect as well, both before and after his conversion. Many of the Quaker works have the same kind of sparseness that marked their other habits of life. They do not have the luxuriant, idiosyncratic notes written by some of the Ranters. George Foxe's books and pamphlets typically have no marginal notes; his *Journal*, edited and published posthumously, is indexed sparsely by means of marginal notes which merely identify the geographic location of the events described. William Penn, credited with the editing of Foxe's *Journal*, indulges in few marginal notes in his pamphlet *The Sandy Foundation Shaken* (1668), a work cited in an appendix to Bunyan's response to Fowler. Of Quaker writings, we know that Bunyan also read Edward Burrough, *Truth Defended* and *The True Faith of the Gospel of Peace Contended For* (both 1656), and responded with *Some Gospel Truths Opened* (1656) and *A Vindication of the Book Called, Some Gospel-Truths Opened* (1657). Whatever Bunyan may have learned from Burrough about religious polemic, he did not borrow from him the convention of marginal notes. Burrough's little booklets, apparently very cheaply produced, are printed edge to edge on very full pages. Sportingly enough, Bunyan's responses also have very bare margins; the second response uses a few marginal notes for emphatic comments to the reader: *"Here my words are corrupted"* (173), or *"*here is another of his false accusations of me"* (*Vindication, MW* 1, 174).

The trial scenes in both the Vanity Fair story in *The Pilgrim's Progress* and *The Holy War* may possibly owe a debt to Richard Bernard's *Isle of Man* (1641), but it must be remembered that there was a whole sub-genre of courtroom scenes published during the Renaissance, and also that Bunyan's first-hand experience in the English courts may have supplied all the antecedents he needed. At any rate, Bernard's margins serve only an indexing or referring function. Even if James Blanton Wharey was right when he observed of Bernard's *Isle of Man* that, "It is highly probable that Bunyan was familiar with this little book, and that he was induced by it to write his second great allegory,"[26] this book would have had little effect in Bunyan's developing sense of how and when to use marginal notes as a part of his story-telling art.

Tindall insists that Bunyan "found encouragement and possibly material for *The Holy War* in two allegories of spiritual conflict by Benjamin Keach, *War with the Devil* (1673) and *The Glorious Lover* (1679), and considers that Bunyan imitated Milton's *Paradise Lost* "at either first or second hand."[27] But Keach's *The War with the Devil* is a dialogue in rhyme rather than an allegory; it bears a much greater resemblance to Dent's *The Plaine Man's Pathway* than to anything written by Bunyan, and while it might have suggested dialogue as a form, it is less certain as an influence than Dent's work. As for *The Glorious Lover*, this long allegorical poem in rhymed couplets has little in common with either *Paradise Lost* or *The Holy War*. The scenes of consultation in Heaven and in Hell which all three works share are probably more reasonably traced to a common sermonic tradition than from one literary work of nearly the same time period to another. Bunyan was certainly not the sort of reader Milton had in mind when he dictated his lines for "a fit audience though few." And there is no compelling reason to assume either that Keach had read Milton or that Bunyan had read Keach. At any rate, Keach is representative of the same literary culture as Bunyan, and their works — margins and all — are evidence of shared literary antecedents and impulses rather than traces of direct but unacknowledged influence.

On even slighter evidence, Tindall claims that Bunyan had read Hobbes' *Leviathan* (1651), claiming as "a hitherto unnoticed allusion" to *Leviathan* Bunyan's claim in *Justification by Faith*, to have "broken the head of your Leviathan."[28] Bunyan's use of the term is much more likely to have been derived from the Bible than from Hobbes' work.[29] Should he have had opportunity to look into it, he would have found *Leviathan* to be an excellent model for the use of summarizing and indexing marginal notes, these being provided consistently throughout the folio volume. However, given that Hobbes' work was widely refuted by Nonconformist writers, Bunyan may have known it, if at all, only by reputation.

IV

There was certainly no scarcity of models for Bunyan's use of margins, especially in religious literature of his day. But however wide we draw the circle of Bunyan's reading, and however pervasive we find the convention of marginal notes accompanying central texts, we will probably still draw our most important conclusions concerning Bunyan's precedents when we focus on the five works which dominated his mental and spiritual formation as an adult: Dent's *A Plaine Mans Pathway to Heaven*; Bayly's *The Practice of Pietie*; Luther's *Commentary on Galatians*; Foxe's *Book of Martyrs*; and, of course, the Bible. To these we now turn.

In *Grace Abounding*, as we have seen, Bunyan names the two religious books which comprised Bunyan's wife's dowry and initiated him into serious spiritual reading. An examination of the marginal notes in each of these works brings us close to actual precedents for the textual format which Bunyan later elects for his narratives. Both Bayly's and Dent's works were immensely popular religious books; between them, they set the style for popular religious writing in the period of Bunyan's formation as a writer.

Dent's *A Plaine Man's Pathway to Heaven* (which went through some twenty-seven editions between 1601 and 1684) has some marginal notes offering biblical references; citations for quotations embedded in text, usually from the church fathers; and titles of lists in the text, such as "Six common oaths" (125), "Nine signs of a sound soul" (202), "St. Peters Eight signes of Salvation" (203), "Six great dangers in sin" (299), and "Nine profitable considerations" (302). There are a few comments to the reader, such as, "Note how God in all ages hath punished the breakers of his law" (300), and asides to the reader such as, "This is most mens case" (303).[30] In general, however, the use of marginal notations in this book is quite sparse. When, later, Bunyan adopts the convention of notes, he does it with considerable While

While notes occur frequently in his margins, they are never extensive or luxuriant (as they are, say, in Baxter's works, where they often dominate a page); perhaps he learned the grace of sparseness in the margins from such works as Dent's.

Bayly's *The Practice of Pietie*, another sturdily popular religious book reprinted in forty-two editions from 1612 to 1695, is somewhat more profuse in its use of marginal notes.[31] The marginal notes are linked to the central text by miniature lower-case letters in super-script, as are the notes to the early editions of *The Pilgrim's Progress*. Bayly's notes are frequently Latin quotations or Greek transcriptions and explanations, suggesting that the audience addressed by the margins is more learned than is the audience of the central text. In some notes, the reader is offered bibliographic references. For assistance in explicating the meanings of the various names of God, for instance, the reader is advised, "See Master Wilson's Dictionary of the Bible, most profitable for this purpose" (46). Sometimes the margins perform the same function as scholarly footnotes do today, as when Bayly states that his analysis about the age of the world is: "After Mr. *Robert Pont* his computation. Treatise of the last decaying age of the world, published, Ann. Dom. 1600. *Robert Pont* Treatise of the last age, page. 17" (414).

The reader of Bayly's book is also offered explanatory notes about everything from biblical geography (131) to theology (601-02). The margins include asides to the reader, such as, "This place, well urged, had grinded *Arius* in pieces,"(28) and, "Papists dare not deny this" (758). An indexing function is served with such notes as, "The damned soules Apostrophe to her body at their second meeting,"(92) contrasted to "The elect Soules Apostrophe to her body at her first meeting in the Resurrection"(127). Bayly offers biblical references, usually to buttress or support the teaching he is offering rather than merely to annotate quotations. And while his tone is usually that of the cool cleric, when he becomes really exercised—as in recounting the story of the two fires in the godless town of Teverton, he places a dramatic summary in the margin:

> Whilest the Preachers cryed in the Church, prophanenesse, profanenesse, *Gain* would not suffer them to heare: there-fore when they cryed fire, fire in the street, God would not suffer any to helpe (433).

This marginal note operates as a miniature narrative, complete with direct speech in a formal choral form, and a cast of characters including collectively-presented preachers and the allegorical character of "Gain."

Luther's *Commentary on Galatians* (1545, trans. 1575) is another book in which the convention of marginal notes is a very significant feature. Since this book was highly influential in Bunyan's spiritual quest and intellectual development, it is of particular interest. Assuming a 1644 edition (admittedly rather later than the one which Bunyan read so raptly) to be representative of the seventeenth-century presentation of this work, a number of observations are of interest to our discussion. For one thing, the marginal notes to Luther's *Commentary* are not the work of the original author, but rather, as in the Authorized Version of the Bible, are the interpretive and explanatory notes of the translators, identified only as "certaine godly learned men [who] refuse to be named, seeking neither their own gaine nor glory."[32]

These "godly learned men" operate as mediators between Luther's translated text and the reader. They offer explanations of unusual words in the text, as, for example, "The *Alcoran* is a book containing the *Turks* religion..."(Fol. 16). They explain a difficult—and for Bunyan, highly important—figure of speech, *prosopopoeia*, explaining it as "a figure, whereby things that have no life are fained personally to speak, or to be spoken to"(Fol. 184 a.v.). Such explanatory notes indicate that the assumed audience of the marginal notes is not erudite, but rather the common reader in need of further simplification of the text. This is an important difference between the marginal notes in this work and Bayly's. The model of addressing the common reader in the margins is one which Bunyan follows.

The teaching of the central text is summarized in pithy adages such as, "The Divell troubleth not those that are dead and biried in sin, but those that are godly and hate sinne;"(Fol. 2 a.v.) or, "Christian righteousness not wrought by us, but wrought in us"(Fol. 7). Here, too, one occasionally finds a miniature drama: "Sin and conscience, two fiends vexing and tormenting us;"(Fol. 15) or visualization: "Christian divinity beginneth at Christ lying in the lap of the Virgin Mary"(Fol. 17 a.v.). This is the kind of precisely drawn miniature or drama Bunyan later uses to good effect in his margins.

Since the voice in the margins is entirely different from the authorial voice of the central text, the marginal notes in Luther's *Commentary* continuously modify the text. Luther writes, for instance, "We are contented to eat the same meats that they eat, we will keep their feasts and fasting daies, so that they will suffer us to do the same with a free conscience." The translators comment, not a little condescendingly: "Luther was content in the time of blindnes to beare with those things which now in the light of the Gospell are utterly to be rejected" (Fol. 47 a.v.).

Luther's text with marginal notes is significantly different from the text without marginal notes; the somewhat condescending English voice in the margin directs the reader's response and earnestly contends, if not for the faith itself, at least for the most Puritan and English expression of it. The voice of the translators in the margins also makes direct application of Luther's words. Asides and warnings are directed to the reader: "See what we fall into when we neglect this doctrine..."(Fol. 8). Where the text is specifically directed to the "Germanes," the translators appropriate it for their English audience. For example, Luther writes,

> when the light of the Gospell, after so great darkness of mens traditions began to appeare, many were zealously bent to godliness: they heard Sermons greedily and had the Ministers of God's word in reverence. But now ... many which before seemed to be earnest disciples, are become plain hogs and belly-gods.... (Fol. 27)

The translators make a direct application in the margins to their English audience: "This may well be said of us Englishmen, for our heart is soon cooled, and that may appear by our cold proceedings at this day"(Fol. 27). When one considers the urgent personal motivation with which Bunyan came to the text of Luther's *Commentary*, one can imagine how he read it, text and margins, margins and text, with a kind of zeal which would have endeared him both to Luther and to the translators. What he found there, along with spiritual reassurance, was yet another way of using marginal notes: as a place for a voice mediating the text to the reader. In such a mediating voice, he would use his margins to interpret, explain, expand, and apply his allegorical narratives.

Bunyan found comfort in counting himself among the faithful witnesses whose stories are told in Foxe's *Actes and Monuments of the Christian Martyrs* (Latin 1554, trans. 1563), a book which he reportedly had with him in prison.[33] The narrative of religious persecution gave an inverse form of consolation to suffering Nonconformists, making this massive work immensely popular, with expanded editions appearing in 1570, 1576, and 1583. Telling, as it does, stories of Christian martyrs from the first century to the sixteenth, this work became, next to the Bible, a staple of Protestant family reading with editions appearing throughout the seventeenth century. While admittedly this monumental work lies outside the reach of Spufford's study of "penny books"available to the poor, it really is hard to talk, as she does, about "the nature of the world of imagination ... opened to the unlettered reader of the seventeenth century,"[34] without taking into account the influence of Foxe's *Book of Martyrs* and the Bible.[35]

Foxe's *Book of Martyrs* is central to Bunyan's works. For Bunyan and the many like him who were part of a persecuted church, reading this work placed suffering and exclusion in a context that extended to the earliest days of the church. Nonconformists were a minority, marginal in the society in which they lived. Through the *Book of Martyrs* they were offered an identity, a way of belonging to something great and heroic. For Bunyan, there were themes here that could suffuse twelve years of imprisonment with a sense of sharing in the long life of the faithful and suffering church. Foxe would be just the thing for a man who could imagine himself dying for his faith,

> mak[ing] a scrabling shift to clamber up the Ladder.... with the Rope about my neck; onely this was some encouragement to me, I thought I might now have an opportunity to speak my last words to a multitude which I thought would come to see me die.... (GA paras. 334-35)

The impact of Foxe's *Book of Martyrs* on Bunyan's narrative style would bear careful study; doubtless it is a more immediate and influential source for his writing style than *Bevis of Southampton*. And he would have read these stories of heroic martyrdom, margins and all. The margins are an impressive aspect of this huge work, indexing the pages of dense black letter print with the names of the martyr whose story is being told. Sometimes, what is most noticeable is the tone of the voice in the marginal notes. For example, at the beginning of Volume III, before continuing with stories of post-Reformation martyrs, a complete English text of the Mass is annotated with marginal notes in a particularly biting and sarcastic tone. Of the instructions in the Mass, "... here may the priest commend all his friends to God," the gloss asks "And why not his enemies also?"(III, 3). The same tone is heard in the margins when the mass-book text instructs, "Here let him hold two pieces in his left hand and the third piece in the right hand upon the brink of the chalice, saying this with open voice: World without end." The sarcastic voice in the margin comments: "It is time to speak at last, for he hath gone a mumming all this while"(III, 5).

In the narrative, too, or alongside inserted documents such as letters or the texts of sermons, the marginal notes "speak" to the reader outside of the voice of the narrative text, supplying additional information, and sometimes building anticipation. Adjacent to the story of the martyrdom of Thomas Cranmer, Archbishop of Canterbury, for example, the margins supply this word concerning a monk mentioned in Cranmer's "Letter of Purgation ... against certain slanders": "This Monke was Doctor Thronton, a cruell murtherer of Gods people, of whose horrible end ye shall reade hereafter ..."(III, 94).

V

After examining the format and the use of marginal notes in seventeenth-century literature which most certainly influenced Bunyan's own work, we still must acknowledge that the overwhelming influence on his work was the Bible, and the Bible in the format familiar to a late seventeenth-century English commoner. While the format of the pages of his narratives is not nearly so dense as the double-columned heavily annotated biblical page, the concept of marginal notes in interaction with the text would be endlessly reinforced by Bunyan's study of the Bible. In the first edition to *The Pilgrim's Progress*, the marginal notes are actually identified with a precise point in the narrative text by means of diminutive letters, "a," "b," "c," and so on, in what appears to be an imitation of the method of linking interpretive notes to precise points within the biblical text.

It is evident that Bunyan used the Authorized King James Version of 1611 for his adult reading, given the overwhelming preponderance of quotations from that version. His acquaintance with the Geneva Bible, probably the Bible of his childhood, is clear from occasional distinctive quotations from it.[36] In a prefatory essay to a facsimile edition of the 1560 Geneva Bible (1969), Lloyd Berry says, "The single most important feature of the Geneva Bible consisted in the marginal notes."[37] These notes became much more Calvinistic in flavour when the notes by Laurence Tomson were added to later editions, along with the Junius notes to the Revelation. The Geneva Bible was much loved by the English Protestants, especially because of these interpretive notes. "When the version was disappearing, they complained that they 'could not see into the sense of Scripture for lack of the spectacles of these Genevan annotations.'"[38]

This image of the marginal notes as "spectacles" is of particular interest to our study, suggesting as it does the way in which the original readers of seventeenth-century texts "saw" marginal notes—or rather, "saw through" marginal notes to the main text. It also reminds us that marginal notes were not mere accessories to text. Bunyan's marginal notes may seem irrelevant or distracting to some twentieth-century readers, but to his original, intended audience, they were a means to understanding, a way of "seeing into" his text.

The Tomson and Junius notes were added to the Authorized Version in a 1642 edition, meaning that Bunyan undoubtedly had the best of two worlds from an English Calvinist point of view: the new translation with its excellent translation notes, together with Tomson's stoutly Calvinistic interpretive notes. This annotated edition of the Bible presents the reader with a dense and complex text which invites active, involved reading and virtually precludes passive or casual reading. The complexity of the text compels the reader to engage in study. Evidence that Bunyan used this particular edition of the Bible may be found in his mention of marginal readings of the Scripture which exactly conform to Tomson's notes. For example, "*David* was called a man after Gods own heart; to wit, because he served his own generation, by the will of God, or as the Margent reads it, after he had in his own age served the will of God," (*Holy Life*, *MW 9*, 316), Bunyan here quoting precisely the Tomson note accompanying Acts 13:36.[39]

In the annotated 1642 Bible, the notes to the main biblical text are of several kinds. First, there are the "translatours notes" which are a standard part of the Authorized Version. Variant readings are indicated within the text and in the margins with distinctive printer's marks: daggers indicating Hebrew equivalents; vertical parallel bars indicating alternative translations. The translators defend their notes in the preface, "The Translatour to the Reader," itself a document accompanied by marginal notes. The marginal note which summarizes their defence begins, "Reasons moving us to set diversity of senses in the margine," and in the text, the translators ask the reader, "[D]oth not a margine do well, to admonish the Reader to seek further, and not to conclude or dogmatize upon this or that peremptorily?"[40]

The translators are clearly aware that marginal notes offering variant readings may be seen to destabilize text. They anticipate the concerns of such modern critics as Valentine Cunningham, who see that, "[M]argins, glosses ... will perhaps always have an undermining effect ... on determinate meaning."[41] But the translator's notes also expand the range of possible meanings, creating a text which opens out on a range of meanings, all of which are potential in the original text. This possibility of expanding or opening-out meanings creates in the reader the necessity of critical reading, weighing and considering and holding final judgement in a kind of continuous tension with present reading. It keeps the reader aware that the meaning which is being arrived at in the interaction with text is merely a reading, one of the many possible ways of responding to the richness of meaning which is potential in the text. The effect of presenting a text with such paratextual apparatus is that the text is seen as inexhaustibly rich, accessible at many different levels, and continuously inviting further scrutiny and reflection.

Besides the translators' notes of possible variant readings, to which it is clear Bunyan gave careful attention and thought, there are several other types of marginal notes in the 1642 edition of the Bible. There are cross-references to verses containing the same word or touching on the same theme, indicated by an asterisk in the text matching an asterisk in the margin. And there is the extensive commentary in marginal notes by Tomson and Junius. These explanatory and doctrinal notes are linked to the appropriate point in the text by means of superscript lower-case alphabet letters, a method which Bunyan adopted in the earliest editions of *The Pilgrim's Progress*.

The whole effect of the extensive annotations is the creation of a richly pointed, very complex text, daunting to the modern eye. To read this text with understanding was the great challenge of the newly, and often barely, literate reading public of England. So totally would such a task involve the reader in the making of meaning that it is not surprising that the Bible was fundamental to the experience of reading—and, indeed, of meaning—for centuries to come.

VI

In his use of marginal notations alongside the central text of his narratives, Bunyan is producing books which share conventions with those he has read. This inherited convention for both producing and interpreting text is a complex one which Bunyan uses artistically and intentionally. His margins are a part, not only of the visual format which presents itself to the reader, but also of the entire reading experience which Bunyan offers his readers.

Not all of Bunyan's works look alike, indicating that he is aware of a decorum which dictated the use or non-use of marginal notes. His autobiography or "confession," for example, is not glossed with marginal notes, perhaps because Bunyan there speaks in only one voice, whereas in his narratives he is speaking in the voice of a narrator within the narrative proper and in his *persona* as preacher and guide in the margins.[42]

In sermonic materials, Bunyan follows the sparsely annotated format of the published Puritan sermon or even dispenses with notes entirely. In polemic, the sparseness of his margins may be as much a result of the speed with which he enters a fray as of any observed decorum. When he turns to fiction, Bunyan uses the margins as an artist. He discovers that the use of marginal notes supplies a device which heightens the verisimilitude of the story by placing the author's voice, as distinct from the narrator's voice, just outside the frame of the narrative. In his allegories, Bunyan exploits the convention of marginal notes to its fullest, finding in it a form which allows him to separate the voice of the narrator from that of commentator, of the dreamer from that of the interpreter, and to involve his readers in the active process of coming to meaning and discovering significance. In this, the format of marginal notes and central text, together forming a dual, interactive text, plays a vital role.

CHAPTER 3

Self-Construing Artifice:
Form and Function of Bunyan's Marginal Notes

It is intriguing to ask why marginal notes, so insistent a characteristic of Renaissance and Early Modern texts, should have flourished as a literary convention throughout the seventeenth century, and then disappeared in the eighteenth century. "[O]verall," Slights notes, "the amount of marginal annotation increases over the period ... from 1475 to 1640."[1] But during the next century marginal notations disappear. Apparently, when the conditions under which text was seen to require commentary ceased to exist, other methods of dealing with the pragmatic functions for which they existed were developed.

In this chapter, we will first examine the convention of the dual Renaissance text, trying to locate some of the ways in which philosophy and form may be interrelated, and then move on to consider the pragmatics of the convention as Bunyan used it.

I

C. S. Lewis states that, "literary phenomena ... spring from the whole mental life of the period in question."[2] The literary phenomenon of the Renaissance book page, with its dual text comprising narrative or expository text flanked by additional notes, unified by the page itself, conforms to a vision of reality. The unity-in-duality of text and comment on each page gives a visual reproduction of a view which sees the visible world connected to an invisible underlying reality. The human being was, as Sir Thomas Browne memorably proposed:

> That great and true *Amphibium*, whose nature is disposed
> to live ... in divided and distinguished worlds; for though
> there bee but one world to sense, there are two to reason;
> the one visible, the other invisible.[3]

According to this prevailing understanding of reality, man lives in two realms at the same time, the material or created world and the spiritual or immaterial world. The material-temporal world is linked to the spiritual-eternal world by a whole range of analogies; consequently, the spiritual-eternal world could be grasped and understood through a system of correspondences. A late Puritan expression of these correspondences exists in notes written by Jonathan Edwards between 1716 and 1758, some of which remained unpublished until 1948. Perry Miller, who edited the manuscript, sees Edwards as deeply influenced by both Newtonian physics and Lockean sensationalism, yet continuing the tradition of Renaissance thought in seeking to decode the exact language by which God speaks through Nature. Edwards attempts to systematize the "real correspondences" between natural and spiritual reality.

> [I]t is apparent and allowed that there is a great and remarkeable analogy in God's works. There is a wonderfull resemblance in the effects which God produces, and consentaneity in His manner of working in one thing and another throughout all nature. It is very observable in the visible world; therefore it is allowed that God does purposely make and order one thing to be in agreeableness and harmony with another. And if so, why should not we suppose that He makes the inferiour in imitation of the superiour, the material of the spiritual, on purpose to have a resemblance and shadow of them?[4]

In an important essay which traces the decline of this belief in nature as a "divine analogy" by which the spiritual and ethical world could be understood, Earl R. Wasserman explains the system of analogical correspondences which was familiar and commonly held in the Renaissance:

> [This] system of analogical correspondences ... was accepted as 'scientific,' not fictitious, for it was assumed that God, expressing Himself in all creation, made the physical, moral, and spiritual levels analogous to each other and to Himself.[5]

Wasserman sees that, from the late seventeenth century onward, the "intricate network of analogical relationships" was gradually replaced by psychological associations. These psychological associations were much weaker than the earlier analogies, and were expressed more easily in similes than in the metaphors used so readily by Renaissance writers.

It is interesting that at about the same time the clear sense of a dual and analogically connected universe gradually passed away, the dual, interactive text also passed out of use. One could not, of course, argue a simple cause and effect relationship: numerous other factors most certainly enter in. Tribble is convincing in her argument that changing attitudes towards claiming ownership of the text itself influence the development towards a unified solo text replacing the multivocal text of the Renaissance. There were also physical inducements to simplify the presentation, including changes in book size. Obviously, the format of text plus notes, developed for such large-scale volumes as Foxe's *Acts and Monuments* (the Book of Martyrs), was less suitable for the small octavo and even smaller duodecimo books which began to dominate the popular literary scene in the later part of the seventeenth century. The increase in number of volumes being published and the decrease in the cost of books also would have put negative pressure on maintaining the fashion of marginal notes. As we have noted, marginal notes presented a complication for typesetters, one which printers were no doubt quite happy to get rid of for the sake of efficiency as the demand for books increased.[6] However, even such small-format volumes as *The Pilgrim's Progress*, printed "at a low ebb in regard to the art of printing ... for those who could purchase but inexpensive books,"[7] persisted for some time in being annotated. So it may be more than mere historical coincidence that a pervasive conceptual construction of reality and a form of textual presentation which so accurately reflected it should have thrived and faded away together.

Bunyan, who writes at a time when he could have chosen to produce bare and unmarginated texts like John Owen's, or richly marginated texts like Richard Baxter's, chooses the latter. He also chooses to write three of his four major narratives in the allegorical mode. There is a metaphysical dimension to this format of text-plus-marginal commentary that makes it harmonious with the allegorical impulse: the reality is greater than the appearance; the allegory is the sum of what is shown and the invisible reality to which the signifiers of the story point. It is both dream and interpretation. Allegory as a literary mode bears witness to a belief structure which relates the seen and known to an unseen, all-encompassing reality. Edwin Honig says,

> [A]llegory is an ... instrument of thought and belief. Essentially part of the impulse Aristotle calls metaphysical ... allegory reveals a fundamental way of thinking about man and the universe.... It constantly reappears ... on the borders between religion or philosophy and art, serving to frame significant questions about the nature of illusion and reality.[8]

By using a standard, conventional form, Bunyan finds a way, as Langland had before him, to present a visual representation of the inner reality of allegory. The format of text plus notes is mimetic of the analogical mode of thought which underlies allegory. As an imaginative construct, allegory creates mimesis not so much by the naturalistic representation of scene or character as by a faithful rendering of a view of a dual reality. For Bunyan and those who share with him a world-view shaped by the Bible, the temporal and eternal worlds exist side by side, the material world reflecting the spiritual. As twentieth-century readers, we tend to find the "truth" of Bunyan's narratives in his faithful rendering of human speech and character and experience. That is, we tend to locate truth within human experience. Bunyan's first readers, however, would have more likely found the "truth" of his narratives in the marginal notes which linked the fiction of the story to the spiritual reality mediated by biblical texts, locating truth in scriptural revelation as it stands, marginally but nonetheless authoritatively, alongside human experience. In the margins, Bunyan answers what J. Hillis Miller calls the question crucial to allegory: Which way does the action go across the bar separating the material realm from the spiritual? Is meaning received as a gift from Heaven or does man offer it to Heaven as the greatest gift he can give to God, the gift of imaginative love?[9] For Bunyan and his readers, meaning, like salvation for his pilgrims, is a gift received in the texts and contexts of sacred Scripture.

Bunyan's initial unease about using an allegory to present truth, anxiously expressed in his "Apology" for *The Pilgrim's Progress*, is occasioned by more than an intellectual debate about the relationship between fiction and truth. However little formal rhetorical training he may have had, Bunyan is heir to a rhetorical definition of allegory as "dissimulation." Puttenham had defined *Allegoria* as "the figure of [*false semblant or dissimulation*]."[10] Because it said "under covert and darke terms" one thing while meaning another, this figure represented a potential subversion of signification. Spenser uses the term, "darke conceit," as a synonym for allegory, drawing on a tradition which sees truth as too lustrous to be viewed directly by the eyes of fallen man, and therefore requiring the "veil of allegory" in order to be apprehended.[11]

Medieval and Renaissance allegory is written in the belief that because there is a possibility of apprehending truth, there is a corresponding possibility of error in interpretation. The potential for a wrong interpretation in any reading of allegory means that allegory requires commentary, as Spenser acknowledges in his letter to Sir Walter Raleigh:

> Sir knowing how doubtfully all Allegories may be construed, and this booke of mine, which I have entituled the Faery Queene, being a continued Allegory, or darke conceit, I have thought good as well for avoyding of gealous opinions and misconstructions, as also for your better light in reading thereof, ... to discover unto you the general intention and meaning.[12]

Allegory and commentary are so intrinsically related that Frye makes authorial commentary a defining condition of allegory, stating, "We have actual allegory when a poet explicitly indicates the relationship of his images to example and precepts, and so tries to indicate how a commentary on him should proceed."[13] Angus Fletcher also sees the control of interpretation as fundamental to allegory: "[A]llegorical works present an aesthetic surface which implies an authoritative, thematic, 'correct' reading, and which attempts to eliminate other possible readings."[14] Whether embedded within the narrative, as in Dante's *Divine Comedy* or Spenser's *Faerie Queene*, or set forth in a dual, interactive format as in Langland's *Piers Plowman* and in Bunyan's narratives, authorial comment as a control on the interpretation of the allegory is an essential aspect of the mode.

To ignore or resist the commentary which is an intrinsic part of the allegorical mode is to fail to enter into a full engagement with an allegorical work. When a work presents a belief structure which is incompatible with the reader's beliefs, as Bunyan's narratives do to many modern and post-modern readers, attentive recapturing of the vision of the nature of truth and reality which informs the work may be as important as re-evaluating the significance of the convention which represents that vision. Without recapturing something of the vision of the nature of truth and reality which governs Bunyan's thought, the reader may find the marginal notes intrusive or merely distracting, rather than enriching the reading of Bunyan's narratives.

For Bunyan, as for earlier writers in the allegorical tradition, telling truth by means of fiction meant harnessing a potentially deceptive mode for the service of truth—a daring act of redemption by which *"feigning words / Make truth to spangle, and its rayes to shine"* ("Apology", *TPP*, 4, lines 1-2). Bunyan justifies this use of "feigning" words by claiming a "biblical poetics," adopting modes and forms of narrative which are sanctioned by their use in the Bible.[15]

The allegorical frame of thought would doubtless have come to Bunyan from folk-sources, especially from the sermon, in which the use of allegory was a tradition that went back at least as far as the Franciscans.[16] Bunyan's formal introduction to the biblical literary mode of allegory may possibly have come through his study of the Epistle to the Galatians in Luther's commentary. The allegorical mode is operative in several places in Galatians: the Covenant of Law is depicted as jailer and as pedagogue; under that covenant, humanity is depicted respectively as prisoner and as child (Gal. 3:23; 4:1-3). And in Galatians 4:22-26, St. Paul makes use of a particularly convoluted allegory, one over which even Luther would scratch his head.

The Pauline allegory sets up a contrast between the covenant of law and the covenant of grace, setting the two covenants up as parallels to the two sons of Abraham, "the one by a bondmaid, the other by a free woman" (Gal. 4:22). St. Paul goes through a chain of identification which links earthly Jerusalem to Mount Sinai, where the law was given; and Mt. Sinai in turn to "Agar," or Hagar, apparently associating the wilderness into which she fled with the wilderness around Mt. Sinai (Gen. 16; 21:9-21). Ishmael, the child born through human effort rather than by God's promise, comes to stand for human effort to fulfill God's purposes. By an amazing twist, St. Paul defies the customary historical association of the Jewish nation with Abraham's other son, Isaac, and identifies first-century Judaism as of the spiritual lineage of Ishmael. He goes on to identify the heavenly or spiritual Jerusalem with Sarah, the mother of Isaac (Gen. 18:1-14; 21:1-8). St. Paul identifies Isaac, the miraculously-born child of promise and grace, with the Christian Church, born of the new covenant of grace. The complex allegorical and typological equivalencies are:

A.

Hagar = by association, Mt. Sinai
Mt. Sinai = by metonymy, the Covenant of Law
The Covenant of Law = by association, earthly Jerusalem
Jerusalem = by metonymy, Judaism
Judaism = by analogy, Ishmael, Abraham's son as fruit of human effort.

B.

Sarah = by extension, heavenly Jerusalem
Heavenly Jerusalem = by association, the Covenant of Grace
The Covenant of Grace = by association, the Church
The Church = by analogy, Isaac, the son of Abraham as fruit of God's gracious intervention.

St. Paul in turn links this exceedingly complex allegory to an allegorical passage from the prophet Isaiah which depicts Israel as a previously-barren wife called into a celebration of motherhood. St. Paul appropriates the text and imagery of the Isaiah allegory to the Sarah = heavenly Jerusalem = Church equation which he has developed (Isa. 54).

With his love of words and riddles, Bunyan could not but have been fascinated by this complex allegory. In addition to the sacred text, he had a triple commentary to respond to. First, the Tomson notes alongside the biblical text identify and draw attention to the allegory, and comment upon it in a series of numbered notes to verses 21 and 27:

> [6] ... the apostle ... bringeth forth an allegory, wherin he saith, the holy Ghost did shadow out to us, all these mysteries....[7] He sheweth that in this allegorie, he hath folowed the steps of Esay....

At the next remove from the text, Bunyan had Luther's *Commentary on Galatians*. In this text, Luther expresses some uneasiness with St. Paul's identification of both "Sinai" and the earthly "Jerusalem" with "Agar."

> I durst not have been so bold to handle this allegory after
> this manner, but would have called Jerusalem *Sara* or the
> New Testament ... and I would have thought that I had
> found a very fit allegory. Wherefore it is not for every man
> to use allegories at his pleasure: for a goodly outward
> show may soon deceive a man and cause him to erre.[17]

By this comment, Luther draws attention to the unusual and puzzling geographic and thematic linkages in this allegory, and at the
same time points out difficulties inherent in the literary form of the
allegory.

A third level of commentary with which Bunyan had to deal in his
formal encounter with the biblical art of allegory was the cryptic cautionary marginal note of the translators, adjacent to Luther's discussion of the allegory: "It is not for every man to dally with allegories."
No wonder, then, that Bunyan felt a need to write not only an "Apology" but also a continual marginal commentary for *The Pilgrim's Progress*. If the interpretation even of a biblical allegory written under
divine inspiration had to be hedged in with warnings and precau-
tions, an allegory of human devising would need to be carefully explained.[18]

Bunyan relies on the use of marginal notes to guide the interpretation of his narratives. With each explanation, an episode in the allegory becomes an explained emblem or parable, accessible to the
reader at an immediate and consciously verbal level; with each biblical reference, the story is linked to the biblical text, both clarifying and
enlarging Bunyan's own application while ascribing a powerful authority to his constructed text.

II

In the layout of the page, the marginal notes occupy the edges, the
space that would otherwise be a white frame. It is clear enough that
the marginal notes affect the progress of the eye across the line from
left to right. If the reason for the margin around a page is to frame the
words and limit the motion of the eye at the ends of a line to aid legi-
bility, the inscribed margin has the effect of continually breaching this
frame, tugging the eye past the story into another discourse mode
signalled by a different size of print, another length of line — and thus
continuously teasing the mind of the reader to consider meaning beyond the frame of the narrative being read.[19]

By pointing beyond the story to the biblical text and beyond the biblical text to the spiritual reality which it represents and illumines, the biblical references in Bunyan's narratives continually assure the reader that there is meaning beyond the immediate apprehension of the story. These references are the "drag against the narrative" which Paul Salzman believes allows time for the discovery that "no event in *The Pilgrim's Progress* is contingent; a purpose rules all action."[20] By means of the many scriptural references, the narrative is explicitly linked to the universal history of the Bible, drawing the narrative — and the individual who "reads himself" in it — into the great universal history of creation, fall, and redemption, the whole grand story of "that famous *Continent* of *Universe*" (*HW*, 8).

The marginal notes are points of intensely important intersection, operating in intermediate space between human, imaginative text and the sacred text of the Bible. In the margins, metaphor and interpretation, word and Word, narrative and metanarrative meet. Through the insistent presence in the marginal notes of biblical references, the reader is confronted with the authority of the Bible. In Bunyan's work, this is not merely the summoning of an external authority to grant some sort of legitimacy to the narrative he is presenting, but rather a continual referring of the narrative to the Bible as the source of meaning, the ground of story, the literature in which the larger meaning of life and language is to be found.

The marginal notes also operate in an intermediate space between the narrator of the story and the reader of it. Through the marginal notes, the reader is invited into an ongoing encounter with the author of the story — either in his own proper self as writer, or in his *persona* as pastor. The experience of the story is mediated and interpreted, even "translated," by the voice in the margins. The reader is continuously reminded of authorial intention, and is continually granted authorial assistance and guidance.

This aspect of the marginal notes reflects the Protestant conviction that one is not alone in approaching the sacred text, but enabled by the Holy Spirit to apprehend the spiritual truth that is there. Jesus had promised his disciples "the Comforter" who "w[ould] guide [them] into all truth" (John 14:26; 16:13). The Greek word translated "comforter" is *parakletos*, one "called to one's side, i.e., to one's aid."[21] In his authorial alongsideness in the marginal notes, then, Bunyan imitates the function of the Holy Spirit whose authorial presence makes Scripture "plain and perspicuous."[22]

As the reader is never unaware of the author, so the narrative is never autonomous, divorced from the author. It is owned, commented upon, interpreted by the author or translator. The author's presence is explicit, as it continues to be in fictional narration until late in the nineteenth century. The apparent "quaintness" of such insistent authorial presence is a result of a change in literary conventions which, by the turn of the twentieth century, mandated that the author attempt to create the fiction of his or her own non-presence. Postmodernist metafictional writing is demonstrating again the vitality of authorial intrusion and comment; familiarity with these techniques will recover conventions and make the techniques of early fiction such as Bunyan's seem less strange.[23]

Bunyan stands at the end of a very long tradition in the writing of religious allegory. After his work, allegory falls into a long eclipse from which it is only now emerging, both in criticism and as a fiction form. Bunyan's use of allegory is much more anxious than that of the earlier allegorists who could assume that the necessary analogical connections existed and therefore could draw on a vocabulary of symbol even without the aid of the marginal notes, relying on embedded clues and a shared repertoire of symbolic imagery and accepted correspondence to guide the reader's interpretation. Bunyan is writing at the end of one tradition of mimesis and the beginning of another. His text-plus-note presentation, with its insistent identification and explanation, visually confronts the reader with a unity maintained against a widening fissure. For even as Bunyan writes, the two realms of reality, the material and the spiritual which throughout the Middle Ages and deep into the Renaissance had coexisted in unity, have begun to divide. Paradoxically, the format of Bunyan's allegories affirms at once unity-in-duality and the duality itself.

III

We now turn to the pragmatics of function. Because marginal notes are such highly complex literary elements, it is useful to have some method of classifying and discussing them. While previous attempts at bringing order to the discussion of marginal notes have been made, they are, at best, incomplete. Although Slights lists fifteen functions of Renaissance marginal materials, he does not consider his list to be comprehensive, stating: "[T]he list of functions for marginalia is not intended to be complete, and some items in it overlap others."[24] The fifteen functions which Slights identifies are: amplification, annotation, appropriation, correction, emphasis, evaluation, exhortation, explication, justification, organization, parody, pre-emption, rhetorical gloss, simplification, and translation.

Another classification of marginal notes is made by Keeble. Discussing Bunyan's marginal notes specifically, Keeble links marginal note functions with the various authorial *personae* speaking in the margin. When the author speaks in the margins in the *persona* of interpretive guide, he supplies biblical texts to serve as interpretive key or to comment on the story, adds a gloss on a particular symbol or character, draws out the thematic drift of incidents, or sharpens the satirical bite of the narrative. When the author speaks in the margins as preacher, he directs a passage to a particular sector of his audience, admonishing, encouraging, and exhorting. And when the author speaks as writer, he establishes his own integrity by identifying outside sources, draws attention to his art by summarizing or signposting the plot, or indicates to the reader an appropriate response to story.[25]

Salzman also offers a classification of Bunyan's marginal notes, closer to the one which will be developed here. "Bunyan uses three types of gloss: a pure description of the narrative ... ; an interpretation of an event ... ; and, by far the most numerous, the citation of biblical references."[26]

The taxonomy of functions for marginal notes which is proposed here is simpler than the list of functions suggested by Slights or the categories according to *persona* suggested by Keeble, and is somewhat more comprehensive than Salzman's three categories. Developed to classify the marginal notes in Bunyan's narratives, it might well do for categorizing marginal notes in many other Renaissance works as well. For each marginal note, it allows a classification according to function, and according to effect. The four functions are: to refer, to index, to interpret, and to generalize. Any particular marginal note may perform one or more of these functions in its position adjacent to text. In its effect on the narrative with which it is juxtaposed, the marginal note may be either text-reflexive or text-extensive — and in some cases, may operate in both of these ways. Text-reflexive notes reflect further attention to the nearby narrative text. They may modify, intensify or ameliorate the effect of the adjacent narrative text. Text-extensive notes invite the reader's attention to move beyond the narrative. They extend the narrative by amplification or application.

The most frequently used marginal notes are those which *refer*. In terms of Slights' list of functions, reference may be seen as amplification by means of additional evidence or examples; as appropriation of a text to the narrative at hand; as annotation of material quoted or alluded to in the narrative text; or as providing additional evidence or examples. Annotations of scripture texts embedded or alluded to within the narrative text comprise the greatest number of Bunyan's marginal notations. However, Bunyan often goes beyond quoting to giving references which expand on allusions or hints in the text, embroidering his narrative with marginal biblical references which, rather than merely annotating pericopes, operate to bring to mind themes, ideas, or motifs.

To see how complex the interaction is between marginal notes and narrative text in even quite straightforward annotation, we can look at an example from *The Pilgrim's Progress*. Christian is asked by Obstinate "What are the things you seek, since you leave all the world to find them?" Christian replies:

*1 Pet. 1.4	I seek an *Inheritance, incorruptible, undefiled, and that fadeth not away; and it is laid up in Heaven, *and fast there, to be bestowed at the time appointed on them
*Heb.11.16	that diligently seek it. Read it so, if you will, in my Book. (*TPP*, 11)

The first biblical reference in the adjacent margin annotates the italicized, embedded quotation. The "inheritance" spoken of in the annotated quotation is, we are told, "laid up in Heaven," Bunyan here choosing to use an unannotated phrase closely akin to the phrase "reserved in heaven for you," which he might have quoted from I Peter 1:4, but which, in a slightly differing form, occurs twice in the AV: "the hope which is laid up for you in heaven," in Colossians 1:5; and "there is laid up for me a crown of righteousness," in II Timothy 4:8. The passive voice of the verb places the emphasis on the agency of grace. This inheritance is not something which Christian is going to lay up for himself, like the treasure which Jesus told his disciples to lay up for themselves in heaven (Matt. 6:19,20). The "inheritance" which is spoken of here is the free gift of God — already laid up for the believer in Heaven.

The inheritance referred to is not only "laid up," however. It is also "fast there," secure and ready "to be bestowed at the time appointed on them that diligently seek it." Again, the verb is passive; the believer's inheritance is a grant of grace—laid up for him, secured for him, bestowed on him. The marginal annotation to this phrase is problematic. Although the first two editions of *The Pilgrim's Progress* annotate it with "Heb. 11.62," this is an error, there being only forty verses in the eleventh chapter of Hebrews. The emendation in the definitive edition to "Heb. 11.16" will do, but that verse does not have the precise turn of phrase which one would expect, reading: "But now they desire a better country, that is an heavenly: wherefore God is not ashamed to be called their God: for he hath prepared for them a city." What we seem to have in the annotated sentence is a collation of phrases from Hebrews: the "hope ... both sure and steadfast" of Hebrews 6:19; the time "appointed unto men once to die" of Hebrews 9:27; and the God who "is a rewarder of them that diligently seek him" of Hebrews 11:6. One might expect that the reference intended is this last one. Here, then, is an example of a single annotation for several texts collated within the text. The erroneous reference may well be an example of Bunyan's working from memory without taking time to check the reference in his Bible. But it may, in this case, be a printer's error caused by misreading the author's note. Bunyan might quite possibly have written "Hebrews 11:6" followed by a comma which was interpreted by the typesetter as a "2," with the resultant erroneous reference, Hebrews 11.62.

Turning to *The Holy War*, we find an example of a different type of marginal biblical reference: one in which the citation is not for specific scriptural words or phrases quoted within the text, nor for a collation of such quoted words and phrases as in the example above, but rather in which the citation serves as a reference for a related theme or idea. In the description of the original state of Mansoul, Bunyan writes:

Gen 1:26

[T]he founder, and builder of it, so far as by the best, and most Authentick records I can gather, was one *Shaddai*; and he built it for his own delight. He made it the mirrour, and glory of all that he made, even the Top-piece beyond any thing else that he did in that Countrey ... (9)

The Scripture reference is to a verse which reads in part, "And God said, Let us make man in our image, after our likeness.... " The annotation is not for any specific word or phrase within the adjacent descriptive paragraph, but rather for the idea lying behind it: humankind as the mirror of God's glory and the crowning act of creation.

We might postulate that what was happening for the intended reader was that the marginal gloss was operating alongside the narrative, almost subliminally creating a sense of authority and trustworthiness which would have added a sense of significance to every line; presenting a context for the many scriptural pericopes, and thereby widening and extending the meaning of the quoted phrases by placing them in association with the greater whole from which they are taken. The use of any biblical reference confers authority upon the narrative text adjacent to it. As with the paragraph we have just looked at from *The Pilgrim's Progress*, the invitation in *The Holy War* is to go beyond the story to the Bible. "Read it so, if you will, in my Book," says Christian to Obstinate (*TPP*, 11), implying: "Don't take it on my word. Read it in the source." Similarly, the reader of *The Holy War* is implicitly invited to consult "the best, and most Authentick records" available—that is, to refer to the Bible itself.

The reader is also expected to care about that larger context, and, if need be, to "search the Scripture" in the same way in which congregations were expected to go home after a sermon and "prove" the teaching by reading the text within its biblical context, and to evaluate carefully the teaching received. While Bunyan takes scripture texts out of their contexts and trims or collates them to fit his narrative passage, he is at pains to indicate by means of the references where the greater whole can be found, inviting the reader to check on the legitimacy of his use of each text.[27]

By far the greatest number of referential marginal notes are biblical references. But in *The Life and Death of Mr. Badman*, Bunyan also makes use of Samuel Clarke's *Looking Glass for Saints and Sinners*, and a number of anonymous sources of anecdotal illustrations. In *The Pilgrim's Progress, The Second Part*, the referring function becomes circular as Bunyan refers to page numbers in *The Pilgrim's Progress* where the prior, parallel narrative events occur, making *The Pilgrim's Progress, The Second Part*, an extension of *The Pilgrim's Progress* as well as *vice versa*.

The second major function of the marginal notes is to *index* the narrative. Indexing marginal notes perform at least three of the functions which Slights identifies: they create emphasis, provide organization, and simplify the text. One-way indexing is done is by supplying titles which indicate, in outline, the structure of a segment of the work. An example of this may be found in the headings which mark the "causes of the hubbub" and the main events in the trial of the pilgrims in Vanity Fair (*TPP*, 90-97). The titles of the third and fourth "causes of hubbub" were added to the second edition; many of the marginal notes which identify parallel elements throughout *The Pilgrim's Progress* were added to the third edition, suggesting that without them there was an observable deficiency in the indexing of the text. In *The Holy War*, parallel elements are identified and emphasized with rubrics such as "The speech of the Lord Willbewill" and "The speech of Forget-good the Recorder" (49). In the trial of the Diabolonians, the trial of each of the vices follows a standard format signalled in the margin by "[X] set to the bar"; "His Indictment"; "His plea" (119-124). These titles at once index the story and emphasize the repetitive pattern of its structure.

Marginal notes also index the narrative by means of titles or summaries supplied for main events within the narrative sequence. Examples of titles abound: in *The Pilgrim's Progress, The Second Part*, for example, we find such headings as, "Talk at Supper" (205); "A fight betwixt Grim and Great-heart" (219); "Greatheart's Resolution" (258). We can establish a distinction between summary and title on the basis of summaries having a verb or verbs in them, while titles are phrases without verbs. Succinct summary statements are abundant. "Christian findeth his Roll where he lost it" (*TPP*, 44) will serve as an example. A series of telegraphic indexing summaries occurs in the margins adjacent to the narrative of the battle for the conquest of Mansoul: "The Battel joined, and they fight on both sides fiercely"; "Eargate broken open"; "The Princes Standard set up, and the Slings are plaid still at the Castle" (*HW*, 87-91).

Marginal notes which *interpret* the allegory to the reader make up the third group of marginal notes. Functions which Slights identifies as explication and rhetorical gloss I subsume under the general function of interpretation. There is some overlap with other functions: biblical references sometimes offer interpretive clues to the allegorical or emblematic elements in the adjacent text, thus serving both the referring and the interpreting function. Interpretive marginal notes may also be seen to serve an indexing function. Interpretive marginal notes occur frequently at the beginning of *The Holy War*. Beginning with marginal notes to the preface ("To the Reader"), and continuing through to the end of the narrator's prologue, a series of notes identifies and interprets allegorical elements. "[M]y Master" in the narrative text is identified in the margin as "Christ"; the "fair and delicate Town ... called Mansoul" is interpreted in the margin as "Man." "[A] famous and stately Palace" in the centre of the town is glossed "The heart," (7,8) and so on. After this initial flurry of interpretive activity to ensure that the reader has the "key" to the allegory (and is turning it rightly), the marginal notes settle down to their more pedestrian referencing and indexing functions. Nonetheless, the large number of specifically interpretive glosses which occur in *The Holy War* (the Captain, Wall, and keepers of the Gates of Mansoul are identified as "Heart," "Flesh," and "Senses" respectively [22], for example), suggest that Bunyan is aware of the new level of difficulty which his more ambitious allegorical epic presents to his readers. Whenever new elements are introduced into the allegory, there is another rush of interpretive marginal notes (see, for example, 103-105).

Such interpretive notes are noticeably more prevalent in *The Holy War* than in the other, more accessible, allegories. However, such notes appear in the other works at each point at which Bunyan may feel that the reader needs additional help with interpretation. Thus, the parchment roll given to Christian by Evangelist is explained by a marginal note as the "Conviction of the Necessity of Flying" (*TPP*, 10); a note in *The Pilgrim's Progress, The Second Part*, serves both to index the arrival of the divine messenger to Christiana and to interpret the spiritual meaning of both messenger and message: "*Convictions seconded with fresh tidings of Gods readiness to pardon" (179).

Interpretation is also given by notes which indicate that the narrative text is to be taken ironically, as in the twice-repeated aside "O brave Talkative" (*TPP*, 77); or to warn that the narrative text contains untruth, something which seems to make Bunyan particularly uncomfortable and anxious to gloss to ensure correct interpretation: "Thats false Satan," charges a marginal note—a charge not so much directed against Satan as a warning to the possibly unwary reader (*HW*, 39). So, too, the note beside Diabolus' speech, identifying it as "Satanical Rhetoric"(*HW*, 20), is designed to keep the reader reading critically and not acceptingly. Since, according to a cryptic marginal note, "Satan reads all backwards" (*HW*, 193), the reader is warned to keep alert and to read the narrative under the author's guidance and in accord with his intended meaning.

The fourth class of marginal notes are those which *generalize* the message of the narrative into epigrammatic exhortations for the edification of the reader. An exhortation may be directly addressed to the reader, or indirectly given through a warning or instruction to a character within the allegory, as in the frequently repeated "Take heed, Mansoul" and "Look to it, Mansoul," which operate as advance warnings in *The Holy War* (167-70), alerting the reader to areas of spiritual difficulty.

Many of these didactic generalizations are terse and pithy enough to stand individually as adages or epigrams. Rather than quoting generalizations from classical or other sources, Bunyan draws conclusions from the story itself, or, perhaps, sometimes illustrates an adage by means of the elaboration of the story. "No great heart for God, where there is but little faith" is the didactic generalization drawn from the story of Little-Faith (*TPP*, 129). A common-place observation in *Mr. Badman* is succinct and rhythmic, if somewhat obvious: "A bad Master, a bad thing." Doctrine is stated tersely, often sounding like the response to catechetical questioning: "Original sin is the root of actual transgressions" (*Mr. B*, 17). In *The Holy War*, the generalizations are often in the form of warnings, common-place statements which state a generally accepted fact and, at the same time, imply a warning: "Cumberments are dangerous" (*HW*, 173); or "Satan cannot weaken our Graces as we ourselves may" (*HW*, 143).

Marginal notes which interpret and those which generalize occur much less frequently than marginal notes which refer to other texts and those which index the narrative text. They have, however, attracted greater critical interest, simply because such notes are more obviously interesting in themselves. However, all the functions of the marginal notes are worthy of attention. And it is worth remembering that some of the most complex and interesting interactions between marginal notes and narrative text occur when marginal notes function in more than one way at a time, as when reference notes offer interpretation, or interpretive or generalizing notes also index the story.

Marginal notes can further be characterized in terms of their effect on the adjacent text. They may interact with the adjacent narrative by emphasizing, intensifying, or ameliorating the effect of the text. Marginal notes which thus direct the reader back to the text for another reading may be called *text-reflexive*. Marginal notes may draw the reader into considerations beyond the text, expanding the meaning of the text by linking it to the Bible or other intertext, or by applying the text to the reader's own experience of life. These marginal notes may be termed *text-extensive.*

These two effects of marginal notes on the adjacent text reflect the inherent duality of the act of reading. "Whenever we read anything," Northrop Frye points out,

> we find our attention moving in two directions at once. One direction is outward or centrifugal, in which we keep going outside our reading, from the individual words to the things they mean.... The other direction is inward or centripetal, in which we try to develop from the words a sense of the larger verbal pattern they make.[28]

In Bunyan's texts, as the reader re-creates the links between episodes and engages with the adventures of the characters, the ongoing narrative of the main text carries the centripetal impulse. This centripetal impulse is aided by text-reflexive marginal notes which continuously force the reader back into text, emphasizing elements within the narrative and aiding interpretation of it. Text-extensive marginal notes, on the other hand, are related to the centrifugal pattern of reading by which the story is linked to larger conventions of meaning, the signifiers of the story forged into association with signified concepts, doctrines, and the spiritual experience of the reader.

The "ideal reader" of Bunyan's margins is one who is well versed enough in the Bible to be able to summon the scripture text, together with its context, from the reference supplied. And such a reader is not an unreasonable construct. Margaret Spufford cites the *Rural Recollections* of one George Robertson, who describes minutely details of life in the Lothians from his earliest memories, before 1765. In describing the reading habits of the farmers of the area, Robertson wrote:

> [N]o book was so familiar to them as the Scriptures; they could almost tell the place of any particular passage, where situated in their own family Bible, without referring to either book, chapter, or verse; and where any similar one was situated.[29]

To be "well-versed" in the Scriptures by the standard of the Nonconformists of the seventeenth century—and for a long while thereafter—was to know biblical texts and their location within the Bible, chapter by chapter and verse by verse. Robertson's description seems to imply a sort of mental concordancing of one's "own family Bible," knowing where to look for a particular passage without having to be told a biblical reference for it. It seems probable that Bunyan expected his reader to be able to summon from memory the entire text and immediate context of the scriptures to which he refers in the margins. To be sure, the actual reader of Bunyan's narratives may not always have been so well-versed as this; for some, the marginal notes may have made a sort of Bible study guide. But the assumption on which the notes are based seems to be that the verses referred to are accessible to the reader and continuously add meaning or interpretation to the narrative passage to which they are adjacent.

Biblical references are most often text-extensive. As quotations draw the intertext of Scripture into the text of the narrative, so the annotations draw the text of the narrative back into the biblical intertext, causing a sort of knitting up of the two texts, Bible and narrative. Marginal notes may amplify the narrative text by providing a link to a biblical *exemplum*: Lot, urged to flee from Sodom despite the mocking of his family, is set up, by means of a reference note, as a parallel to Christian in his flight from the City of Destruction (*TPP*, 10).[30]

The marginal references may extend the meaning of the text by relating it to an inter-testamentary flow of meaning. Bunyan switches easily back and forth between the Old Testament and New Testament; his view is clearly the Reformation one which sees the Bible as one unified book. Bunyan's extension of his narrative texts by linking them with the entire, unified canon of Scripture is very clear in the "reference strings" which occur in the margins alongside collations of quotations within text or as supplements to the text itself. To take just one example, the eclectic list of textual references which accompany the description of the work of grace in the soul in Faithful's discourse with Talkative would be a challenge for anyone to link together without the aid of the adjacent text. The references are: John 16:8, Romans 7:24, John 16:9, Mark 16:16, Psalm 38:18, Jeremiah 31:19, Galatians 2:16, Acts 4:12, Matthew 5:6, Revelation 21:6 (*TPP*, 83). The antiphonal effect of this "reference string" in interaction with the narrative text will be discussed in Chapter 4. In such marginal collections of references, however, each scriptural text amplifies a phrase embedded in the narrative and places it in the larger context of the Bible and in creative juxtaposition with other scriptural texts.

Sometimes Bunyan supplies a "wide-net reference" rather than a precise textual reference — annotating a passage with a whole chapter reference. While some of these "wide net" references may be the result of a slip in memory, and may have indicated a place where Bunyan meant to look up the verse number to complete the marginal note, some seem to be intentional invitations to the reader to consider not just a specific verse but an entire passage. This seems to be the case when a paragraph in *The Pilgrim's Progress* is attended by four full-chapter references: Heb. 10, Rom. 4., Col. 1 and I Pet. 1, each chapter in its entirety applicable to the discussion carried on within the narrative (141).

Early in *The Pilgrim's Progress* when Evangelist, "pointing his finger over a very wide Field," asks Christian, "Do you see yonder *Wicket-Gate?*", the adjacent marginal note is to the whole chapter of "Mat. 7" (10). By annotating the "Wicket-Gate" with a chapter reference rather than with the specific verse reference, Bunyan encourages the reader to get to the text about the strait gate and narrow way by way of earlier texts in the chapter, and so greatly expands the implications of the "wicket-gate" image. The chapter referred to begins with a warning against judging: "Judge not that ye be not judged" (7:1); goes on to encourage asking, seeking and knocking: "Ask, and it shall be given you; seek, and ye shall find; knock, and it shall be opened unto you" (7:7); and only then actually creates the image of the gate: "[S]trait is the gate, and narrow is the way, which leadeth unto life, and few there be that find it" (Matthew 7:14).

By means of the whole-chapter annotation, the reader is invited to form an image of a small gate, difficult to see with the "natural" eyes of human reason, but also a gate at which entry is available to every one who "asks, seeks, knocks." Bunyan's attention to "knocking" is clear: Christian knocks, "more than once or twice" (*TPP*, 25); and Christiana, in *The Pilgrim's Progress, the Second Part* knocks urgently "as her poor husband did" (*TPP* 2, 188). It is the timid Mercie who knocks loudest and longest:

> Now *Mercie* began to very impatient, for each *minute* was as long to her as an Hour, wherefore she prevented *Christiana* from a fuller interceding for her, by knocking at the Gate her self. And she knocked then so loud, that she made *Christiana* to start. (*TPP* 2, 189)

With this repeated narrative detail, Bunyan demonstrates to the reader the importance of "asking, seeking, knocking," and the great importance of not pre-judging whether one is called or not. All of this is implied in the original whole-chapter marginal reference to "Mat. 7," with the full significance of the "strait gate" placed in a larger biblical context and gradually worked out through the two parts of the allegory.

Biblical references can also operate text-extensively by providing a scripture which is itself admonitory — such as the reference to "I Cor. 5.8" in the margins adjacent to a description of the feasting with Prince Emmanuel in the early days of the conquest of Mansoul (*HW* 148). The biblical text to which reference is made is a warning: "Therefore let us keep the feast, not with old leaven, neither with the leaven of malice and wickedness; but with the unleavened bread of sincerity and truth." This admonition is quite additional to the material in the narrative text, and supplies a warning note in the midst of the joyful feasting of the narrative. Similarly, in the margin adjacent to the passage in which "Christian bewails his foolish sleeping.... '*O wretched Man that I am*, that I should sleep in the day time'" (*TPP*, 44), a reference to "I Thess. 5. 7, 8" calls up an admonition which helps to explain the level of Christian's grief: "For they that sleep, sleep in the night .... But let us, who are of the day, be sober." The pilgrim's sleeping identified him with the non-elect ("they that sleep"), rather than with the elect ("[we] who are of the day"); thus, it was unseemly behaviour for Christian.

As these examples demonstrate, Bunyan's highly creative ways and usage of the Bible is evident only through a careful study of his marginal notes. The many biblical references in the margins represent an important extension of his narrative text.

Marginal notes offering didactic generalizations are also most often text-extensive. They, however, extend the text not into the realm of another text, but in the direction of a reader's own experience of life — yet another "text" to which Bunyan consciously links his works. Bunyan's generalizing marginal notes are in the spirit of the "application" of the Puritan sermon. The *Westminster Directory for the Publique Worship of God* (1645) specifies six types of application or "use": instruction or information; confutation of false doctrines; exhorting to duties; dehortation, reprehension and publick admonition; applying comfort; trial or self-examination.[31] Bunyan's hortatory notes encourage application, or extension of text into the life of the reader, in all of these ways.

The didactic generalizations very often offer instruction and information: "*There is no perswasion will do, if God openeth not the eyes" (*TPP* 2, 39); "When Faith and Pardon meet together, *Judgment* and *Execution* depart from the heart" (*HW*, 107); "*Death is not welcome to nature though by it we pass out of this World into glory*" (*TPP* 2, 156); "Satan greatly afraid of Gods Ministers, that they will set *Mansoul* against him" (*HW*, 40); "Mortification of sin is a sign of hope of life" (*HW*, 196). The marginal generalizations also "confute" false doctrines or misconceptions. For example, the marginal note, "Christ would not have us destroy ourselves thereby to destroy our sins" (*HW*, 144), is a brief warning against either extreme asceticism or spiritual despair which might lead one to contemplate suicide.[32] "*Angels help us not comfortably through death*" (*TPP* 2, 157) dispels a popular misconception that the proof of one's calling is a quiet and peaceful death.[33]

Exhortation to Christian duties is frequently found in the marginal notes as well: "*Pray, and you will get at that which yet lies unrevealed*" (*TPP* 2, 203); "*Notice to be taken of Providence*" (*TPP* 2, 269); "*True Knowledge attended with endeavours*" (*TPP* 2, 82); "The world are convinced by the well ordered life of the godly" (*HW*, 39). What the *Westminster Directory* terms "Dehortation, reprehension & publick admonition" can be found in such generalizing marginal notes as, "A Lie knowingly told demonstrates that the heart is desperately hard" (*Mr. B*, 18); "*Swearing and Cursing are sins against the light of Nature" (*Mr. B*, 32); "*Stupified ones are worse then those merely Carnal*" (*TPP* 2, 247).

The didactic generalizations in the margin also sometimes apply comfort, as when Bunyan cheerfully observes, "Christians are well spoken of when gone, tho' called Fools while they are here" (*TPP*, 175). And for people whose lives were disrupted by one wave of persecution after another, there would be some comfort to be derived from knowing that theirs is the common lot of pilgrims: "*The ease that Pilgrims have is but little in this life*" (*TPP*, 106).

In all of these ways, Bunyan's generalizing marginal notes, often finely-worked literary elements in themselves, operate text-extensively, condensing aspects of the message of the allegory into epigrams intended to be readily understood and remembered, and to be directly applied to the reader's own life.

As compared with the text-extensive effect of many referring and generalizing notes, indexing notes are text-reflexive. They draw attention to elements which exist within the text, creating emphasis by reiteration of allegorical names or by focusing on parallel elements. Indexing notes may intensify the narrative by repeating elements that are there. In *The Pilgrim's Progress*, when the text says, "you must note, that tho the first part of the Valley of the shadow of Death was dangerous, *yet this second part ... was, if possible, far more dangerous," the already emphatic text is given further intensification by the explanatory marginal note: "*The second part of this Valley very dangerous" (65). In *The Life and Death of Mr. Badman*, Bunyan emphasizes the stories he believes to be true on the evidence of reliable reports by means of the "index" or pointing finger device. If one is looking for a juicy seventeenth-century anecdote, one need only slide one's eyes down the margins to the first available pointing finger, the device serving in its traditional *nota bene* role. And, given the nature of the *exempla* which are designated by this device, the pointing finger gradually takes on the nature of a gesture of accusation.

Interpretive marginal notes are also most often text-reflexive. In some cases, the interpretation of the margins ameliorates the effect of the adjacent text, as when, during the second onslaught of Diabolus, the "young children ... dashed in pieces" are explained as, "Good and tender thoughts" destroyed by the enemy of Mansoul (*HW*, 204).

Even as little as a single word may create a marginal note which has the effect of modifying the adjacent text by offering an explanation which might not naturally spring to mind. This happens in *The Holy War* when Emmanuel charges the inhabitants of the Town of Mansoul to "love ... nourish [and] ... succour" his "valiant Captains, and couragious men of war." The passage is glossed with a marginal note: "Words" (143), which by its ambiguity forces a re-reading of the passage in order to determine whether it is the Captains who are to be seen as "words," or whether "words" describes the method of nourishing them. The intention seems to be that "words," probably as used in preaching or polemical writing, are to be equated with "Captains and couragious men of war." The single-word interpretive note modifies the effect of the adjacent narrative by forcing, through a slowed reading, a less-than-obvious allegorical equivalency on the reader.

IV

When considering the welter of marginal notes in Bunyan's narrative texts, a consideration of these four functions (referring, indexing, interpreting, and applying) and two basic relationships to and effects upon the adjacent narrative (text-reflexive and text-extensive), can provide a useful and relatively simple way of categorizing the marginal notations so that some sort of useful consideration can be taken of them.

There are, of course, still a number of interesting questions to be asked about a marginal note. One is to ask in which direction each marginal note is turned: does it look toward the reader or toward the text? Marginal notes with referring and indexing functions are oriented toward the text. Interpretive or didactic statements are directed toward the reader.

Another kind of inquiry would be to consider how lines of reference run. In the intermediate zone between narrative and reader in which the marginal notes operate, lines of reference run in a number of directions: from a quotation or allusion in the narrative to its corresponding reference in the specific text quoted; from the narrative to the reader's experience; or from a marginal note across to the narrative at hand, as in indexing statements of various kinds.

The marginal notes to Bunyan's narratives are clearly very complex in their functions and interactions with the narrative text. They are also frequently artistically wrought, producing their own special effects at the edge of the narrative, and it is to the art in the margins that we now turn our attention.

CHAPTER 4

Art in the Margins

In understanding the appeal and impact of Bunyan's narratives, we have seen the importance of recognizing that many of Bunyan's originally intended readers would have been highly biblically literate, their inner ears trained by hours of exposure to the cadences of the King James Bible and to the sounds and structures of the Nonconformist Puritan sermon. They would also have had their imaginations stocked with the images and landscapes both of rural England and of the Bible. So the original readers came to Bunyan's narrative text with a rich auditory and visual repertoire on which Bunyan was able to draw by means of both the central narrative and the marginal notes. Having emphasized the function of the marginal notes in the previous chapter, in this chapter we will look at the art of the marginal notes, considering the aural and visual appeals they add or emphasize. We will also consider two affective responses evoked in the reader by means of the interaction of some of the marginal notes and the corresponding narrative text: the devotional response evoked by iconography, and the playful response evoked by puzzle and game elements present in marginal notes.

I

However much the Puritans may have urged a plain style, the demands of the oral form of the long sermon and the resources of the language encouraged them to make abundant use of such devices as word and sound-play and syntactical emphasis. Trained through exposure to the cadence and pattern of innumerable sermons, Bunyan's readers would quickly detect the aural appeal, reminiscent of pulpit stylistics, of such marginal notes as, "The Worldly Man for a Bird in the Hand" (*TPP*, 31). This marginal note is replete with the repetition of sounds: the "ir" sound in "worldly" and "bird"; the final "d" in "bird" and "hand"; and the rhyme of "man" and "hand." To all of

101

this sound play is added wordplay in the form of an inverted proverb. The folk proverb being played on says, "A bird in the hand is worth two in the bush." Bunyan, by implication, denies the validity of that proverb when applied to the spiritual world in which man-made proverbs often work out all wrong.

There is also an aural appeal in such phrases as, "Things that are first must give place, but things that are last are lasting," (*TPP*, 31) with the repeated "st" sounds and the play on meaning: "being last" (in position or rank) played off against "to last" (as a condition of duration). And again, as with the proverb cited above, the entire adage is itself an inversion of the common-sense view of things. It is, of course, an allusion to Jesus' paradoxical statement that "the first shall be last, and the last first" (Mark 10:31).

"He whose lot it will be to suffer will have the better of his brother" (*TPP*, 87) is another paradox, this time offered in the form of a miniature poem with the near-rhyme of "suffer" and "brother" and the repetition of "t" and "b" sounds binding what is in effect a couplet in trochaic tetrameter. But it is also, in total, a word-game of the tongue-twister variety, again revealing the inverted order of things when the spiritual view is taken. From a this-worldly point of view, suffering is always bad, and it is better not to suffer. But from the point of view of spiritual progress, suffering can be an advantage; at its worst it can do no more than provide a short cut to the Celestial City, as it does for Faithful at Vanity Fair (*TPP*, 97).

Didactic generalizations are often polished epigrams or aphorisms. An important element in the effectiveness of such miniature forms is the aural effect of a play on sounds. In considering one of any number of examples, "Christ makes not War as the World does," (*HW*, 71) we immediately become aware of alliteration, vowel modulation, and the consonantal rhyme of the sequence, "war" and "World." Emphasis is created by alliteration in a didactic generalization such as, "Sin, and the soul at odds" (*HW*, 59). Sound-play occasionally grants emphasis to even something as simple as a brief summary of action. This is the case with the internal rhyme in "They chide on both sides," (*HW*, 59) or in the repeated, military staccato of hard "c," "t," and "s" sounds in, "The Captains call a Council and consult what to do" (*HW*, 62). Even in the small space of a marginal note, syntax is used for artistic and emphatic effect. The periodic sentence structure of the marginal note, "'Tis not grace received, but Grace improved, that preserves the soul from temporal dangers"

(152), is further enhanced by the use of parallel elliptical noun clauses, the whole epigram replicating in miniature the parallelism and periodicity which are key features of seventeenth-century preaching.

The multitudinous scriptural references would also have had an aural appeal, now very difficult to reconstruct. Where a late twentieth-century reader sees only a string of references in the margins, for many of the original readers each reference would call up an entire text. As a result of rote memorization and slow, methodical, often oral reading, such texts would be voiced in the readers' minds. In Chapter 3, we referred to the list of textual references which accompany the description of the work of grace in the soul in Faithful's discourse with Talkative (*TPP*, 83) as representative of many such strings of references. Perhaps we can recover something of the effect that the original audience might have experienced by writing out the passage in two columns, with the scripture written out in full as it would probably be "heard" and responded to on the cue of the references in the margins. The effect would have been a sort of antiphonal reading, with the words of the Scripture voicing themselves over against the words of the narrative text. This passage, then, would actually be read with the attention of the reader moving from the collation of ideas in the narrative text across to the marginal reference and the text it calls to mind, and then back to the narrative text (in this presentation represented in italics):

A work of grace in the soul ...
gives him conviction of sin,

John 16:8:
 And when he [the Holy Spirit] is come, he will reprove the world of sin, and of righteousness, and of judgment.

especially of the defilement of his nature,

Romans 7.24:
 O wretched man that

I am! who shall de-
liver me from the
body of this death?

and the sin of unbelief,

John 16.9:
 He will reprove the
world of sin ... be-
cause they believe not
on me.

*(for the sake of which he is sure to
be damned, if he findeth not mercy
at Gods hand by faith in Jesus
Christ.)*

Mark 16.16:
 He that believeth and
is baptized shall be
saved; but he that be-
lieveth not shall be
damned.

*This sight and sense of things
worketh in him sorrow*

Psalm 38.18:
 For I will declare
mine iniquity; I will
be sorry for my sin.

and shame for sin;

Jeremiah 31.19:
 Surely after that I
was turned, I re-
pented; and after that
I was instructed, I
smote upon my thigh:
I was ashamed, yea,

even confounded, be-
cause I did bear the
reproach of my
youth.

he findeth moreover revealed in
him the Saviour of the World,

Galatians 1.16:[1]
 It pleased God ... to
reveal his Son in me.

and the absolute necessity
of closing with him, for life,

Acts 4.12:
 Neither is there sal-
vation in any other:
for there is none other
name under heaven
given among men,
whereby we must be
saved.

at the which he findeth hungrings
and thirstings
after him,

Matthew 5.6:
 Blessed are they
which do hunger and
thirst after righteous-
ness: for they shall be
filled.

to which hungrings, &c. the prom-
ise is made.

Revelation 21.6:
 I will give unto him

that is athirst of the
fountain of the water
of life freely.

In the reading I have attempted to demonstrate here, the reference
as it stands in Bunyan's text cues the recall of the entire text, creating
a voice in the margins which may be seen as similar to the kind of
voiced texts that Bunyan describes in *Grace Abounding* as calling after
him or "hollowing" at him (*GA*, e.g., para. 93). In such passages, Bunyan invites the reader to share his own personalized and voiced experience of the Scripture through hearing and responding to the
voices of Scripture as they occur in the interplay between narrative
text and marginal gloss, the text sometimes given voice within the
narrative, and at other times requiring voicing from within the
reader's memory.

In addition to the antiphonal effect of a marginally summoned
Scripture text in interaction with the narrative text there is, occasion-
ally, an echo effect of the gloss to text. An example occurs in the en-
counter between Atheist and the pilgrims in *The Pilgrim's Progress*.
After the pilgrims have told Atheist that they are going "to the Mount
Sion," the text is as follows:

He Laughs at them.	Then *Atheist* fell into a very great Laughter.
	Chr. *What is the meaning of your Laughter?*
	Atheist. I laugh to see what ignorant persons you are....
	(*TPP*, 135)

The scornful laughter in the text, emphasized by a triple repetition
("Laughter," "your laughter," "I laugh,") and intensified by adjectives
("very great"), is echoed from the margin by yet another repetition
offered by the indexing summary note. The effect is that the reader,
together with the pilgrims, is surrounded by Atheist's mocking laughter. When one adds to the repetition of "laughter" within the text the
mocking laughter which may well have been lodged in the memory of
many of the readers, this passage of the narrative takes on a painful
intensity.

Another example in which the margin sets up an echo to the narrative demonstrates an even more complex and subtle effect. In *The
Holy War*, an attempted uprising in favour of Shaddai is termed
within the narrative text as a "heavy riotous Rout in *Mansoul*." An indexing marginal note summarizes the action: "The two old Gentlemen

put in prison as the authors of this revel-rout" (*HW*, 62). The repetition from the margin subtly draws attention to the ironic reading required of the words "heavy riotous Rout," a judgment of the event made from the Diabolonian point of view. In this case, the auditory echo functions to cue the sarcastic Diabolonian tone in the narrative and the ironic attitude of the narrator implied by the narrative text.

II

The marginal notes operate as visual cues as well as auditory ones. Some of the marginal notes, complete with an allegorical cast of characters and a summary of action, function as miniature scenes from a morality play. While the morality plays themselves had long been extinct on the English stage, the sermon had continued a long-standing tradition of embedding morality-play type dialogue or action within it.[2] Bunyan and his readers, schooled in the art of the sermon though debarred from the theatre, were sensitive to scenes in which the moral aspects of character were personalized, and in which the essential drama of the *psychomachia* was played out.[3]

In *The Pilgrim's Progress*, such a morality drama occurs at the Slough of Despond. Here, the summarizing-indexing note heightens the sense of drama in a few words: "Christian *and* Obstinate *pull for* Pliable's *Soul*" (12). The moral qualities embodied by the characters are emphasized by contrasting type-face, Roman type used for the allegorical proper names and italics for the other words of the note. (This emphasis by contrasting type-face is a frequent, if unintentional, feature of the marginal notes.) In this single marginal notation, with three allegorical characters and specific directions for action, Bunyan creates the summary of a scene which would be perfectly at home in a morality play.

Another instance of this sort of miniature drama occurs in the glosses to Little-faith's story where, again, characters and action are locked in a sequence of precisely drawn scenes of intense drama: "Little-Faith *robbed by* Faint-heart, Mistrust, *and* Guilt" (125); "*They got away his Silver, and knockt him down*" (126); "Littlefaith *lost not his best things*" (126); "Little-faith *forced to beg to his Journeys end*" (126). In each note, the two primary elements of the drama within the narrative, character and action, are given further emphasis. Even some stage properties (Little-faith's Silver, and "his best things," identified in the narrative text as his Certificate and "Jewels") are identified for easy visualization. And, as always in these brief dramatic summaries in the margins, the moral of the drama is clarified by the bare repetition of allegorical names from the main narrative.

The action summaries in *The Holy War* are also sometimes highly dramatic. The attack of Diabolus in his attempt to regain Mansoul is attended with marginal notes which are full of action verbs and which, taken in sequence, amount, if not exactly to such miniature dramas as those we have found in *The Pilgrim's Progress*, at least to stage directions for a larger drama. Thus, we read in the margins of Diabolus that "He makes an assault upon *Eargate*, and is repelled," that "He retreats and intrenches himself," that "He casts up Mounts against the Town," that "He bids his Drummer to beat his Drum," and that "*Mansoul* trembles at the noise of his Drum" (*HW*, 188-89).

There are other tiny dramatic moments. Some are created by vivid verbs in the marginal notes: "Talkative *flings away from* Faithful," (*TPP*, 84) or "Christian *snibbeth his fellow*" (*TPP*, 127); some by tight sketches of characters in dramatic situations, as in the readily-visualized description, "Captain *Experience* will fight for his Prince upon his Crutches" (*TPP*, 220).

As we have noted earlier, Bunyan and his readers were familiar with the emblem books which were popular throughout the seventeenth century. The marginal notes serve to emphasize the emblematic character of some scenes, cuing the reader to visualize a particular scene in an emblematic mode. The three parts of an emblem (title, picture, and epigram) afford opportunity to use the marginal note as title, as description of or commentary upon the picture, or as epigram, with the central narrative text supplying a verbal delineation of the picture, and, perhaps, an elaboration of the epigram.[4] The most obvious example of "emblematization" is the marginal note to the narrative of Christiana's boys cringing back behind Great-heart as they encounter the Lions. This scene, the marginal note tells us, is "An Emblem of those that go on bravely, when there is no danger; but shrink when troubles come" (*TPP* 2, 218).[5] The marginal note operates here as epigram to the verbal picture in the narrative which, by means of the marginal note, is frozen into emblem. This "freeze-frame" effect is the most distinctive difference between emblematized scenes and the rest of the narrative, in which the characters are in motion. With a marginal note which offers either an emblem title or epigram, the motion is stopped, the characters suddenly "frozen" in their allegorical relationships.

The "Picture of a very grave Person" which Christian encounters as he first enters the House of the Interpreter is a characteristic emblem, with its elements emphasized by the margins (*TPP*, 29). This emblematic vision of the true minister of the gospel has all three of the elements of an emblem: title ("a Picture of a very grave Person") answered with a rhyming indexing marginal note, *"a brave Picture"*; a description of the picture itself, indexed with the marginal note, *"*The fashion of the Picture"*; and an explanatory epigram, indexed in the margin by the note, *"*The meaning of the Picture."* The strategies acquired by the reading of emblem books are here directly transferred to a narrative text, with the marginal notes signalling the various stages of the process by which meaning is achieved through the elements of the emblem form (*TPP*, 29).[6]

The epigram of the emblem is accompanied in the margin with appropriate Scripture references, which significantly modify the response to the description in the text, systematically translating physical detail into more abstract metaphoric terms. "The Man whose Picture this is ... can *beget Children," says the Interpreter, and the margin answers the asterisk with "*I Cor. 4. 15": "[I]n Christ Jesus I have begotten you through the gospel." The pictured man can "Travel in birth with Children," and the startling physical image conjured by this statement is quickly ameliorated by its translation into spiritual terms by the reference, "*Gal. 4. 19," where St. Paul addresses the Galatians as, "My little children, of whom I travail in birth again until Christ be formed in you." Finally, the pictured man can "*Nurse them himself when they are born," with the cued visualization again ameliorated by the reference to "*I Thes. 2. 7," where St. Paul reminds the Thessalonians that "we were gentle among you, even as a nurse cherisheth her children."

The narrative text at this point shifts from describing the emblem to offering a point-by-point explanation which is indexed by the marginal note, *"The meaning of the Picture."* Later, the marginal gloss *"*Why he shewed him the Picture first"* alerts the reader to a transition to be made from the inset pictorial emblem back to the larger narrative frame. Throughout the House of the Interpreter passage, and other emblematic passages such as the discourse with the Shepherds at the Delectable Mountains (*TPP*, 119 ff.) and the feast at Gaius' Inn (*TPP 2*, 261 ff.), the reader is required to switch frequently from the mode of reading and visualization appropriate to an emblem, to the more generally allegorical reading of the story as a whole. In *The Holy War*, the emblematic nature of the descriptions of the colours and scutcheons of the commanders of both Emmanuel's and Diabolus' armies (*HW* 36-7; 186-7) are emphasized by the marginal notes, which supply text-extensive interpretive biblical references. These references afford the reader the opportunity of more fully explicating each of the emblematic elements.

Another form of visualization to which the margins contribute is the creation of motif. We have already referred to the story of Lot fleeing from Sodom as an important biblical counter-point to the story of Christian's pilgrimage. A similar Old Testament story occurs as a motif in *The Pilgrim's Progress: The Second Part*. Although Christiana sets out on her pilgrimage accompanied by two neighbours, only one is prepared to go the distance with her: "Timorous *forsakes her; but* Mercie *cleaves to her*" (*TPP* 2, 183). With the parallel structure and particular word choice of this marginal note, Bunyan uses the language of the book of Ruth to set up a parallel to the story of Christiana and Mercie.

> Orpah kissed her mother in law; but Ruth clave unto her. And she said, Behold, thy sister in law is gone back unto her people, and unto her gods; return thou after thy sister in law. And Ruth said, Entreat me not to leave thee.... "
> (Ruth 1:14-16)

The allusion in the marginal note establishes a biblical analogue to the Christiana-Mercie relationship. This implicit Naomi-Ruth motif in the background of the Christiana-Mercie pilgrimage is made explicit when the two women reach the House of the Interpreter, where the Interpreter says to Mercie:

> Thy setting out is good, for thou hast given credit to the truth, Thou art a *Ruth*, who did for the love she bore to *Naomi*, and to the Lord her God, leave Father and Mother, and the land of her Nativity to come out, and go with a People that she knew not heretofore. (206-7)

The Bible story creates a backdrop of visual imagery against which the Christiana-Mercie pilgrimage is set. A long and dangerous trip made by two women issues in a romance set in a barley field and resulting in a wedding celebration. It is a story full of the promise of new life. A typological reading of this story, familiar to Bunyan's readers, saw in its events a foreshadowing of the union of the Church (Ruth = Wife = Church) with Christ (Boaz = Husband = Christ). This pictorial motif creates the artistic conditions in which Christiana and Mercie's becoming mother-in-law and daughter-in-law by means of the marriage of Mercie and Matthew (261) fulfils the typological design, even if the marriage does not seem particularly apt in connection with the foreground of the pilgrimage narrative itself.

There are cases in which Bunyan uses a marginal note to create small, precise mental pictures, similar to the vignettes drawn in the margins of medieval manuscripts. Vignettes are a particular aspect of textual margins, defined as:

> [A]n ornamental or decorative design on a blank space in a book ... usually one of small size or occupying a small proportion of the space; spec. an embellishment, illustration, or picture uninclosed in a border, or having the edges shading off into the surrounding paper ....
>
> (*OED*, s.v. "vignette.")

A few examples will suffice to indicate the technique of marginal vignette to which I am referring. "Christ Crucified seen afar off" (*TPP* 2, 191) is a marginal note which invites the reader to envision a miniature but distinct crucifix. "Old Honest asleep under an Oak" (*TPP* 2, 246) conjures, with some explicitness, a traditional picture of a senex.[7] "*A good woman and her bad son" (*Mr.B*, 63) creates a mental cartoon of a caricatured and stereotypically care-worn matron with an evil-looking son.

III

Frequently, marginal notes have affective overtones which create or intensify the emotional colouration of the adjacent narrative. For example, the step-by-step narrative of Emmanuel's withdrawal from Mansoul is emotionally heightened by the marginal notes which offer foreshadowing, "Christ withdraws not all at once" (*HW*, 153). In the narrative, the motion of the present-tense verbs and the almost breezy folk-narrative style keeps the story going: "Wherefore what does he but in private manner withdraw himself ... and so away from Mansoul he goes." But opposite this is the stark summary of absence in the margin: "He is gone" (*HW*, 154). In the three words of the marginal note Bunyan recreates the emotion of a great loss: "He is gone" is capable of being read as a groan, or a gasp of realization—as well as a succinct summary of a major narrative event. It represents, with stark simplicity, an inexpressible loss and grief, with an impact like that of the "She ys ded!" spoken by the narrator late in Chaucer's *The Book of the Duchess*.[8] The marginal note creates a significant intensification of the affective quality of the narrative at this crucial point.

In one kind of interaction with the narrative, the marginal references may significantly ameliorate the visualization invited by the narrative. An example of this is the marginal amelioration of the harsh action within the text in the scourging of the forgetful pilgrims by a "shining one" (*TPP*, 134). The marginal chain of references explains the nature of God's chastisement of his elect people (134). The scriptures cited are "Deut. 25. 2" in which a limited, judicial scourging is established as a suitable punishment: "[I]f the wicked man be worthy to be beaten ... the judge shall cause him ... to be beaten according to his fault, by a certain number." This is followed in the margin by a reference to "2 Chron. 6. 26,27," which establishes the idea of affliction as a means God uses to bring about repentance: "If they pray ... and turn from their sin, when thou doest afflict them; Then hear ... and forgive." And finally, the pericope in the text, "*As many as I love, I rebuke and chasten; be zealous therefore, and repent*" is annotated in the margin with its scripture source, "Rev. 3. 19."[9] All of these scriptures need to be taken into account if the intended affective response is to be experienced by the reader. Rather than experiencing only a withdrawal of sympathy from the "ministering angel," the reader who responds to the margins as well as to the text reflects God's mercy as it operates judiciously in chastisement.

Sometimes a marginal note illumines the corresponding narrative passage in a way which is analogous to the way in which a pictorial illumination might affect an adjacent passage in a medieval book. This occurs in *The Pilgrim's Progress* when Bunyan describes Christian at the cross. Within the narrative, the passage is almost disappointingly sparse. Anticipation of this event in the narrative has been carefully built. The "great burden upon his Back" is one of the first things we note about the pilgrim (*TPP*, 8). It is this burden which almost drowns him at the "Slow of Dispond" (*TPP*, 15). And when at last Christian reaches the gate, we are as eager as he for relief, listening as he asks the gatekeeper, Goodwill, "If he could not help him off with his burden that was upon his back." This Goodwill cannot do, telling him, "As to the burden, be content to bear it, until thou comest to the place of *Deliverance; for there it will fall from thy back it self." The marginal note which answers the asterisk in the narrative gives a doctrinal statement: "There is no deliverance from the guilt, and burden of sin, but by the death and blood of Christ" (*TPP*, 28). So, coming to this place of "deliverance" becomes an important delayed event much anticipated in the story.

But when, finally, Christian comes to the cross, the scene is very bare of detail. A little hill. A bare cross. The burden loosed and tumbling, rolling into a tomb, open as a symbol of resurrection:

*When God releases us of our guilt and burden, we are as those that leap for joy.

*Zech.12.10.

He ran thus till he came at a place somewhat ascending; and upon that place stood a *Cross*, and a little below in the bottom, a Sepulcher. So I saw in my Dream, that just as *Christian* came up with the *Cross*, his burden loosed from off his Shoulders, and fell from off his back; and began to tumble; and so continued to do, till it came to the mouth of the Sepulcher, where it fell in, and I saw it no more.

Then was *Christian* glad *and lightsom, and said with a merry heart, *He hath given me rest, by his sorrow; and life, by his death.* Then he stood still a while, to look and wonder; for it was very surprizing to him, that the sight of the Cross should thus ease him of his burden. He looked therefore and looked again, even till the springs that were in his head sent the *waters down his cheeks. (*TPP*, 38)

Even with the description of Christian's joy within the narrative, and the didactic generalizing note in the margin explaining the doctrinal significance of the event, the passage feels inadequate to the anticipation which has been built up in the story. It is marginal note which, when fully attended to, supplies the pictorial detail and emotional colouration that seem to be lacking from the text. The verse referred to in Zechariah says:

And I will pour upon the house of David, and upon the inhabitants of Jerusalem, the spirit of grace and of supplications: and they shall look upon me whom they have pierced, and they shall mourn for him, as one mourneth for his only son... (Zech. 12:10)

The referring, text-extensive note in the margins supplies the emotional component so understated in the narrative. The verse from

Zechariah invites a reader who reads the Old Testament text as prophetic of the sufferings of Christ to envision or "look upon" the
suffering Christ, "whom they have pierced." The attention to the
wounds of Christ implied by this text would be capable of evoking
within the spiritually sensitive reader emotions of closely-related grief
and joy parallel to those experienced by the pilgrim.

The Zechariah reference, long assimilated into the Christian repertoire of Messianic prophecies, would have also suggested mirroring
passages in the New Testament. One of these passages refers the
reader to the historic moment of the crucifixion:

> ... one of the soldiers with a spear pierced [Jesus'] side, and
> forthwith came there out blood and water. And he that saw
> it bare record, and his record is true.... For these things
> were done, that Scripture should be fulfilled ... 'They shall
> look on him whom they pierced.' (John 19:34-37)

The other New Testament echo of the Zechariah reference refers
the reader forward to the *eschaton*:

> Behold, he cometh with clouds; and every eye shall see
> him, and they also which pierced him: and all kindreds of
> the earth shall wail [cf. "mourn"] because of him. Even so,
> Amen. (Rev. 1:7)

The Zechariah reference in the margin invites the reader to a
meditation upon the whole meaning of the cross. On the one hand, it
significantly intensifies the emotional potential of the scene in the narrative, potentially cuing an affective response in the reader much
more profound than that suggested by the narrative passage alone.
On the other, it also opens Christian's own experience at the Cross
outward onto a panoramic view of the entire scope of God's saving
act in Christ's death: as it was foretold, accomplished, and is yet to
find final fulfillment. "*A Man *cloathed with Raggs ... a Book in his hand,
and a great burden upon his Back*" (*TPP*, 8) is, at the Cross, included in a
cosmic drama. And with him, the common reader is invited, by way
of a marginal reference which illumines the narrative, to experience
sorrow for Christ's suffering, joy at its outcome in one's own salvation, and anticipation of Christ's final and still-awaited victory. Without attention paid to the marginal reference at this point in the

narrative, the full significance of the scene at the Cross can scarcely be appreciated.

IV

As we have seen, the marginal notes to Bunyan's narratives assist the reader in the creation of aural and visual effects which subtly enrich and enhance the narratives and which are capable of ameliorating or intensifying the reader's affective response to events and scenes within the narratives. But the marginal notes also elicit a deliberate and conscious effort on the part of the reader, frequently inviting the reader to enter into the delights of pun, puzzle, and riddle. Word-games of various kinds, from the basic game of allegory through the specific games of solving word-puzzles and understanding proverbs or riddles, are features of the narrative text as a whole.[10] The intense reader involvement Bunyan elicits is not quite as solemn as proposed by Iser, that is, caused only by a reader's search for certainty of salvation,[11] or as burdensome as Haskin suggests, bearing the load of the reader's need to gain a personal mastery of biblical interpretation. The intense reader engagement with the texts is also the intensity of play.

A careful reading of the marginal notes turns up numerous interesting examples of marginal notes as puns, riddles, or enigmas, or as succinct solutions to riddles or enigmas in the narrative, the marginal note operating rather like a riddle solution which in a modern children's book may be printed upside-down at the bottom of the page on which the riddle appears. The marginal biblical reference—"I Pet 5. 8"serves as the solution to an in-text riddling allusion to "he that goeth about as a roaring lion" (*TPP*, 39) Nothing in the narrative text identifies this "he," but the marginal notation turns the reader to the scripture which says, "Be sober, be vigilant, because your adversary the devil goeth about seeking whom he may devour." The reference to "Hos. 14. 9" placed adjacent to the narrative describing the discourse of the shepherds at the Delectable Mountains provides another example of a riddle being solved by a text (*TPP*, 119). In this case, the verse referred to says:

> Who is wise, and he shall understand these things? prudent, and he shall know them? for the ways of the Lord are right, and the just shall walk in them: but the transgressors shall fall therein. (Hosea 14:9)

In other words, the riddling style of the shepherds is designed as a "code" which can be "unscrambled" by those who have spiritual insight. By being able to play the game of recognition of references, the reader discovers herself to be an insider to information that is closed to others.

Enigmatic marginal notes set up puzzles for the reader: "Knowledge and knowledge" (*TPP*, 82) and "A way and a way" (*TPP*, 132) are examples of such puzzles, solved only by previous "inside knowledge" or a close reading of the text. For the reader who can identify the two kinds of knowledge, spiritual and carnal, or who understands that the two ways refer to the true way of salvation, *via* Christ and the cross, and the false way by means of human effort, there is the pleasure of "getting the right answer." For the reader puzzled by an enigmatic marginal note, of course, the marginal notes operate text-intensively, offering the reader the invitation to go back into the narrative text to read again for a fuller understanding.

The marginal gloss "*Award of grace" (*TPP*, 42) seems at first glance to be a straightforward indexing gloss on the adjacent narrative, where it is linked by asterisk to the "*Arbour*, made by the Lord of the Hill, for the refreshing of weary Travailers." But it also may be a pun on "a word of grace" which would be another way of saying "gospel." It is through the speaking of the word of grace that those who have been attempting to gain assurance of salvation by their works—"weary travailers"—learn that it is "by grace you are saved through faith ... not of works lest any man should boast," (Eph. 2: 8, 9) and thus find the refreshing Reformation Arbour of salvation through grace alone.[12]

Another example of a punning marginal note occurs in *The Holy War* when Mansoul discovers that the Prince has withdrawn. A marginal note describes the condition of the Mansoulians: "They are all agast" (*HW*, 156). This is an ironic pun, powerfully played alongside the narrative text where, "my Lord *Secretary* [i.e., the Holy Ghost] ... whom they had grieved with their doings" was inaccessible to them (157). The very serious problem is that they are not "a-ghast" in the sense of being filled with the Holy Spirit, but rather "aghast," shocked, at his having withdrawn from them.

It is not hard to imagine that there may well have been family games based on the shared oral reading of a segment of *The Pilgrim's Progress* followed by the quotation of marginally cited scriptures by various family members. But at every reading a more subtle kind of game was certainly being called for by the referring notations, a serious game to be sure, but a game nonetheless. The self-affirming pleasure of recognition leads to the mental effort of remembering the text or, perhaps, the physical act of looking it up, and then of relating the marginal note to the narrative text, or of relating marginal notes one to the other. The marginal notes create intense reader involvement by inviting the reader into games of "Can you recall?" "Get it?" "Go back and check."

The referring notes also invite vigorous mental activity as the reader is challenged to relate scripture to scripture, scripture to narrative text, and then both scripture and narrative to life. The continually present words, characters, and Bible stories open out at the side of the ongoing narrative like a mirrored hall through which the reader can go from Bunyan's narrative to biblical narrative and back again with ease. Linking of Old Testament texts with New Testament texts in accordance with the internal rules of any particular reference string is in itself a mental exercise demanding considerable sophistication. Related passages from the Hebrew and Christian Testaments are often cited together, with lexical or thematic links to be established by the reader. "*Mich 7. 8" is cited together with "*Rom. 8. 37" after Christian's battle with Apollyon (*TPP*, 60). The text from the Hebrew prophet says, "Rejoice not against me, O mine enemy: when I fall, I shall arise; when I sit in darkness, the Lord shall be a light unto me" (Micah 7:8). The New Testament assertion is that "[I]n all these things we are more than conquerors through him that loved us" (Romans 8:37). Here, the link between the two passages is thematic: the idea of a spiritual victory over an enemy is repeated in the two passages. In other reference chains, the reader might find a key word linking all of the texts, or texts which represent type and antitype, prophecy and fulfillment.

With every set of references which goes beyond providing direct annotation for quotations within the narrative text, there is room for the "game of the margins" to be played: recalling a text within its immediate, local context, and juxtaposing it with other texts related to it, and then determining the implied relationship to the narrative. Discovering the thematic, linguistic, or typological links between cited scriptures, or between Scripture and narrative text, would have been a challenging mental game for the attentive and competent reader.

It is not necessary to accept the theory that Bunyan had covert political intentions expressed through his writings to find some interesting "hidden messages" in the narrative text and marginal notations which would have been private messages of hope and comfort to a persecuted people. Christopher Hill makes an interesting comment concerning the relationship of biblical commentary and political statement: "Seventeenth-century use of Biblical commentaries to make covert political suggestions has never, I believe, been properly studied. It could be a way of discussing the undiscussable."[13] The game element of detecting and responding to such consoling messages may have been an important part of reading for those who, like the author himself, were experiencing persecution that ranged all the way from scorn to imprisonment and confiscation of property.[14]

A marginal note, "*Christian *had into the Study, and what he saw there*," (53) identifies the point in *The Pilgrim's Progress* at which Christian is initiated into his role as part of a suffering people.

> Then they read to him some of the worthy Acts that some of his servants had done: As how they had subdued King-doms, wrought Righteousness, obtained Promises, stopped the mouths of Lions, quenched the *violence of Fire, es-caped the edge of the Sword; out of weakness were made strong, waxed valiant in fight, and turned to flight the Ar-mies of the *Aliens*. (*TPP*, 53)

At House Beautiful, both Christian and the reader gain the comfort of a lineage of persecuted believers. Later, the indictment of Faithful and Christian by the court at Vanity Fair affords the sense of continuity between the current persecutors known to Bunyan and his fellow Nonconformists and great persecutors of the past. The Judge in his speech to the jury makes reference to the legal precedence of persecu-tion established by Pharoah, Nebuchadnezzar, and Darius, with men-tion of them respectively annotated in the margins by references to "Exod. 1," "Dan. 3" and "Dan. 6" (*TPP*, 96). By identifying these per-secuting kings as servants to the prince of Vanity Fair, "our noble Prince *Beelzebub*," (94) Bunyan places the contemporary persecuting king, Charles II, in rather dubious company and in disreputable ser-vice.

In the account of his pilgrimage prior to meeting up with Chris-tian, Faithful talks of an encounter with one who is called "this bold faced *Shame*," a swiftly-sketched character of oxymoronic name, who embodies the general contempt and opprobrium which Nonconform-ists had to endure. Shame "objected *the base and low estate and condition of those that were chiefly the Pilgrims," (*TPP*, 72) and an asterisk in the narrative at this point is answered by the marginal notation, "*John 7. 48." This textual citation, obliquely connected to the narrative rather than referring to anything within the quotation, is added to the second edition. The verse cited asks: "Have any of the rulers … believed on him?" — most surely a question which those of Bunyan's persuasion would have been asking about the contemporary religious and political leadership of England.

A similar subtle reference to the spiritual impercipience of those in power occurs in the passage of narrative describing the fall of "Vain-confidence." A marginal reference beside the narrative describing "a deep Pit … to catch *vain-glorious* fools withall" is to "Isa. 9. 16." The text referred to, rather than merely echoing the adjacent passage, states: "For the leaders of this people cause them to err; and they that are led of them are destroyed" (*TPP*, 112).

Twentieth-century readers probably do better with the larger game of Bunyan's narratives than with the specific interplay of references and narrative. We can, at least in theory, still respond to the game of allegory, in which the concrete sign stands for a generalized or abstract referent. (Or, to use Bunyan's own definition, "Doth call for one thing to set forth another" (*TPP*, 6, line 15).[15]

Bunyan grows into the game of language as he grows in confidence as a thinker and a writer. In the preface to *Grace Abounding*, the convert who had been called from his game of cat into an experience of God is very serious in his use of language:

> God did not play in convincing of me; the Devil did not play in tempting of me; neither did I play when I sunk as into a bottomless pit … : wherefore I may not play in my relating of them, but be plain and simple, and lay down the thing as it was. (*GA*, para. 3, 4)

It is obvious from this statement that Bunyan has had to fight against a powerful impulse to "play" in his presentation.[16] Fortunately for his readers, the play impulse in language and life was too great to be held in check permanently. By the time he writes the "Apology" for *The Pilgrim's Progress*, Bunyan is able to defend his choice of playful language vigorously, if anxiously. Admitting that his original intention was merely "mine own self to gratifie" (*TPP* 1, line 24), he acknowledges the fun element of creating story: "I set Pen to Paper with delight" (*TPP* 1, line 29). He asserts boldly that, on the basis of biblical precedents, "I have leave" to write in an allegorical mode (*TPP* 5, line 33), announcing a new freedom both in the exercise of his craft and in his relationship to a "God ... /[Who] guide[s] our Mind and Pens for his Design" (*TPP* 6, line 11).

After the success of *The Pilgrim's Progress*, Bunyan accepts play as a legitimate mode of conveying truth, and the apologies to his later allegories become increasingly confident. In the prefatory verse "To the Reader" of *The Holy War*, no apology for the allegorical method is offered; indeed, the voice in the verse speaks from within the allegorical mode, affirming "*That* Mansoul's *matchless Wars no Fables be*" (*HW* 4, line 7). Thus, in *The Holy War*, Bunyan plays the game of allegory from the very outset. By the time he "sends forth" *The Pilgrim's Progress, The Second Part*, Bunyan dismisses any disagreement with his mode of story-telling with a playground taunt:

> *Some love no Cheese, some love no Fish, & some*
> *Love not their Friends, nor their own House or home;*
> *Some start at Pigg, slight Chicken, love not Fowl,*
> *More then they love a Cuckoo or an Owl.*
> (*TPP* 2, 171, lines 29-33)

Bunyan is quite explicit about the double role of his allegorical mode. It both reveals and conceals the truth.[17] "Wisdom's covered/With its own mantles," (*TPP* 2, 171, lines 35-6) he says, and advises his Book to "*shew to all / That entertain, and bid thee welcome shall / What thou shalt keep close, shut up from the rest*" (*TPP* 2, 172, lines 2-4). In this revealing and concealing function, the marginal notes, particularly the scripture references, play an important part, for the biblical texts "speak" only to those who already have put them into their memory, and serve as a distraction or as an obfuscation to those who do not at a glance understand the verse to which reference is being made — or who are unwilling to expend the effort to make themselves acquainted with the biblical intertext.

Bunyan is especially sensitive to the spirit of play in his young readers, who may well have had to struggle to wrest the meaning from his stories. He offers to double the profit "*to their paines/ Of reading*" (*TPP* 2, 170, line 3): the pleasure and fun of opening "*pretty riddles*" (*TPP* 2, 170, line 2) added to the value of spiritual instruction. To appeal to the reader's "*nimble Fancies*" (*TPP* 2, 173, line 27) is to invite them to play his game with him. Throughout his "Apology" and

"Sending Forth," one hears echoes of the village green not only in the taunting chant noted above, but also in the cries of blindman's buff, (*"The blind also, delightful things to see"* (*TPP* 2, 7, line 1), hide-and-go-seek (*"a search after what it fain would find,/ Things that seem to be hid"* (*TPP* 2, 171, line 3), mumming or play-acting (*"Present thee to them in thy* Pilgrims *guise"* (*TPP* 2, 171, line 1), and music and dance (*"these strings,/ ... if but touched will such Musick make,/ They'l make a Cripple dance"* (*TPP* 2, 173, lines 22-23).

R. Rawdon Wilson argues that literary texts differ from games in some primary respects, particularly in that conventions which govern the creation and recuperation of literary texts are not as rigid as are rules in games, but he sees a number of ways in which texts may be playful:

> They may be thought of as the result of play — an author's, a reader's or an entire culture's ... [P]lay may seem delib-
> erate ... or as welling up ... from an author's unconscious
> in paronomasia, word games, and wit.... [P]lay can be seen
> to become game when the presence of a constitutive rule
> exists.[18]

If allegory as a whole can be seen to be a sort of linguistic and literary game, then Bunyan's narratives can be seen as games in themselves which also contain many other elements of game and play: word and sound play, pun, wit, and parody; games of recall and recognition; games of cross-matching from narrative to intertext and back again. For an author who set out renouncing play, Bunyan has produced very playful works. And, for that reason, they are deeply engaging, thoroughly delightful works which continue to yield double profit for the reader's pains.

Bunyan's marginal notes add artistic detail to his narratives, prompting the reader to embellish the stories in ways which range from responding to aural appeal and summoning visualization to entering into affective meditation or solving puzzles. The notes convey aural, visual and affective appeals. At many points, they offer the intellectual challenge of recognition and application. And at others, they afford the reader the opportunity to verify the conclusions and generalizations reached during the reading of the narrative against the summaries and epigrams in the margin. At every point, the marginal notes involve the reader in the serious play of allegory as well as in the solving of particular referential or interpretive puzzles. The notes are not only functional aids to understanding, but also adornments to the story and invitations to play.

CHAPTER 5:

Reading out to the Edges:
The Opening of The Pilgrim's Progress

In our study so far, we have considered many specific local effects created by the marginal notes in interaction with the central narrative text. We have yet to demonstrate how to exegete an entire narrative passage, taking into full account the marginal commentary.

It is, of course, our contention that a reading which is fully informed by the authorial marginal voice will be distinctively different from other readings. For one thing, more careful attention to the marginal notes produces a more alert reading of the narrative itself, the text-reflexive function of the marginal notes forcing attention again and again to salient points at which interpretive choices must be made.

With an attentive, marginally guided reading, aspects of the text which are problematic often become clear, the text-extensive function taking the reader to explanatory intertextual material. Assimilations of Bunyan's narrative to points of view quite incongruent with his inscribed intention can also be challenged on the basis of the marginal notes.

In this chapter, I will attempt to demonstrate how a close reading of the narratives, taking full account of the margins, can revitalize our readings of Bunyan's works. The method of demonstration is to give a close and marginally-informed exegesis of the first paragraph of *The Pilgrim's Progress*. This will, I believe, show how integral the notes are to an understanding of the text, and how they enrich, guide and enable the interpretation of the narrative.

The opening paragraph of *The Pilgrim's Progress*, often praised for its purity of plain English style, ought also to be praised for the way in which the active use of the marginal space amplifies the narrative, so that in the interaction of the marginal notes and the narrative text, the major themes of the book are introduced. Here is the text:

The *Gaol.

*Isa.64.6.
Lu.14.33.

Psal.38.4.

Hab.2.2.

Act.16.31.
*His Out-cry

As I walk'd through the wilderness of this world, I lighted on a certain place, where was a *Denn; And I laid me down in that place to sleep: And as I slept I dreamed a Dream. I dreamed, and behold *I saw a Man *cloathed with Raggs, standing in a certain place, with his face from his own House, a Book in his hand, and a great burden upon his Back.* I looked, and saw him open the Book, and Read therein; and as he read, he wept and trembled: and not being able longer to contain, he brake out with a lamentable cry; saying, *what shall I do?* (8)

While the swift sequence of simple, active verbs in this opening paragraph (walked, lighted, laid me down, slept, looked, saw, open, read, wept, trembled, brake out), moves us directly into the action of the narrative, the margins slow the reading, forcing the reader to stop and consider, to take time to grasp the "keys" with which the meaning of the story will be unlocked. With the very first paragraph of the story, Bunyan establishes a tension between forward narrative motion and the drawing aside of the reader or the pilgrim for further instruction, a tension which is an essential element of Bunyan's story-telling. Throughout *The Pilgrim's Progress*, Bunyan uses the technique of the oral raconteur in setting an action in motion and then heightening the listener's anticipation by repeatedly delaying realization of the goal through deferrals, digressions, and discourses.

Both Salzman and Keeble note the "braking" or "dragging" effect of the marginal notes against the forward thrust of the narrative. Keeble sees the marginal notes as functioning to keep the reader alert to the didactic purpose of the narratives.

> [I]n the margins of his allegories, Bunyan is there, pointing up the moral and taking us off from a preoccupation with the outside of his dream. Even as the imaginative power of his text invites the suspension of our critical faculties in involvement and identification with the tale and its characters we are inhibited from making this reponse by being alienated from the text.... Moments of tension in the plot are never allowed to pass without our absorption in the detail of the allegory being disturbed in this way [i.e., by marginal commentary].[1]

Salzman sees the marginal glosses as being in "tension with the narrative momentum: the descriptive glosses summarize narrative events; the interpretative glosses pull the reader up and reinforce the didactic point of the allegory; the biblical citations, if the reader follows them up (as Bunyan's contemporaries certainly did), drag against the narrative. The didactic, the expository, the interpretative, balance the narrative surface, the 'action.'"[2]

The marginal notes to the first paragraph of *The Pilgrim's Progress* slow the plunge into story while the author offers interpretive keys to important elements which will thematically dominate the narrative. The warning made explicit in Bunyan's preface to *The Holy War* is here implicitly set out by the format: the reader who goes to work "without [the] key" (*HW*, 5) is likely to be set off on a misreading.

The marginal notes beside the narrative text at the beginning of *The Pilgrim's Progress* are structurally analogous to the four notes played by the violins at the start of the *Finale* to Mozart's "Jupiter" Symphony. As Mozart gives instrumental voice to four notes and then goes on to build a "structure from that four-note measure that is truly awe-inspiring,"[3] so Bunyan here sounds distinctive thematic notes which are then played out in dramatic scenes, imagery patterns, and doctrinal discourses throughout *The Pilgrim's Progress*.

I

A careful reading of the first marginals will be as fruitful in interpreting the entire work as is an attentive listening to the opening notes of Mozart's work. Essential, unifying themes and recurrent motifs are introduced. In the standard edition, as in editions after the third, the first marginal note is an interpretive gloss, identifying the "Denn" within the narrative text as "The *Gaol," and thus fusing for the reader the dream-narrator within the story with John Bunyan himself as a prisoner. "The *Gaol" is among the many marginals added to the third edition, printed in 1679. Whether the marginal notes and narrative passages added after the first edition reflect a temporarily eased political climate,[4] or whether they were added in response to misunderstandings or questions on the part of Bunyan's earliest readers, the verbal glosses (as distinct from the biblical references) to the first paragraph represent a whole class of "afterthoughts" added to the second and third editions as the author again re-read and interacted with his text as it appeared in print and its no longer merely presumed audience.

In opening the story with the narrator in "the wilderness of this world" before shifting to a "Dream" landscape, Bunyan frames his narrative in a way which has a long literary tradition, however he may have come to know of it. Both *The Divine Comedy* and *The Fairie Queene* have early wilderness scenes.[5] *The Divine Comedy* opens with the narrator "alone in a dark wood," about which he asks,

> How shall I say
> what wood that was! I never saw so drear,
> so rank, so arduous a wilderness!
> Its very memory gives a shape to fear.[6] (Canto I, 3-6)

This "arduous wilderness," identified by Dante as "the Dark Wood of Error" into which he has strayed from the True Way, is part of the traditional landscape of the courtly romance tradition, which in turn developed through elaboration of the epic landscape of classical antiquity.[7] Such wilderness scenes are usually relieved by a *locus amoenus*, complete with a refreshing spring, within them. Spenser's forested wilderness in *The Faerie Queene* is also a "wandring wood"; the deceptively attractive *locus amoenus* is "*Errours den*" (Bk I, Canto 1, stanza 13).[8]

Bunyan's "wilderness of this world" is somewhat different from these wild forests, both in landscape and significance. Like the later "Wilderness" through which the pilgrims pass just before arriving at Vanity Fair (*TPP* 85, 88), the "wilderness of this world" is named rather than described. The demonstrative pronoun separates "this world" from another landscape, the landscape of "That [world] which is to come," as the full title of the book tells: *The Pilgrim's Progress from This World to That which is to Come, Delivered under the Similitude of a DREAM Wherein is Discovered, The Manner of his setting out, His Dangerous Journey, and Safe Arrival at the Desired Country*. Bunyan does not compare, as does Augustine, "The City of Man" and "The City of God," but, rather, "the wilderness of this world" with the shining, populous, ordered City, lyrically described in the glimpse framed by opening and closing gates at the end of the story:

> Now just as the Gates were opened to let in the men, I looked in after them; and behold, the City shone like the Sun, the Streets also were paved with Gold, and in them

> walked many men, with Crowns on their heads, Palms in
> their hands, and golden Harps to sing praises withall....
> And after that, they shut up the Gates: which when I had
> seen, I wished my self among them. (*TPP*, 162)

The story, then, is framed by "the wilderness of this world" and "the Celestial City." The motion of the narrative is from one landscape to a radically different one.

The "wilderness of this world" is more closely related to desert wildernesses of the Bible than to the treed wildernesses of medieval and earlier Renaissance literature: the wilderness to which the Spirit led Jesus "to be tempted of the devil" after his baptism is empty but for "wild beasts"(Mark 1:12,13). Even Milton is sparse in his description of this wilderness, "A pathless Desert, dusk with horrid shades."[9] Bunyan may also have been summoning the image of the desert wilderness which the children of Israel traversed, "the waste and howling wilderness" of Deuteronomy 32:10. As interpreted in the Psalms, this desert landscape stands for testing, reproof, and also for God's providential care: "They wandered in the wilderness in a solitary way.... Then they cried unto the Lord in their trouble, and he delivered them out of their distresses"(Ps. 107:4-7). It is thus a suitable image for tribulation and persecution seen, as Bunyan is wont to see it, in a dual aspect, both as God's chastisement and as the opportunity for his people to experience his provision (*Seasonable Counsel, MW 10*, 96-97).

Whether the wilderness of Bunyan's opening paragraph is a forest or a desert, the narrator "walks through" it rather than wandering in it, taking a purposeful trajectory through it. The wilderness is not, as in Dante or Spenser, a place of wandering in a labyrinth of error; nor, is it, as in the re-interpretation of the Pentateuchal record in Psalm 107 or Paul's appropriation of the wilderness imagery for the Christian experience in 1 Corinthians 10, a place of doubt and murmuring against God. It is, rather, a place of "going on," of steadfast purposefulness, as well as of weariness, suggested by the plodding motion of the opening line, with its many monosyllabic words trudging one after another.

As in *Faerie Queene*, the "Denn" in the opening lines of *The Pilgrim's Progress* is an inverted or reversed image of the traditional *locus amoenus*. This "Denn" suggests a place suitable for wild beasts rather than for a human, a place of dangerous rest rather than of refreshment. Bunyan's contemporary, Benjamin Keach, does not have an entry for "wilderness" in his index of symbols. He does, however, define "Den" as follows: "A [Den] is a Cavity or hollow place of Stones or great Rocks in which Thieves and Robbers hide themselves."[10] This connection of "Den" as a place for thieves would add another dimension to Bunyan's one-word sketch, with its marginal interpretation, of "the Gaol." Gerald Cragg comments on conditions in British jails during the Puritan persecution:

> [M]any of the prisons were fit only for beasts.... In theory
> the felons were segregated from the other prisoners but ...
> [a]ll too often, every distinction between prisoners disap-
> peared, and those who suffered for conscience' sake were
> thrust in among those who were punished for crime.[11]

From this same "Den" Bunyan wrote *Grace Abounding*: "*I being taken from you in presence ... now from* the Lions Dens *... do look yet after you all*" (*GA*, 1). The "Lions Den" image invokes the story of Daniel and a complete range of associations concerning God's faithfulness to his exiled people whom he protects despite malicious political opposition and tyrannical kingly decrees (Dan. 6). Evidently, this link was made by early readers; the frontispiece added to the third edition and repeated for many successive editions thereafter, shows the Author lying asleep above a "denn" complete with a lion.

After the interpretive gloss, "*Gaol," we find in the margins a list of biblical references. Three of these biblical references are interpretive in function; they identify elements of the initial emblematic description of "the Man" who becomes the central character of the allegory. The "Raggs" in which the Man is "cloathed" are to be identified by means of the reference to Isaiah 64:6; the man's stance, "with his face from his own House," is to be interpreted in the light of Luke 14:33; and the "great burden upon his back," is to be explained by the reference to Psalm 38:4. The fourth scripture reference, Habakkuk 2:2, functions, as we shall see, not only interpretively, by identifying the "Book" the man is holding as Holy Scripture, but also to offer, text-extensively, an apologetic for the work and a miniature version of the story line. The fifth reference, Acts 16:31, serves as a text-reflexive interpreting note, emphasizing the narrative question with which the paragraph ends and the story actually begins. The story which follows upon this brilliant opening is an expansion and exemplification of the themes cryptically indicated by the marginal reference.

According to Northrop Frye, "We have actual allegory when a poet explicitly indicates ... how a commentary on him should proceed."[12] With the string of marginal notes referring the opening paragraph to biblical antecedents, Bunyan makes a strong indication of the equivalencies he wishes the reader to establish in understanding and appropriating *The Pilgrim's Progress*. Each of the texts opens out on a wider biblical context and invokes the entire Bible as intertext.

The marginal references to the first paragraph also explicitly link the images of the first paragraph with an expanded Puritan discourse later in the book. All of the biblical references introduced alongside the first paragraph are again referred to marginally or quoted in the passage near the end of *The Pilgrim's Progress*, in which Hopeful retells the story of his conversion to faith in Christ (*TPP* 137-44). In Hopeful's "testimony," all of the major themes of the work which are introduced in the opening paragraph are brought together and explicated.[13] Much of the doctrine implicit in the first paragraph of *The Pilgrim's Progress* and developed throughout the rest of the story is made explicit in this discourse. Indexing summaries in the margins added to Hopeful's story in the second edition indicate very clearly the stages in the progress of the soul towards salvation, serving to emphasize and make even clearer the Calvinistic conversion paradigm that is employed throughout the entire story. Owen Watkins, deriving a paradigm from a wide review of Nonconformist spiritual autobiographies, presents the sequence of events as follows:

> [C]onviction of sin usually led a man to diligent attendance on the means of grace (sermons, prayer, Bible reading, meditation) which he afterwards recognized as a period of 'legal work,' since it was an attempt to satisfy God's justice through the performance of dutied.... A reformation of outward behaviour was one of the earliest signs of an awakened conscience.... Release came when the gospel was experienced in the heart as well as with the understanding, and this was the high-water mark of the conversion process.[14]

Hopeful's testimony is framed by two discourses with Ignorance (*TPP*, 123-25, 144-49), throwing into sharp contrast the difference between assurance of salvation and the illusion of it. In our discussion of the biblical marginal references to the first paragraph, we need also look at their further use in the Hopeful and Ignorance passages to see the unfolding significance of each of the scriptures cited.

The first of the marginal references to the opening paragraph is Isaiah 64:6, glossing the "Raggs" in which the man is "cloathed." Its significance becomes easier to grasp when we set out the narrative with its answering marginal text in the antiphonal form we introduced earlier as being something like the way in which a biblically literate reader might actually have encountered the passage:

But we are all as an unclean thing, and all our righteousnesses are as filthy raggs, and we all do fade as a leaf, and our iniquities like the wind have taken us away. *Isa. 64.6	I dreamed, and behold *I saw a Man* *cloathed with Raggs …

The twin components, "dream" and "interpretation" are placed before the reader as Bunyan transfers the reader into a spiritual realm, where all physical elements have spiritual significance. Whereas the "Denn" is a physical place located in "the wilderness of this world," the dream sets up a new set of equivalences, to be worked out in the interaction of the marginal notes and the narrative text. As with biblical dreamers like Joseph (Gen. 37, 41) and Daniel (Dan. 2, 5, 7, 8), being able to interpret correctly is a sign of divine favour to the reader, and Bunyan gives as many hints as he can to help the reader into a favoured role as dream interpreter.

Identification of clothing as "outering" the inner spiritual condition of the Man is the first step in placing the entire narrative in the appropriate conceptual space, of finding appropriate equivalences between sign and signification, which is necessary in reading allegory. Clothing, of whatever kind, in whatever world, signifies status; since the dream frame has taken us into a particularized experience mode to be understood in the light of the marginal notes, it becomes clear that the "Raggs" in which Bunyan's introduced character is clothed indicate his status in the "dream world" in which the rest of the story will take place. Some recent readings have seen the rags as representing the man's social and economic status: Hill, for example, says: "When we first see him the Pilgrim is in rags—allegorical rags, to be sure, but they also represent his real poverty."[15] More deliberately literal and materialist is what Michael McKeon characterizes as his "willful 'misreading' of the text," in which he sees *The Pilgrim's Progress* as reflecting the gradual rise of the English lower class: "Christian's progress recapitulates the rise of the new gentility of early modern England: from common laborer or *noblesse d'epee* to *noblesse de robe*, from medieval military knighthood to Restoration administrative bureaucrat, from knight-at-arms to Whitehall courtier." [16]

But with the "key in the window," the Nonconformist reader for whom Bunyan wrote would quickly know within what frame of reference to construct primary meaning. No matter how ragged the reader or the writer in material terms, the margin informs that the man is clothed with the inadequate moral covering provided by one's own righteousness or good deeds. The concept underlying this imagery of man's righteousnesss as no better than a covering of filthy rags seems to be that God "sees right through" man's best attempts at moral goodness, and finds such efforts to be "full of holes."

When we compare the emblematic "Man" at the beginning of the book with Hopeful's description of conversion, or with Bunyan's account of his own conversion in *Grace Abounding*, we discover that we have plunged, *in medias res*, into the story of a man who has already come through a number of preliminary stages of dawning spiritual illumination. An initial stirring of "some desires to religion" and awareness of sin, followed by attempts at moral reformation, would have been already experienced before the man could be found standing, burdened and in rags, desperate and ready to run. [17] Of Hopeful, the margin notes, "*When he could no longer shake off his guilt by sinful courses, then he endeavours to mend*" (TPP 139). It is only after Hopeful has taken up "Religious Duties, as Praying, Reading, weeping for Sin, speaking Truth to my Neighbours, etc." that he begins to experience real conviction of sin, "and that over the neck of all my Reformations" (*TPP* 139). Attempts at reformation serve only to convince him that he cannot achieve righteousness through his own efforts. And it is at this point in Hopeful's narrative that Bunyan re-introduces the Isaiah 64:6 text, this time quoting it twice within Hopeful's narrative:

Reformation at last could not help, and why. Isa. 64.6	*Hope.* There were several things brought [conviction] upon me, especially such sayings as these; *All our righteousnesses are as filthy rags* ... with many more the like: From whence I began to reason with my self thus, If *all* my righteousnesses are filthy rags, if by the deeds of the Law, *no* man can be justified .... Then 'tis but a folly to think of heaven by the Law.... [I]f I look narrowly into the best of what I do now, I still see sin, new sin, mixing it self with the best of that I do. (139, 140)

The image of "*a Man *cloathed with Raggs*" is, therefore, that of a man who has had sufficient spiritual illumination to accept as truth the declaration of the Book as recorded in Isaiah 64:6: that his best attempts at moral goodness are ragged and inadequate. This man has come to see himself as he is figured in the Book that is in his hand, rather than as he appears to his family and neighbours. And the reader who is able to "see" this man as the Dreamer does, through the lens of the biblical "spectacles" in the margin, is being granted a spiritually illumined view of the initial moral condition of humankind within Bunyan's Calvinistic view.[18] By checking one's own interpretation against that offered by the marginal reference, the reader can immediately determine whether or not he or she has entered into the "dream-world" of spiritual reality constructed by the narrator.

This biblically-illumined view of humanity in a beggarly spiritual and moral condition is opposite to the view of Ignorance. When Christian puts to Ignorance the proposition that our thoughts of ourselves are good or true only to the extent that they agree with the Scripture, "*When we pass the same Judgement upon our selves which the Word passes,*" he clarifies the nature of such a judgement by quoting from Romans 3: "*The Word of God saith of persons in a natural condition, There is none Righteous, there is none that doth good*" (*TPP* 146). The reply Ignorance makes is informed by an English Pelagianism: "I will never believe that my heart is thus bad" (*TPP* 146). Ignorance represents an unenlightened state of mind about the natural condition of the human heart, a condition which Bunyan intends to correct in his readers from the very first biblical reference in the margins.

The emblematic vision of the Man in Rags sets out for the reader a doctrinal and moral concept which the reader must grasp if the kind of progress the pilgrim makes is ever to be understood. This is a rags-to-riches story, but both the rags and the riches belong to a scheme of meaning with its point of reference in a spiritual realm.

It is at the point of misunderstanding the kind of progress which the pilgrim is supposed to make that Stanley Fish's reading of *The Pilgrim's Progress*, perceptive in many ways, breaks down. The pilgrim certainly makes no progress if "a growing sense of accomplishment and self-satisfaction" is seen to be a goal of the narrative.[19] But there is no reason to suggest that this is the progress which is in view. The full title of *The Pilgrim's Progress* tells us that the progress is a movement across an invisible line which separates two realities; it is a progress in the sense of motion, "from this World to That which is to Come." The narrative also works out an internal progress of the soul toward holiness, describing not only the experience of justification but also the process of sanctification. To whatever degree the pilgrim is "progressive," it is in these directions. A reading which takes into full account the interpretive guidance of the marginal references from the outset of the book will bring the reader to conclude with Knott that significant shared celebrations of progress and insight are clear evidence that there is progress in the course of the story.[20]

As a one-word description of clothing, "Raggs" also introduces an imagery pattern which will run from the opening sentences to the closing paragraphs of the book, a pattern in which clothes operate as signifiers of spiritual states. At every crucial spiritual development in the book, clothing is mentioned and its significance is stressed both within the narrative and by means of the marginal notes. It is part of the still-ragged Christian's initial hope, based on "*the words of [his] book*" that, in the Kingdom to which he is travelling there will be given "**Garments that will make us shine like the Sun in the Firmament of Heaven*" (*TPP* 13). The marginal reference here emphasizes the equivalency between garments and righteousness by referring the reader to Revelation 3.4: "[Those] which have not defiled their garments ... shall walk with me in white."

At the Cross, after Christian's burden falls from his back, he is met by three "shining ones" who grant him, in true fairy- and folk-tale fashion, three boons, one of which is a "change of Raiment" signifying an alteration in status and spiritual state:[21]

*Mark 2. 5	[T]he first said to him, *Thy sins be forgiven.* The second stript him of his Rags, and *cloathed him
*Zech. 3. 4	with change of Raiment. The third also set *a mark in his fore-head, and gave him a Roll with a Seal
*Eph. 1. 13	upon it...that he should give it in at the Cœlestial Gate. (*TPP*, 38)

In this passage, there is a highly important further development of the imagery pattern in which clothing = spiritual state. A "change of raiment" indicates the granting of righteouness, not on the basis of the individual's good deeds, but by an act of God's grace, symbolized by the passive receiving of a change of raiment.[22]

Fletcher draws attention to the importance within allegory of the distinctive ornamentation by which an allegorical figure or character can be known. He uses the Greek word for ornament, *kosmos*, in his discussion of clothing or ornament as metonymic of the entire order of the universe in which the allegory operates and to which it refers. In Fletcher's discussion, *kosmos* signifies both a macrocosm (a universe which implies large-scale order) and a microcosm (a small-scale sign of that order which indicates rank in a hierarchy). As a noun, *kosmos* "could be used of decoration, embellishment, costume, especially if significant of status ... related to hierarchic rank ... or ... indicating membership in a secret society."[23] As an adjective or adverb, it implies the propriety and decorum suitable to one's place in the larger scheme or order. Thus *kosmos* points from the significant detail of dress to the entire order for which it stands.

In *The Pilgrim's Progress*, the robe received at the Cross can be seen to be this distinguishing ornamentation or *kosmos*. The importance of this "costume" is that it represents both the entire universe of meaning to which the allegory relates and the character's particular place or rank within that realm. The robe received at the Cross represents the imputed righteousness of Christ granted as a "covering" to the believer.

J. I. Packer adequately summarizes the Reformers' position:

> [T]he "sole formal cause" of justification is not *God's* righteousness *imparted*, but *Christ's* righteousness *imputed*; and to make their meaning more clear they drew a distinction between Christ's *active* obedience to God's law, in keeping its precepts, and his *passive* obedience to it, in undergoing its penalty, and insisted that our acceptance as righteous depends on the imputing to us of Christ's obedience in both its aspects.... [I]t is on the ground of his obedience, as our representative and substitutionary sin-bearer, and that alone, that righteousness is reckoned to us and sin cancelled.[24]

Bunyan has thoroughly assimilated what both Luther and Calvin had taught: that the "righteousness of faith" is a righteousness attributed to the believer as a free gift by which Jesus Christ's personal righteousness is attributed or "imputed" to the believing individual. Calvin explains this in a passage in which the symbolism of clothing is implicit:

> If you look to yourself damnation is certain: but since
> Christ has been communicated to you with all his benefits,
> so that all which is his is made yours ... [h]is righteousness
> covers your sins—his salvation extinguishes your condem-
> nation; he interposes with his worthiness, and so prevents
> your unworthiness from coming into the view of God.[25]

This teaching is clearly reformulated within the Westminster Confession,[26] and permeates Puritan doctrine as encountered in sermon
and print. Bunyan may have developed his concept of this doctrine
from childhood catechism as well as from sermon and "godly discourse." We know that he encountered it directly in Luther's discussion of Galatians. Luther taught:

> [T]his most excellent righteousness, the righteousness of
> faith, which God imputes to us through Christ without
> works, is neither political nor ceremonial nor legal nor
> work-righteousness but is quite the opposite; it is a merely
> passive righteousness, while all the others, listed above, are
> active. For here we work nothing, render nothing to God;
> we only receive and permit someone else to work in us,
> namely, God.... [T]his is the righteousness of Christ and of
> the Holy Spirit, which we do not perform but receive,
> which we do not have but accept, when God the Father
> grants it to us through Jesus Christ.... [T]hat divine, heav-
> enly, and eternal righteousness ... we can obtain ... only
> through the free imputation and indescribable gift of God.[27]

It is in perfect keeping with Luther's theology that Bunyan's pilgrim is passive both in the removing of the old and in the conferring
of the new *kosmos* or identifying sign.

The text-extensive marginal reference which accompanies Christian's "a change of raiment" is Zechariah 3:4. By recalling or looking
up this text, the reader finds a highly pictorial prophetic vision set as
a parallel to the experience of justification which Christian experiences. In the Old Testament passage, a high priest-elect stands before
God, apparently for confirmation of election:

> [1]And he shewed me Joshua the high priest standing before
> the angel of the Lord, and Satan standing at his right hand
> to resist him. [2]And the Lord said unto Satan, The Lord re-

buke thee, O Satan . . . ³Now Joshua was clothed with
filthy garments, and stood before the angel. ⁴And he answered and spake unto those that stood before him, saying,
Take away the filthy garments from him. And unto him he
said, Behold I have caused thine iniquity to pass from thee
and I will clothe thee with change of raiment. (Zech. 3: 1-4)

The important inference to be drawn from the marginal reference is
that when God grants imputed righteousness, Satan's accusations are
silenced and the "elect" becomes fit to be a member of the "priesthood of believers."[28] The robe given to Christian at the Cross becomes
the sign of both his change of status and of his new destiny.

Not only does the robe externalize the changed spiritual condition
of the pilgrim and indicate his new status; it also represents the visible
part of his Christianity. Bunyan speaks elsewhere, using similar imagery, of holiness of life as the "badge" or "livery" of the Christian:
"[W]e should hide our faith in Christ from *no man*, but should rather
make a discovery of it, by a life that will do so. For our profession
thus managed is the *badge*, and the Lords livery, by which we are distinguished from other men" (*Seasonable Counsel, MW 10*, 51). As such
a distinguishing livery, the garment of the pilgrim plays an important
role in several key scenes in *The Pilgrim's Progress*.

Almost immediately after the scene at the Cross, Christian encounters two other approaches to righteousness personified as Formalist and Hypocrisie who "come tumbling over the Wall on the left
hand of the narrow way" (*TPP*, 39). When Christian denies that they
are truly in the way, the two characters reply sulkily that the only difference they can see between themselves and Christian is "the Coat
that is on thy back, which was, as we tro, given thee by some of thy
Neighbours, to hide the shame of thy nakedness" (*TPP*, 41). Their
comment is highly ironic, since Christian's garment has indeed been
given him by some of his "Neighbours" in the new spiritual community of which he is now a part, which includes "an innumerable company of Angels," a thought which Bunyan found immensely
comforting during his own crisis of faith (*GA*, para 262).

Because from their "natural" or unregenerate point of view, Formalist and Hypocrisie can see the "coat" of imputed righteousness
only in its external manifestation of godly character and upright
moral behaviour, they find the distinction made by Christian as to the
nature of true righteousness and its imputation both trivial and irritat-

ing. Christian's reply indicates the extreme importance of his garment:

*Gal. 2. 16

*Christian *has got his*
Lords Coat on his back,
and is comforted therewith,
he is comforted also with
his Mark, and his Roll.

Chr. By *Laws and Ordinances, you will not be saved, since you came not in by the door. And as for this Coat that is on my back, it was given me by the Lord of the place whither I go; and that, as you say, to cover my nakedness with. And I take it as a token of his kindness to me, for I had nothing but rags before; and besides, *thus I comfort my self as I go: Surely, think I, when I come to the Gate of the City, the Lord thereof will know me for good, since I have his Coat on my back; a *Coat* that he gave me freely in the day that he stript me of my rags. (41)

In text and marginal summary in this passage, the garment is identified as a "Coat," creating an allusive connection to Joseph's "coat of many colours" in the Old Testament. Christian later describes the garment as "this Broidred Coat" (*TPP*, 49). It is this description which informs the woodcut illustrations in the thirteenth edition, in which the long cloak that flows down from the pilgrim's shoulders appears to be patterned like a damask.

For Christian, as for Joseph, the coat is a sign of a father's favour: "I take it as a token of his kindness to me," says Christian, picking up a further echo of the Joseph story: "Now Israel loved Joseph more than all his children ... and he made him a coat of many colours" (Gen. 37:3). For Christian, as for Joseph, the symbolic garment which speaks a father's special love makes him an object of envious hostility heard in the growing surliness of Formalist and Hypocrisie—"[T]hey made him but little answer; only they bid him look to himself" (*TPP*, 40)—and by the implicit hostility of their scorning laughter: "To these things they gave him no answer, only they looked upon each other, and *laughed*" (*TPP*, 41).[29]

While the "Coat" causes envy and resentment among the religious attitude personified by Formalist and Hypocrisie, it creates another kind of hostility in the irreligious or secular society. This we discover when the bestowed garment plays an important part again in the scenes at Vanity Fair. The first reason for the stir caused by the pilgrims is their distinctive garb:

The first cause of the hubbub.   First, the Pilgrims were cloathed with such kind of was diverse from the Raiment of any that traded in people therefore of the *fair* made a great gazing up said they were Fools, some they were Bedlams, an Outlandish-men. (*TPP*, 89-90)

In this reference to the special clothing of the pilgrims we can detect another oblique reference to the earlier allusion to Joseph's many-coloured coat. To the inhabitants of Vanity Fair the coat is merely seen as the motley of "Fools," the bizarre dress of "Bedlams," or, at the very least, the barbarian mode of another realm.

The early woodcut illustrations do not pick up on this identification of the pilgrims as "Fools" because of their clothing; the pilgrims are usually shown in the typical plain garb of contemporary Puritanism. But in a very interesting "reading" of the Vanity Fair passage provided by an uncompleted watercolour illustration by William Blake, the two pilgrims are sketched standing, apparently shackled, on a pedestal; in the foreground below them, in the multi-coloured garb of fools are two mountebanks performing antics. The pilgrims as fools for Christ's sake are made a gazing-stock (cf. m.n., "*They that fly from the wrath to come, are a Gazing-Stock to the world*," [10]); the real fools play out their little acts in front of them. The inhabitants of Vanity Fair demonstrate by their reaction to the pilgrims and their clothing that they are "natural men," unable to receive "the things of Spirit of God: for they are foolishness unto [them]" (1 Cor. 2:14).[30]

The clothing of the pilgrims is, in fact, so distinctive and so offensive to the men of Vanity Fair that it becomes the focus of the first examination of the pilgrims. Christian and Faithful are asked to explain "whence they came, whither they went, and what they did there in such an unusual Garb" (*TPP*, 90). The end result of the first examination is that the pilgrims are beaten and besmeared, an attack made on their "apparel" as it is represents their godly moral character.[31]

The pilgrim's distinctive *kosmos* or ornamentation is envied and resented by Formalist and Hypocrisy, mocked and ridiculed and besmeared by the citizens of Vanity Fair. But in their attacks, they at least acknowledge that the garment exists and has significance. Ignorance, on the other hand, refuses even to acknowledge the need of such a garment. His "False Faith" relies not on Christ's perfect righteousness but on his own (*TPP*, 147). He fails to understand that it is Christ's "*personal obedience*" accepted by grateful faith which is the distinctive covering garment by which the pilgrim who has come by way of the Cross can be known, "*under the skirt of which, the soul being shrouded, and by it presented as spotless before God, it is accepted, and acquit from condemnation*" (*TPP*, 148).

This doctrine of imputed righteousness always brings the Christian — whether Bunyan or his pilgrim — up against the charge of antinomianism. Ignorance exclaims:

> What! would you have us trust to what Christ in his own person has done without us? This conceit would loosen the reines of our lust, and tollerate us to live as we list: For what matter how we live if we may be Justified by Christs personal righteousness from all, when we believe it? (*TPP*, 148)

And Bunyan allows Christian an explosion of impatience in reply:

> Ignorance is thy name, and as thy name is, so art thou. Ignorant thou art of what Justifying righteousness is…. Yea, thou also art Ignorant of the true effects of saving faith in this righteousness of Christ, which is, to bow and win over the heart to God in Christ, to love his Name, his Word, Ways and People. (TPP, 148)

To choose to sin in the face of God's love and grace would, for Bunyan and his church, mark a person as among the non-elect. For anyone who has, with Christian, really *seen* Christ dying for him on the Cross, willful sin is merely unthinkable. The meaning of Ignorance's allegorical name is here carefully explicated. He is willfully ignorant on a number of important doctrinal issues: he is ignorant of his own sinful condition; ignorant about the nature of imputed righteousness; and he is ignorant of the way in which a free and gracious justification wins the heart of a person to a loving desire to obey and please God in every aspect of life.[32]

In the end, as the story has foreshadowed all along, the robe of imputed righteousness for which the Man has exchanged the "Raggs" of the first paragraph of the book, becomes the basis of entrance into or exclusion from the Celestial City. It is to *"the Marriage Supper of the Lamb,"* the eternal celebration of the union of the Church with God, that the pilgrims have been called. As Christian and Hopeful and their heavenly entourage draw near the Gate of the city:

> ... a company of the Heavenly Host came out to meet them:
> To whom it was said, by the other two shining Ones, These
> are the men that have loved our Lord ... and that have left
> all for his holy Name, and he hath sent us to fetch them....
> Then the Heavenly Host gave a great shout, saying,
> Blessed are they that are called to the Marriage Supper of
> the Lamb. (*TPP*, 160)

The garment of Christ's imputed righteousness which has distinguished the pilgrims through life is now seen to be a wedding garment. When Ignorance is asked for the Certificate which would have been given him had he gone to the Cross for pardon, "he fumble[s] in his bosom for one" (*TPP*, 163). In describing this single fumbling action, Bunyan's masterful touch is evident: the reader who looks where Bunyan points "sees" that Ignorance is lacking not only the certificate of election but also the robe of imputed righteousness. And when the King "... command[s] the two shining Ones ... to ... take *Ignorance* and bind him hand and foot, and have him away," (163) Bunyan provides for his biblically literate reader a verbal echo from a familiar parable from the Gospels, to help provide an understanding of the basis of Ignorance's exclusion.

The phrase, "bind him hand and foot," occurs in the parable told by Jesus in Matthew 22:1-14. "[T]he kingdom of heaven is like unto a certain king, which made a marriage for his son." By using this verbal echo, Bunyan conflates the picture of the "Marriage Supper of the Lamb" of Revelation 19 with the parable of the "marriage of the king's son."

In that parable, one of the longest and most complex recorded in the gospels, the first-invited guests "ma[k]e light" of the king's gracious invitation to the wedding feast honouring his son (v. 5). The invitation is then widened to include even less worthy subjects, the king commanding his servants to "Go ... therefore into the highways, and as many as ye shall find, bid to the marriage" (v. 9). The pattern within the parable of rudeness, indifference, and arrogant presumption on the part of invited guests reaches its climax when a guest arrives improperly attired:

> [11] And when the king came in to see the guests, he saw there a man which had not on a wedding garment; [12] And he saith unto him, Friend, how camest thou in hither not having a wedding garment? And he was speechless. [13] Then said the king to the servants, Bind him hand and foot, and take him away, and cast him into outer darkness. (Matt. 22:12-14)

Failure to wear the appropriate wedding garment may, to the modern reader, seem a trivial reason for damnation. However, within the context of the parable itself, the man was apparently without excuse ("he was speechless"). According to an oral sermonic tradition, the wedding garment would have been provided for all guests at the host's expense. This is a reading in full harmony with Bunyan's use of clothing imagery throughout *The Pilgrim's Progress* and of this parable at the critical moment of Ignorance's exclusion from the Celestial City. Samuel Bolton, in *The Wedding Garment and the Wedding Supper* (1647) writes: "No man will go naked to a Feast. Your apparel here [i.e., at Communion] is the Wedding Garment; Christ for justification, Christ for sanctification; and he that came without this, you see what became of him."[33]

The applicability of this parable to Ignorance's arrogant and presumptuous attitude is evident. He does not merely fail to have the garment of imputed righteousness, which is the *kosmos* of the pilgrim; he has willfully and deliberately rejected that garment and chosen to present himself on the basis of his own righteousness. When he fumbles in his bosom, he is fumbling among what we suddenly realize can only be "filthy Raggs."

Bunyan makes his point: willful, arrogant ignorance of one's own sinfulness and of Christ's righteousness cannot be brought into the Celestial City. Despite the realism of the portrayal, within the allegorical frame of reference of *The Pilgrim's Progress*, Ignorance is not an individual but an attitude. "The fault of Ignorance ... is pride, ... a belief in one's own righteousness leading to a rejection of the means of grace offered in Christ."[34] Bunyan seems to indicate in the damnation of Ignorance not a deficiency of grace on God's part, but a lack of response to that grace. When we recognize the understated but highly significant "garment" motif that runs through *The Pilgrim's Progress*, keyed by the first marginal reference, we come closer to understanding what Bunyan's authorial audience would have quickly grasped: that Ignorance *must* be cast out from the Celestial City.

For the pilgrims who have received the covering of Christ's right-eousness, imputed to them by God's grace in response to their faith, the "rags to riches" theme has its grand finale played off against the minor chords of Ignorance's damnation. It is the final vision of the dream, the moment toward which the entire narrative has been yearn-ing, when the King having examined "each man his Certificate which they had received in the beginning," the Gate is opened:

> Now I saw in my Dream, that these two men went in at the
> Gate; and loe, as they entered, they were transfigured, and
> they had Raiment put on that shone like Gold." (161-162)

Better than in a fairy-tale, the theme of transformation by which "*Christ makes Princes of Beggars*" (*TPP*, 53) begins at the Cross and is completed in the final transfiguration at the reception into the Celes-tial City of "the Man" once "cloathed with Raggs." Both the rags and the robe which replaces them are fundamental to the narrative in its embodiment of important Reformation themes. It is not by accident that Bunyan gives "Isa. 64. 6" as his first interpretive key; in doing so, he introduces both his central doctrinal theme — the radical moral fall-enness of humanity and God's gracious reponse to that necessity — and the garment motif which exteriorizes and explains it.

II

The second interpretive key to *The Pilgrim's Progress* is also impor-tant, counterbalancing what has long been seen as an artistic defect in it: Christian's apparent heartlessness in leaving his family behind. Mark Twain has Huck Finn describe *The Pilgrim's Progress* as being "about a man that left his family, it didn't say why."[35] Rupert Bridges writes: "Bunyan's artistic awkwardness is prodigious.... The facts of the story are that a man learning that the town in which he lived was damned to destruction thereupon ran away and left his wife and chil-dren to their fate." Christopher Hill says, "It is a dramatic opening. Allegorically it is very telling, based on the Biblical adjuration to leave one's family for Christ's sake. But taken literally it is horrifying." The marginal reference cues us to an understanding of the passage. Like the damnation of Ignorance, the urgency of the "effective call" of the emblematic, still unmoving Man is placed at the borderline between "the natural" and "the spiritual" planes of understanding. Read with the accompaniment of the marginal reference, the passage is as follows:

Lu. 14. 33:
So likewise, whosoever he be of you,
that forsaketh not all that he hath, he
cannot be my disciple.

I saw a Man ... standing in a certain place,
with his face from his own House ... (8)

Once again, not just a text, but an underlying construction of reality is introduced. As with the damnation of Ignorance, we here need the biblical intertext to guide us in the creation of allegorical equivalences. If the biblical and theological framework is not reconstructed, and the narrative is read "naturally" rather than "spiritually," the whole artistic edifice crumbles under the miscontruction.

The marginal reference is text-extensive, summoning for the reader a text in St. Luke's gospel which occurs in a passage to which reference is made at several other critical junctures in *The Pilgrim's Progress*. In its biblical context, the text has Jesus speaking of choice and priorities:

> 26 If any man come to me, and hate not his father, and mother, and wife, and children, and brethren, and sisters, yea, and his own life also, he cannot be my disciple. 27 And whosoever doth not bear his cross, and come after me, cannot be my disciple.... 33 So likewise, whosoever he be of you that forsaketh not all that he hath, he cannot be my disciple. (Luke 14: 26-27, 33)

The importance of this passage in Bunyan's vision of the Christian life can be seen by his repeated references to it throughout the rest of the narrative. When the Man begins to run, and his Wife and Children cry after him to return, "the Man put his fingers in his Ears, and [runs] on crying, Life, Life, Eternal Life" (*TPP*, 10). The action of Christian is again to be interpreted in the light of a marginal reference to Luke 14:26. The citation occurs again in the margin, this time together with parallel passages from the other Gospels, opposite a *verbatim* quotation of the text within the monologue in which Evangelist reprimands Christian for giving ear to Mr. Worldly-Wiseman. Part of Worldy-Wiseman's appeal to the pilgrim has been his statement that, "[T]hou mayest send for thy wife and Children to thee to this Village [Morality], where there are houses ... which thou mayest have at reasonable rates" (*TPP*, 19). Evangelist admonishes Christian:

Mark 8. 34.
John 13. 25.
Mat. 10. 39.
Luke 14. 26.

... [T]he King of glory hath told thee, *that he that will save his life shall lose it: and *he that comes after him, and hates not his father and mother, and wife, and children, and brethren, and sisters; yea, and his own life also, he cannot be my Disciple.* (*TPP*, 23)

Here, by placing the full quotation of the biblical text within the narration, Bunyan entrusts to Evangelist the task of dispelling any lack of clarity on the priority of God's call.

In Christian's discourse with Charity, there is further and fuller discussion about a person's responsibility for and to his family (*TPP*, 51-52). This discourse, added to the second edition, is summarized by a series of marginal notes which both index and intensify the significance of the interchange: "Christian's *love to his Wife and Children*"; "**The cause why his Wife and Children did not go with him*"; "Christian's *good conversation before his Wife and Children*"; and, finally, "Christian *clear of their blood if they perish.*"

For Bunyan's pilgrim, the claims of natural human love present the most painful obstacle to his leaving the City of Destruction; despite his desperation for salvation, he can only escape the clamour of his love for them by "put[ting] his fingers in his Ears" (*TPP*, 10). His love for his family renders him susceptible to Mr. Worldly-Wiseman's offer of being able to have a respectable religion with familial endorsement. But by placing Christian's decision to go on pilgrimage in the context of the radical and absolute claims of Jesus on all who would follow him, and by forcing Christian to account to Charity, representing the highest of the Christian virtues, for his decision, Bunyan endeavours to clear his pilgrim of the very charges which critics have laid. At the same time, by depicting how wrenching such a repudiation is, Bunyan sets Christ's claims into a context of the human experience of conflicting loyalties. Here, at the very outset of *The Pilgrim's Progress*, the reader is tested by the absolute nature of God's call on the pilgrim's life and the relativizing of the claims of kin.[36]

Without doubt, we are *meant* to feel the painfully strong pull of family ties as Christian sets out, to recognize the cost of the commitment he makes, not least of which is to be widely misunderstood. As Keeble says, "This opening does not deny human affection: on the contrary, we miss the real measure of Christian's anguish and the true quality of his commitment if we miss this tension."[37] By means of the marginal reference adjacent to the first paragraph, as well as by the later addition to the narrative of the dialogue with Charity, Bunyan does what he can to ensure that his hero is seen not as a selfish man concerned only with his own salvation, but rather as someone who understands the radical claims of Christ's call into discipleship.

Bunyan will later devote *The Pilgrim's Progress, The Second Part* to a demonstration that salvation for Christian's family is implicit in the costly choice the Pilgrim makes. As Keeble points out, the pilgrim loses his family temporarily to gain it eternally, a true gospel paradox explicated in and linking the two parts of *The Pilgrim's Progress*: "[H]ad Christian *not* abandoned his family in an apparently selfish desire to gain his own salvation, Christiana never would have set out. In other words, Christian has quite literally saved his family by abandoning it; in preferring Christ before the creature he has made possible the salvation of the creature."[38]

The third of the "keys" beside the opening paragraph explains yet another detail of the emblematic image, focusing our attention on the "great burden upon [the Man's] Back." With the adjacent text written out in full, the sentence reads as follows:

Psal. 38: 4.
For mine iniquities are gone over mine head: as an heavy burden, they are too heavy for me.

I saw a Man with ... a Book in his hand, and a great burden upon his Back.

This emblematic symbol with its interpretive marginal scripture reference introduces the theme of conviction. The burden which the man carries is the realization of the extent and seriousness of personal sin. Conviction is another doctrinal theme which is re-worked in the Hopeful narrative in a long and detailed answer to the question, "*And did you presently fall under the power of this conviction?*" (*TPP*, 138 ff.), and again in the early pages of *The Pilgrim's Progress, The Second Part* as Christiana experiences "**Convictions seconded with fresh Tidings of Gods readiness to Pardon*" (*TPP*, 179).[39]

Bunyan would not be surprised to find that such painful conviction as he dramatizes in *The Pilgrim's Progress* might well be seen by some to be pathological. The pilgrim's own family and friends make such a diagnosis, deciding "that some frenzy distemper had got into his head," and offering a number of contemporary cures, which, as an interpretive marginal note added to the third edition says, are ineffective since they are "**Carnal Physick for a Sick Soul*" (*TPP*, 9). Throughout the story, Bunyan introduces people who have no problem with the burden of sin. Pliable has no encumbrance during his brief struggle at the "Slow of Dispond"; it is Christian, who "could not get out, because of the burden that was upon his back" (*TPP*, 15). Mr. Wordly-Wiseman suggests that there are ways less radical than going to the Cross to deal with the troublesome burden. Ignorance certainly does not feel the weight of this burden. For the Puritan, the sense of sinfulness was a part of the "effectual call" which brought about a spiritual awakening. Thus, the burden, however heavy, is a gift, a "godly sorrow [which] worketh repentance to salvation" (II Cor. 7:10).

There is an important link between "the Book" in the man's hand at the beginning of *The Pilgrim's Progress* and "the burden" on his back. It is through reading the Book that he becomes aware of his sinfulness; Hill is at least partly correct when he notes, "The Pilgrim had acquired his burden by reading the Bible." But if a burdensome conviction of sin comes by way of the Book, so, too, come directions for salvation (**Christ and the way to him cannot be found without the Word*, *TPP*, m.n. 10); and even more important, the promise of God's mercy extended to the one who comes to him. Haskin identifies the burden with the need to be able to assure oneself of election by successfully interpreting the Bible; he sees the burden as a hermeneutic task. Luxon refutes this reading by pointing out, "If ... Christian's burden is essentially, a 'burden of interpretation,' we should expect that the Interpreter could remove it." Thomas Luxon offers, instead, "The burden falls from his back as he experiences an image, a 'sight' of the Word made flesh crucified in his place…. The Word Christian experiences at the Cross is the end of a process of signification which invites readers to see all things and all words as signifiers of a single signified—the Word."[40]

In Hopeful's case, too, the Bible both brings about a sense of sinfulness and encourages him to find release. He lists a total of eight means by which his sins were brought to mind, including, "If I have heard any read in the Bible" (*TPP*, 138). Faithful, Hopeful's spiritual mentor, "gave [him] a Book of Jesus his inditing, to incourage me the more freely to come" (*TPP*, 141). The "Book" functions both to bring about a knowledge of sinfulness and to inform the reader of God's merciful inclination and gracious invitation. It thus both produces the burden and provides means for relief from it. The pilgrim's burdened condition in the opening emblem is the beginning of an ongoing narrative preparation for the extremely important scene at the Cross in which he is released from this burden. Christian later describes this release to Piety at House Beautiful: "I saw one, as I thought in my mind, hang bleeding upon the Tree; and the very sight of him made my burden fall off my back (for I groaned under a weary burden) but then it fell down from off me" (*TPP*, 49).

Bunyan makes it clear that Christian's motivation for going on pilgrimage is effectively transformed by this experience of release from the "*guilt, and burden*" of sin (*TPP*, 28, m.n. 28) at the Cross. At first a flight motivated by fear of divine judgement and carried on in the desire to be freed from a "weary burden," the journey continues impelled by love. Piety's question, "*And what is it that makes you so desirous to go to Mount* Zion?" is answered by Christian: "Why, *there I hope to see him *alive,* that did hang *dead* on the Cross.... For to tell you truth, I love him, because I was by him eased of my burden" (*TPP*, 50).

As with the theme of Christ's righteousness imputed to the believer, the theme of conviction and deliverance from its burden is first given pictorial and experiential development; the theme is then worked out in doctrinal terms in the discourses between Hopeful and Christian, and between the two pilgrims and Ignorance. Under the influence of a Scripture-based conviction of his sinfulness, Hopeful discovers that nothing that he does is untouched by his fallenness. He confesses, "[N]otwithstanding my former fond conceits of my self and duties, I have committed sin enough in one duty to send me to Hell" (*TPP*, 140). It is this conviction of sinfulness and the inability to deal, not merely with the outward manifestations of sin, but with its inner root, which drives Hopeful to get spiritual counsel and to "intreat upon my knees with all my heart and soul, the Father to reveal [Christ] to me" (141).

III

The fourth of Bunyan's opening marginal references is to Habakkuk 2:2. This note serves a very complex function of reference and interpretation. Like the other marginal references to the first paragraph, it identifies an element in the initial emblem, in this case, "the Book" the man is holding. Like the other notes, it introduces a central Reformation tenet. But this reference also serves to grant a special, prophetic authority to Bunyan in the writing of *The Pilgrim's Progress*. In its larger context and its later reference in *The Pilgrim's Progress*, the

Habakkuk text reflects on experiences of illumination or revelation, reflecting on the experiences both of reading and writing. Here is the text juxtaposed with the narrative:

Hab. 2. 2:
And the Lord answered me, and said, Write the vision, and make it plaine upon tables, that he may runne that readeth it.

I looked, and saw him open the Book, and Read therein; and as he read, he wept and trembled ...

Like the other references adjacent to the first paragraph, the text which annotates this part of the emblem occurs again in Hopeful's discourse ("Habb. 2. 3," *TPP*, m.n., 142). In Hopeful's discourse, the "Habb. 2. 3" marginal note annotates a direct quotation within the narrative: "*If it tarry, wait for it, because it will surely come, and will not tarry,*" a scriptural fragment which Hopeful applies as an encouragement to go on praying for the inward revelation of Christ: "So I continued Praying untill the Father shewed me his Son" (142). Let us look at the contextual surround of this text.

> [1]I will stand upon my watch, and set me upon the tower, and will watch to see what he will say unto me, and what I shall answer when I am reproved. [2]And the Lord answered me, and said, Write the vision, and make it plain upon tables, that he may run that readeth it. [3]For the vision is yet for an appointed time, but at the end it shall speak, and not lie: though it tarry, wait for it; because it will surely come, it will not tarry. [4]Behold, his soul which is lifted up is not upright in him: but the just shall live by his faith.
> (Hab. 2:1-4)

In addition to the biblical passage on which the one-verse marginal reference opens out, there is a paratextual surround in the 1641 Authorized Version with Tomson's notes which may have conditioned the way in which this passage would have been read by Bunyan himself and by many of his first readers. In this presentation of the text, "The Argument" of Habakkuk is summarized as follows:

> The prophet complaineth unto God, considering the great felicity of the wicked, and the miserable oppression of the godly, which endure all kinde of affliction and cruelty, and yet can see none end.... And lest the godly should despair, seeing this horrible confusion, he comforteth them by this

that God will punish the Caldeans their enemies, when
their pride and crueltie shall be a height: wherefore he ex-
horteth the faithfull to patience.

In the marginal notes to Habakkuk 2, a gloss paraphrases the
opening of the first verse as follows: "I will renounce mine own
judgement, and only depend on God to be instructed what I shall answer them that abuse my preaching, and to be armed against all
temptations." With such explanatory notes, Habakkuk 2 was no
doubt a popular text with the persecuted Nonconformists of the Restoration period; reasons for Bunyan's personal fondness for the passage certainly become clear.

In using Habakkuk 2:2 as a reference beside the opening paragraph, Bunyan offers an interpretive key, identifying the Book the
Man reads as God's written Word, the prophecy which "came not in
old time by the will of man: but holy men of God spake as they were
moved by the Holy Ghost" (2 Peter 1:21), which for Puritan Nonconformists comprised the entire text of the Bible. The referring marginal
note also suggests the reason for God's granting his revelation to man:
in order to prompt a response; to create "*Conviction of the necessity of
flying*" (10) to God for refuge. But the reference has, of course, another
level of application to the text at hand, and that is as a general reference to the entire story, a dream-vision written in order to "*make a
Traveller*" of the reader (*TPP*, "Apology," 6, line 33), or, as Habakkuk
puts it, "that he may run who reads it."

Taken as fragments or, more richly, in their larger context, these
verses from the prophet Habakkuk are appropriated by Bunyan as
authorization for writing theology in the dream-vision mode. Bunyan's demonstrated ability to appropriate scriptures directly to himself would make it possible for him to find a parallel to his own
writing activity in the writing of the prophet; the authorization received by Habakkuk ("the Lord answered me ... Write the vision, and
make it plain") could be "heard" by Bunyan as conferring on both his
writing task and chosen mode a kind of approval by analogy.

The Habakkuk text also offers to the beginning reader an encouragement to keep at the task of reading until the visualization of the
scenes and their spiritual meanings become accessible, "[for] the vision ... shall speak." For the anxious, seeking reader motivated by a
desire to discover in himself signs of salvation, the passage, especially
as cited in the Hopeful discourse, grants the reassurance that one

might well, with Hopeful, have to wait for the inner revelation of Christ, but that "the vision will come."

The theme that it is not the proud but the humble who hear God's word and gain God's favour is struck in the last verse of the Habakkuk passage; while certainly over-materializing Bunyan's allegory, Hill and McKeon have, by their materialistic misreadings, at least helped us to see the degree to which *The Pilgrim's Progress* is a book by and about, as well as for, the poor and humble. The passage concludes with a sentence which sounds the great theme of the Reformation, as of Bunyan's own spiritual illumination: "the just shall live by his faith."

The Habakkuk reference thus sounds a distinctive note with regard to the purpose and authority of *The Pilgrim's Progress*, while at the same time creating a curiously repeating mirrored figure, a sort of verbal equivalent of the *trompe l'oeil* of Renaissance paintings.[41] Not only is this the emblematic Man who will emerge from the freeze-frame of the first paragraph to become the energetic pilgrim of this story; one catches in this image and its marginal note a reflection of writers and readers before this text has been composed — Habakkuk, Old Testament prophet, as a synecdoche for all the writers of Scripture, and the community of readers for whom he wrote; Bunyan himself, the newly-literate reader of the Bible, as we have encountered him in *Grace Abounding*. Caught, too, in the repeating images of reading and writing is the current reader, who becomes a part of a historical succession of those who have read themselves in the Man with the Book. The "Man" with "a Book in his hand" effectively becomes a repeating image by which each reader becomes the person with the book in his or her hand reading about a man with a book in his hand reading about a man with a book in his hand.

This mirror effect of a Man and a Book reflects not only back in time, but also back and forth between margin and narrative, the picture shifting from a prophet writing on tablets to an imprisoned author writing out his story; from the reader of Habakkuk's prophecy, to the reader of the Book within the narrative, to the past and present readers of the narrative itself; the connection even made, tentatively but nonetheless rather audaciously, from the prophetic authority behind divinely inspired Scripture to the inspiring impulse in Bunyan himself.

The fifth marginal reference adjacent to the opening paragraph serves to establish the central narrative question of the work.

Act. 16. 31.
And they said, Believe on the Lord Jesus
Christ, and thou shalt be saved, and thy
house.
*His Out-cry

I saw a Man [with] a Book in his hand ...
and as he read, he wept and trembled:
and not being able longer to contain, he
brake out with a lamentable cry; saying,
what shall I do?

The marginal reference to Acts 16:31 annotates the first direct quotation of the book. The frozen emblem suddenly comes to life as the Man reads, weeps, trembles, tries to hold in his emotions, and finally is forced to utter what is indexed below the marginal reference as "*His Out-cry." His question, "What shall I do?" is the narrative question, the question which the story as a whole sets out to answer. This narrative question sets the terms and conditions for the quest. A reader who cannot care about the Man or "*His Out-cry," can scarcely care about the events of the narrative except by reading them at an adventure story level or by appropriating the narrative to a quite different set of allegorical equivalencies from those set by Bunyan's biblical and theological correlatives.

The specific text cited by the marginal note not only annotates but actually answers the question posed, in the wake of a prison-jolting earthquake, by a jailer at Philippi to the imprisoned missionaries, St. Paul and Silas: "Sirs, what must I do to be saved?" The missionaries' reply summarizes the gospel. The marginal reference in the first paragraph is the answer to the question (v. 31), rather than the question itself (v. 30), encoding for the reader who knows the Bible the whole of the question and, in a very short and pointed form, its answer.

The marginal note, "*His Out-cry," supplies both an indexing rubric to this question and, as a text-reflexive element, forces us to focus on the specific words of the cry as they occur within the narrative text. Again, the stunning integration of narrative and theology which Bunyan has achieved is evident. For in the first instance of asking this question, the Man with the Book does not even know how to frame his question.

"What must I do?" is the central question of all religion; the implied answer would be a list of duties and deeds. But when this central narrative question is repeated just a few paragraphs later, the Man knows, by reading in his Book, a little more of what he needs to ask, and asks the question in a more complete form: "Now, I saw upon a time, when he was walking in the Fields, that he was (as he was wont) reading in his Book, and greatly distressed in his mind;

151

and as he read, he burst out, as he had done before, crying, *What shall I do to be saved?"* (*TPP*, 9)

Evangelist, the pilgrim's spiritual mentor, promises that the pilgrim's question will be answered by Good Will, the Keeper of the Gate, "at which when thou knockest, it shall be told thee what thou shalt do" (*TPP*, 10). But there is an important paradox implied in the long-delayed answer which Christian finally receives to this question.

When Christian reaches the Wicket-Gate, he presents himself, saying: "*Evangelist* bid me come hither and knock (as I did;) And he said, that you, Sir, would tell me what I must do" (*TPP*, 25). Good Will's answer is not in terms of deeds to be done, but in terms of a journey to be taken. After some initial talk, Good Will, the allegorical impersonation of God's attitude of grace, gives an answer which implicitly corrects Christian's question. The significance of a shift from "doing" to "going" is emphasized by the folkloric device of tripling, with the answer which corrects the question repeated the requisite three times: "[C]ome a little way with me, and I will teach thee about the way thou must go. *Look before thee; dost thou see this narrow way? That is the way thou must go. It ... is as straight as a Rule can make it: This is the way thou must go" (*TPP*, 27).

The narrative question, "What must I do to be saved?" is to be answered not by something to *do*, but by a way to *go*, a journey to take; not by a sequence of duties or actions, but by a God-ward direction of life.

This paradox, that what one must do is "not do," is one which Ignorance, thinking religiously, cannot begin to grasp. He simply cannot accept that a person cannot *do* anything for his own salvation except to "fly" from God's wrath to his mercy. The centrepiece of Ignorance's theology is doing: "I believe that Christ died for sinners, and that I shall be justified before God from the curse, through his gracious acceptance of my obedience to his Law: Or thus, Christ makes my Duties that are Religious, acceptable to his Father by vertue of his Merits; and so shall I be justified" (147).

The theme of "doing" *versus* "going" is worked out against negative objections to it in the discourse with Ignorance; it is repeated in a positive way in Hopeful's story. At the absolutely central and crucial discussion of the nature of saving faith, the reference reappears.

Christ is revealed to him, and how.

One day I was very sad, I think sader then at any one time in my life; and this sadness was through a fresh sight of the

greatness and vileness of my sins: And as
I was then looking for nothing but *Hell*,
and the everlasting damnation of my
Soul, suddenly, as I thought, I saw the
Lord Jesus look down from Heaven
upon me, and saying, *Believe on the Lord
Jesus Christ, and thou shalt be saved.* (TPP,
142-143)

Act. 16. 30,31.

The great revelation to Hopeful, as it had been to Christian before him, is that "believing and coming was all one," that all one can *do* is *come*. The narrative question which ends the first paragraph, *"What shall I do?"* is answered dramatically through the events of the narrative of Christian's journey and verbally in Hopeful's recounting of his own journey:

> From all which I gathered, that I must look for righteousness in his person, and for satisfaction for my sins by his blood; that what he did in obedience to his Fathers Law, and in submitting to the penalty thereof, was not for himself, but for him that will accept it for his Salvation, and be thankful. And now was my heart full of joy, mine eyes full of tears, and mine affections running over with love, to the Name, People, and Ways of Jesus Christ." (143)

The narrative question is at this point as fully answered as is possible. The act of believing faith is to "accept [Christ's righteousness] as a gift. Gratitude will be the natural result, and that will be lived out in devotion, fellowship, and obedience.

The sign over the Gate of the Celestial City takes on its full significance both for the characters of the story and for its readers in the light of this revelation. The text under which the pilgrims enter eternal life is written in "Letters of Gold": *"Blessed are they that do his commandments, that they may have right to the Tree of Life; and may enter in through the Gates into the City"* (161). When one *goes* the pilgrim way, one discovers, at the end, that one has *done* God's commandments. The paradox is resolved only at the gate to the Celestial City. The entire pilgrimage is lived in the tension invoked by the phrase, "believing and coming [is] all one."

The whole story is written to convince the reader that, as fallen persons, it is impossible to "do" God's commandments sufficiently fully to gain acceptance apart from the imputed righteousness of

Christ; but that in gratitude for that imputed righteousness, one lives a life which pleases God and fulfills his claims. Any attempt to *do* those commands assumes quite inappropriately an innate ability to *do* them — the error of Ignorance. Bunyan argues in the whole of *The Pilgrim's Progress* that all that anyone who wants to pass through the Golden Gate can do is to go the pilgrim way, actively seeking a revelation or spiritual illumination of the full meaning of Christ's self-offering, and then to keep on going on in loving obedience and gratitude.

In the opening paragraph of *The Pilgrim's Progress*, the references in the margins function in the ways which we discussed earlier (see above, Chapter 3). They interpret, index, and refer. They connect text and the biblical intertext and intensify the narrative by forcing attention to specific thematic and pictorial elements. The scripture passages to which the references direct the reader represent the whole range of literature in the Bible. This initial "reference chain" is extremely rich in its amplification of the allusive adjacent text. The references do not merely annotate words quoted within the text, but rather lead the reader to, or cue in from the reader's memory, scriptures which explain the allegorical symbolism and equivalences, thus introducing the method of interpretation by which the reader is to understand the entire dream-vision. These marginal references sound the main "Gospel-strains" which will form the melodic line of the entire book: man's ragged, burdened condition before salvation, the absolute priority of the claims of the spiritual, the significance of the Word and of words to the experience of salvation, and salvation offered through faith in Jesus Christ.

When "heard" and responded to, these marginal references add immeasurably to the richness of the opening paragraph. They serve the double function of concealing and revealing. In using such cryptic signifiers to elucidate and enrich his meaning, Bunyan speaks like the Shepherds of the Delectable Mountains through whom *"Secrets are reveal'd, / Which from all other men are kept conceal'd"* (123). For the reader who will take the trouble to follow the intertextual leads in the margins, there is an opening out and explication of the text. As with Bunyan's other narratives, the keys to the book are there, "in the window," for the reader who is serious about exploring more fully the richness of the work.

Endnotes

INTRODUCTION

[1] U. Milo Kaufmann, *The Pilgrim's Progress and Traditions in Puritan Meditation* (New Haven: Yale University Press), 25.

[2] See for example: John Bunyan, *The Pilgrim's Progress*, ed. Roger Sharrock (Hartmondsworth: Penguin Books, 1965); John Bunyan, *The Pilgrim's Progress From This World to That Which is to Come and Grace Abounding to the Chief of Sinners*, ed. James Thorpe, Riverside Editions, gen. ed. Gordon N. Ray (Boston: Houghton Mifflin Company, 1969). In "A Note on the Text" to his edition, Thorpe states, "I have . . . omitted the scriptural citations in order to make these works more readable."

[3] Leona Rostenberg, *Literary, Political, Scientific, Religious and Legal Publishing, Printing, and Bookselling in England, 1551-1700*, 2 vols., Preface by Donald G. Wing, Burt Franklin Bibliographical and Reference Series No. 56 (New York: Burt Franklin, 1965); Elizabeth Eisenstein, *The Printing Press as an Agent of Change: Communication and Cultural Transformations in Early-Modern Europe*, 2 vols. (Cambridge: Cambridge University Press, 1979).

[4] Jacques Derrida, *Margins of Philosophy*, trans., Alan Bass (Chicago: University of Chicago Press, 1982).

[5] Most notably for Bunyan studies, see Christopher Hill, *A Turbulent, Seditious and Factious People: John Bunyan and his Church, 1628-1688* (Oxford: Clarendon Press, 1988). Published in the United States as: *A Tinker and a Poor Man: John Bunyan and His Church, 1628-1688* (New York: W.W. Norton, 1990); See also, Margaret Spufford, ed. The World of Rural Dissenters, 1520-1725 (Cambridge: Cambridge University Press, 1995) esp. ch. 1, "The Importance of Religion in the Sixteenth and Seventeenth Centuries," 1-102.

[6] Richard Greaves, *Deliver Us From Evil* (New York and Oxford: Oxford University Press, 1986); Neil H. Keeble, *Richard Baxter: Puritan Man of Letters* (Oxford: Clarendon Press, 1982), and *The Literary Culture of Non-Conformity in Later Seventeenth-Century England* (Athens: University of Georgia Press, 1987); Nigel Smith, ed. *A Collection of Ranter Writings from the Seventeenth Century* (London: Junction Books, 1983) and *Perfection Proclaimed: Language and Literature in English Radical Religion, 1640-1660* (Oxford: Clarendon Press, 1989); John R. Knott, *Discourses of Martyrdom in English Literature, 1563-1694* (Cambridge: Cambridge University Press,1993).

[7] Michael Riffaterre, "Intertextual Representation," *Critical Inquiry* 11 (1984), 142.

[8] As interpreted by Michael Payne, *Reading Theory: An Introduction to Lacan, Derrida, and Kristeva* (Oxford, UK and Cambridge USA: Blackwell, 1993), 241.

[9] John Sturrock, et al., "The Rise of Theory — A Symposium," *Times Literary Supplement* 15 (July 94), 12-13.

[10] Stanley Fish, *Self-Consuming Artifacts: The Experience of Seventeenth-Century Literature* (Berkeley: University of California Press, 1972), 224-64; Wolfgang Iser, *The Implied reader: Patterns of Communication in Prose Fiction from Bunyan to Beckett* (Baltimore and London: John Hopkins University Press, 1974), 1-28.

[11] Fish, *Self-Consuming*, 225.

[12] Wayne Booth, *The Rhetoric of Fiction*, 2d ed. (Chicago: University of Chicago Press, 1983), 71-76.

[13] For critical discussions of Fish's readings, see Gerald Graff, "Interpretation on Tlon: A Response to Stanley Fish," *New Literary History* 17 (1985): 109-27; John R. Knott, Jr., *The Sword of the Spirit* (Chicago: University of Chicago Press, 1980), 185-86, n. 37; Sharon Seelig, "Sir Thomas Browne and Stanley Fish: A Case of Malpractice," *Prose Studies* 11 (1988) 72-84; Joseph H. Summers, "Stanley Fish's Reading of Seventeenth-Century Literature," *Modern Language Quarterly* 35 (1974): 403-17. For exchange between Iser and Fish, see Stanley Fish, "Why No One's Afraid of Wolfgang Iser," *Diacritics* 11.1 (1981): 2-13 and Wolfgang Iser, "Talk Like Whales," *Diacritics* 11.3 (1981): 82-87. For a special issue on Iser, see *Diacritics* 20 (1990).

[14] See for methodology: Robert Darnton, "Toward a History of Reading," *Priceton Alumni Weekly*, 8 April 1987: 19-24; for application to eighteenth-century France, see Robert Darnton, *The Forbidden Best-Sellers of Pre-Revolutionary France* (New York: W. W. Norton, 1995) and *The Corpus of Clandestine Literature in France, 1769-1789* (New York: W. W. Norton, 1995). Eugene R. Kingten also describes method, "Reconstructing Elizabethan Reading, *Studies in English Literature 1500-1900* 30 (1990): 1-18, and applies his method in a full-length study, *Reading in Tudor England* (Pittsburgh: University of Pittsburgh Press, 1996). For work which includes readers contemporary with Bunyan's period, see David Cressy, *Literacy and the Social Order: Reading and Writing in Tudor and Stuart England* (Cambridge: Cambridge University Press, 1980) and Margaret Spufford, *Small Books and Pleasant Histories: Popular Fiction and Its Readership in Seventeenth-Century England* (London: Methuen, 1981).

[15] See, for instance, Seymour Chatman, *Story and Discourse: Narrative Structure in Fiction and Film* (Ithaca and London: Cornell University Press, 1978); Gerald Prince, *A Dictionary of Narratology* (Lincoln and London: University of Nebraska Press, 1987); Peter Rabinowitz, "Truth in Fiction: A Re-Examination of Audiences," *Critical Inquiry* 4 (1977): 121-44.

[16] Gerard Genette, *Narrative Discourse: An Essay in Method*, trans. Jane E. Lewin; foreword by Jonathan Culler (Ithaca: Cornell University Press, 1980); Paul Ricoeur, *Time and Narrative*, vols. 1,2, trans. K. McLaughlin and D. Pellauer (Chicago: University of Chicago Press, 1984, 1985), vol. 3, trans. K. Blamey and D. Pellauer (Chicago: University of Chicago Press, 1998).

[17] Miller, *Death of a Salesman* (New York: Viking Press, 1949; Compas Books Edition, 1958), 56.

[18] Lawrence Lipking, "The Marginal Gloss," *Critical Inquiry* 3 (Summer 1977): 609-55; Valentine Cunningham, "Glossing and Glozing: Bunyan and Allegory," in Neil H. Keeble, *John Bunyan: Conventicle and Parnassus* ed. (Oxford: Clarendon Press, 1988), pp. 217-40; William Slights, "The Edifying Margins of English Renaissance Books," *Renaissance Quarterly* 42.4 (1989): 682-716 and "'Marginall Notes that spoile the Text': Scrip-

tural Annotation in the English Renaissance," *Huntington Library Quarterly* 55 (1992): 255-78.

[19] Evelyn B. Tribble, *Margins and Marginality: The Printed Page in Early Modern England* (Charlottesville: University Press of Virginia, 1993).

[20] Martin Buber writes, "This is the eternal origin of art that a human being confronts a form that wants to become a work through him. . . . The created work is a thing among things and can be experienced and described as an aggregate of qualities. But the receptive beholder may be bodily confronted now and again." *I and Thou*, trans. with notes added, Walter Kaufmann, Scribner Library, Lyceum Editions (New York: Scribners, 1970), 60-61.

[21] Richard E. Palmer, *Hermeneutics: Interpretation Theory in Schiermacher, Dilthy, Heidegger, and Gadamer*. Northwestern University Studies in Phenomenology and Existential Philosophy, gen. ed. John Wild (Evanston: Northwestern University Press, 1969), 44.

[22] Mario J. Valdes, ed. and intro., *A Ricoeur Reader: Reflection and Imagination*, Theory/ Culture Series, ed. Mario J. Valdes (Toronto: University of Toronto Press, 1991), 20.

23 John Bunyan, The Pilgrim's Progress from this World to That Which is to Come, ed. James Blanton Wharey and Roger Sharrock (Oxford: Clarendon Press, 1960, reprint, with corrections, 1967). All quotations from *The Pilgrim's Progress* are from this edition unless otherwise noted, and will be cited parenthetically using *TPP* as the appbreviated title for the first part of *The Pilgrim's Progress* and *TPP2* as the abbreviated title for *The Pilgrim's Progress, The Second Part*. The abbreviated title will be followed by a page number except in the case of references to the poetic prologues ("The Author's Apology for His Book," *TPP*, and "The Author's Way of Sending Forth His Second Part of the Pilgrim," *TPP2*), where both page and line number will be shown.

[24] Valdes, ed., *A Ricoeur Reader*, 60-1.

[25] Jo[hn] Geree, preface to *Directions for the Private Reading of Scriptures...*, by Nicholas Byfield, 4th ed. 1648 (Ann Arbor, Mich.: University Microfilms, Early English Books 1641-1700), Reel 18:9.

[26] One thinks of the phrase, "to pick out a tune," as an analogue, but Bunyan uses food metaphors. "Would'st thou read Riddles, and their Explanation / . . . Dost thou love picking-meat?" (*TPP*, 7, lines 14-16). At the feast at Gaius' Inn, a "dish of Nuts" is explained:

> Hard Texts are Nuts (I will not call them Cheaters,)
> Whose Shells do keep their Kirnels from the Eaters.
> Ope then the Shells, and you shall have the Meat,
> They here are brought, for you to crack and eat.
> (*TPP 2, 263*)

[27] W. Fraser Mitchell, *English Pulpit Oratory From Andrewes to Tillotson: A Study of its Literary Aspects* (London: SPCK, 1932), 115-17; following John Wilkins, *Ecclesiastes: or a Dsicourse Concerning the Gift of Preaching*, 7th ed. (London: n.p., 1646).

[28] Kathleen M. Swaim, *Pilgrim's Progress, Puritan's Progress: Discourses and Contexts* (Urbana: University of Illinois Press, 1993), 114. Swaim's ch. 4, "The Sermonic Word" (106-131) is a useful introduction to Puritan sermonic practice.

²⁹ Hans Robert Jauss, *Toward an Aesthetic of Reception,* trans. Timothy Bahti, Theory and History of Literature, Vol. 2 (Minneapolis: University of Minnesota Press, 1982), 139.

³⁰ Paul Ricoeur, "Between the Text and Its Readers," in *A Ricouer Reader,* ed. Mario J. Valdes, 407-14.

³¹ There is a possible allusion here to the Hebraic script, a fascination with which was part of the literary temper of radical nonconformity. "Many sectarians . . . seem to have revered Hebrew characters because of their initial search for original scriptural accuracy" (Smith, *Perfection,* 287).

³² Shari Benstock, "At the Margins of Discourse: Footnotes in the Fictional Text," *PMLA* 98 (1983): 204.

³³ Michael Murrin, *The Veil of Allegory: Some Notes Toward a Theory of Allegorical Rhetoric in the English Renaissance* (Chicago: University of Chicago Press, 1969), 121.

³⁴ Fish, *Self-Consuming Artifacts,* 243.

³⁵ Barbara K. Lewalski, *Protestant Poetics and the Seventeenth-Century Religious Lyric* (Princeton: Princeton University Press, 1979), 155.

³⁶ Rabinowitz, "Truth," 130-33.

³⁷ Keeble, *Literary Culture,* 139.

³⁸ John Bunyan, *The Holy War* (1682), ed. Roger Sharrock and James F. Forrest (Oxford: Clarendon Press, 1988). All quotations from *The Holy War* used within this work are from this edition unless otherwise noted, and will be referenced parenthetically using *HW* as the abbreviated title, followed by page number.

³⁹ Roger Sharrock, "Bunyan Studies Today: An Evaluation." In *Bunyan in England and Beyond* , ed. M. Van Os and G. J. Schutte (Amsterdam: Vu University Press, 1990), 154.

⁴⁰ John Bunyan, *Grace Abounding to the Chief of Sinners,* ed. Roger Sharrock (Oxford: Clarendon Press, 1962), 1. All quotations from *Grace Abounding* used within this work are from this edition unless otherwise noted, and will be referenced parenthetically using *GA* as the abbreviated title, followed by paragraph number.

CHAPTER 1: BUNYAN AS READER

¹ For discussion concerning the "reader" of and in literary texts are offered by Iser, *Implied Reader,* 27-38; Steven Mailloux, *Interpretive Conventions: The Reader in the Study of American Fiction* (Ithica and London: Cornell University Press, 1982), 20-39; Susan R. Suleiman and Inge Crosman, eds. *The Reader in the Text: Essays on Audience and Interpretation* (Princeton: Princeton University Press, 1980), 3-45; Jane P. Tompkins, ed. *Reader-Response Criticism: From Formalism to Post-Structuralism* (Baltimore: John Hopkins University Press, 1980), ix-xxvi. I shall speak of the contemporary English Nonconformist reader as Bunyan's "intended reader," the reader for whom Bunyan evidently wrote, a member of what Rabinowitz identifies as the "authorial audience," about whom the author makes "certain assumptions ... [concerning] beliefs, knowledge, and familiarity with conventions" ("Truth," 126). To the degree that the characteristic assumptions and attitudes of the intended reader are inscribed within the text itself, we apply Iser's term, "implied reader" (*Implied Reader,* 1-28).

[2] Keeble, *Literary Culture*, 136-7. See also: Cressy, *Literacy and The Social Order*, 73-4; Harvey J. Graff, *The Legacies of Literacy: Continuities and Contradictions in Western Culture and Society* (Bloomington: Indiana University Press, 1987), 162-3; Kenneth Levine, *The Social Context of Literacy* (London: Routledge and Kegan Paul, 1986), 79-82; Spufford, *Small Books*, 1-82 passim.

[3] Darnton, "Toward a History," 20.

[4] Ibid., 23.

[5] Kintgen, "Reconstructing," 13.

[6] This work is called for by Ann Hughes, "The Pulpit Guarded," in Ann Hughes, *John Bunyan and His England: 1628-1688*, eds. W. R. Owens and Stuart Sims (London: The Hambledon Press, 1990), 38, n. 9.

[7] Keeble goes so far as to say, "His marginalia were not incidental additions but an integral part of the design of his allegories" (*Literary Culture*, 146).

[8] Charles Doe, ed. and intro., *The Works of That Eminent Servant of Christ, Mr John Bunyan* (London, 1692), A-1.

[9] Spufford, *Small Books*, xviii.

[10] John Bunyan, *A Book for Boys and Girls* in *The Poems*, ed. Graham Midgley, Miscellaneous Works, Vol. 6 (Oxford: Clarendon Press, 1980). All further references to Bunyan's collected *Miscellaneous Works*, gen. ed. Roger Sharrock, Oxford English Texts, 13 vols. (Oxford: Clarendon Press, 1960-1991) will be cited parenthetically by the abbreviated title, MW and the appropriate volume and page number. In the case of poetry, line numbers will also be given.

[11] Spufford, *Small Books*, 26.

[12] Ibid.

[13] Benjamin Keach, *The Progress of Sin* (1684), 3rd ed. (London, 1715), 59.

[14] Spufford, *Small Books*, 25.

[15] Northrop Frye, *The Great Code: The Bible and Literature* (New York: Harcourt Brace Jovanovich, 1982), xiii.

[16] We will follow accepted seventeenth-century Nonconformist usage in referring to the Hebrew Bible as the "Old Testament."

[17] Hans Frei, *The Eclipse of Biblical Narrative: A Study in Eighteenth- and Nineteenth-Century Hermeneutics* (New Haven: Yale University Press, 1974), 27.

[18] John R. Knott, Jr., *The Sword of the Spirit*, 151.

[19] Or Puritan hermeneutics, see Kaufmann, TPP and Traditions, ch. 2, Knott, *Sword of the Spirit*, ch. 1 and ch. 6; Lewalski, *Protestant Poetics*, ch. 4. Dayton Haskin in "The Burden of Interpretation in *The Pilgrim's Progress*," Studies in Philology 79 (1982)" 256-78, draws attention to interesting links between Bunyan's hermeneutics and those of earlier Puritan writers (e.g., Perkins and Ames). I think Haskin to be wrong, however, in identifying the necessity of personally interpreting the scriptures to be a burden (265). For our discussion of "burden," see ch. 5 of this work.

[20] For a careful distinction between the older allegorical reading which the Reformers rejected and the figural reading which they embraced, see Frei, 27-36.

[21] See translators preface to Martin Luther, *A Commentary on Galatians* (London, 1644), A4.

[22] Bunyan's development as a reader shows interesting parallels to the developmental "roles" which J. A. Appleyard, S.J. identifies in *Becoming a Reader: The Experi-*

ence of Fiction from Childhood to Adulthood (Cambridge: Cambridge University Press, 1990), 14-15, identifies. Appleyard sees a series of roles "which appear to shift as readers mature," and identifies them as: (1) The Reader as Player, "playing in a fantasy world that images realities, fears, and desires"; (2) The Reader as Hero and Heroine, becoming "the central figure of a romance"; (3) The Reader as Thinker, reading "to discover insights into the meaning of life, values and beliefs"; (4) The Reader as Interpeter, able to recognize literature "as an organized body of knowledge with its own principles of inquiry and rules of evidence"; (5) The Pragmatic Reader. The first four of these roles can be clearly seen in Bunyan's development from "playing" at secular adventure stories, to introjecting his own experience into biblical narratives, to increasingly reading to interpret and develop a structure of belief, and finally to being able to approach biblical literature with a clear set of hermeneutical principles. Perhaps Appleyard's development sequence may be applied not only on an age scale from childhood to adulthood but on a developmental scale, from beginning to mature readings, at whatever age those stages may be experienced.

[23] Kaufmann, *TPP and Traditions*, x-xi.

[24] For example: John White of Dorchester, *Directions for the Profitable Reading of the Scriptures* (London: [Rich] Royston to be sold by John Long in Dorchester, 1647), cited commendingly by Richard Baxter in *The Saints Everlasting Rest*, 1st ed. (London: n.p., 1649), 250; Nicholas Byfield, *Directions for the Private Reading of Scriptures* (1648).

[25] John Dryden, "Religio Laici," In *The Poems of John Dryden*, vol. 2, ed. Paul Hammond (London: Longman, 1995), 81-134, lines 413-14.

[26] On "interpretive community" see Stanley Fish, "Interpreting the Variorum," *Critical Inquiry* 2 (1976): 480-85.

[27] See, for example, Baxter, "Dedicatory Epistle" to *Saints Rest* (1649, printed 1650) in which he asks the reader to make allowance for inadequate references due to the author's being separated from his library at the time of writing. "Being in my quarters far from home and had no Book but [my] Bible ... nor had any minde of human ornaments ..." (A2 a.v.)

[28] Ibid., "Dedication."

[29] John Calvin, *Institutes of the Christian Religion*, trans. Henry Beveridge, 2 vols. reprint (Grand Rapids: William B. Eerdmans, 1975). All further references to the Institutes will be from this edition, and will be cited by book, section and page.

[30] Lewis Balyly, *The Practice of Pietie* (1612?) 36th ed. (Edinburgh, 1636), 151.

[31] Dayton Haskin, "Pilgrim's Progress in the Context of Bunyan's Dialogue with the Radicals," *Harvard Theological Review* 77 (1984): 73-94.

[33] See, for example, the personifying of the shadowy mountain in William Wordsworth, *The Prelude, 1799, 1805, 1850*, ed. Jonathan Wordsworth, M. H. Abrams and Stephen Gill (New York: Norton, 1979), lines 90-129. I am indebted to Prof. James F. Forrest for pointing out this likeness between Bunyan's and Worthsworth's imaginative constructs.

[34] George Herbert, "The Holy Scriptures I" and "The Holy Scriptures II" in *George Herbert and Henry Vaughan*, ed. Louis Martz, Oxford Authors, gen. ed. Frank Kermode (Oxford: Oxford University Press, 1986), 50.

[35] Darnton, "Toward a History," 21. See also Joyce Coleman, *Public Reading and the Reading Public in Late Medieval England and France* (Cambridge: Cambridge University Press, 1996), esp. 1-33. While Coleman wrties of an earlier period and Darnton writes

mostly of a somewhat later period than the seventeenth century, both make observations highly relevant to the aural reception of literature which is so clearly indicated in much of Bunyan's work.

[36] The pun on "sound" in the last line of the quatrain (meaning both "doctrinally correct" and "appealing to the sense of hearing") seems too apt to be unintended.

[37] William James, *The Varieties of Religious Experience* (1902) in *The Works of William James*, Vol. 15, ed. F. H. Burkhardt, F. Bowers, K. Skrupskelis (Cambridge, Mass: Harvard University Press, 1985), 132.

[38] Peter Carlton, "Bunyan: Language, Convention, Authority," *ELH* 51 (1984): 22-25.

[39] Graham Ward, "To Be a Reader: John Bunyan's Struggle with the Language of Scripture in *Grace Abounding to the Chief of Sinners*," *Literature and Theology* 4 (1990): 43.

[40] Brainerd P. Stranahan, "Bunyan's Special Talent: Biblical Texts as 'Events' in *Grace Abounding* and *The Pilgrim's Progress*," *English Literary Renaissance* 11 (1981): 330.

[41] Iser, *Implied Reader*, ch. 1, passim; Haskin, "Burden of Interpretation," 257.

[42] Lewis Bayly, *The Practice of Pietie*, B-1.

CHAPTER 2: BUNYAN'S MARGINS

[1] Mailloux *Interpretive Conventions*, 126. See also David Lewis, *Convention: A Philosophical Study* (Cambridge: Harvard University Press, 1969), passim; Jonathan Culler, *Structuralist Poetics: Structuralism, Linguistics, and the Study of Literature* (London: Routledge and Kegan Paul, 1975), 131-60.

[2] Slights, "Edifying Margins," 682.

[3] James F. Forrest, "Between Presumption and Timidity: On Editing Bunyan." In *Bunyan in England and Abroad*, ed. M. Van Os and G. J. Schutte (Amsterdam: Vu University Press, 1990), 67.

[4] In his introduction to *Grace Abounding*, Sharrock states "Bunyan ... did not supervise the reproduction of his text with any care" (*GA*, xxxix), and that therefore "[t]he punctuation has been silently corrected" (*GA*, xli). In editing *The Holy War*, Sharrock and Forrest follow the same line of reasoning regarding the authoria indifference to punctuation: "[I]t has not been thought illegitimate to alter the pointing ... where the reader's need for clarity has seemed paramount; the original accidentals were in any event probably perfected by the printer (*HW*, xlvii). In view of the evidence for Bunyan's close involvement with the printing and proofreading of his work, perhaps such editorial considerations should be reconsidered.

[5] See Baxter, "A Premonition," *The Saints Everlasting Rest*, 2nd and subsequent additions. "I have added many Marginal quotations, especially of the Ancients: which though some may conceive it to be useless, and others to be meerly for vain ostentation; Yet I conceived useful, both for the sweetness of the matter ... and also to free myself from the charge of singularity."

[6] John Moxon, *Mechanick Exercises Applied to the Art of Printing* (London: 1683), 197, 211, 265.

[7] Frank Mott Harrison in his *Bibliography of the Works of John Bunyan* (Oxford: Oxford University Press for the Bibliographical Society, 1932) notes that *A Pocket Concor-*

dance compiled by Bunyan in 1671/72, is noted in a printers' advertisement although no copy appears to be extant; Harrison also suggests that Bunyan may have had a hand in completing Vavasour Powell's concordance (xvii). The printer's advertisement to *Grace Abounding*, 8th ed. (for Nathaniel Ponder, 1694) reads: "This author hath prepared a compleat concordance, to bind it with the twelvs Bible, and is in Mr. Ponders...." The advertisement page in the Bruce Peel Collection, University of Alberta, has been shaved off, but by the tops of letters visible, the final line appears to read, "shop to be printed." This offers further evidence of Bunyan's having written a concordance which may never have been printed, a project Charles De mentions in his introduction to the Folio edition of Bunyan's *Works*.

[8] Forrrest, "Presumption and Timidity," 67.

[9] John Bunyan, *The Life and Death of Mr. Badman* (1680), ed. James F. Forrest and Roger Sharrock (Oxford: Clarendon Press, 1988). All references are from this edition and will be cited parenthetically using *Mr. B* as the abbreviated title.

[10] My hypothesis that adding marginal notes may have been part of the final re-reading and preparation of a manuscript by the author for printing seems to be borne out by Samuel Pepys' entry, 23 January 1662/3, "Finishing the margenting of my Navy-Manuscript" (cited *OED*, s.v. "margent").

[11] Moxon, *Mechanick Exercises*, 266.

[12] On additions to marginalia, see Sharrock, introduction, *TPP*, xlvi, xciv-xcv, ci-cii, cxvi.

[13] William York Tindall, *John Bunyan: Mechanick Printer* (New York: Russell and Russell, 1934, 1964), 209.

[14] Richard Baxter, *Catechizing of Families* (London, 1683), A-6.

[15] Spufford, *Small Books*, 258.

[16] Spufford discusses the content and literary history of *Sir Bevis of Hampton* (*Small Books*, 7-8), broadsheet ballads (Ibid., 11-15) and "George on Horseback," (Ibid., 227-29).

[17] A veiled allusion to "penny merries" may occur within the story of Little-Faith. Christian asks: "Will a man give a penny to fill his belly with Hay? or can you perswade the *Turtle-dove* to live upon Carrion, like the *Crow*?" (*TPP*, 128). Given the identification of Little-Faith's "Jewels" are identified as the Scriptures by means of a marginal reference to 2 Pet. 1:19 [*TPP*, 127]), the subsequent reference to "hay" and "carrion" seems also to refer to reading material, cheap literature that fills, but does not adequately feed the mind.

[18] See Rosemary Freeman, *English Emblem Books* (London: Chatto and Windus, 1948); Sharrock, "Bunyan and English Emblem Writers," *Review of English Studies* 21 (1945): 105-116; Peter Daly, *Literature in the Light of the Emblem: Structural Parallels Between the Emblem and Literature in the Sixteenth and Seventeenth Centuries* (Toronto: University of Toronto Press, 1979). Daly, 60ff, concurs with Sharrock's identification of the emblematic nature of the House of the Interpreter, but critiques his use of the term, "emblem theatre," to describe it, pointing out that emblems are primarily static rather than active, and the two terms "emblem" and "theatre" are, to some degree at least, oxymoronic.

[19] John Dod and Robert Cleaver, *A Plaine and Familiar Exposition of the Ten* Commandements (London, 1604) 253, 259, 33.

[20] Adams' biographer states: "John Bunyan was then only two years old, but it seems certain that the Bedfordshire preacher's quartos and great folio came to be known and devoured by the 'immortal dreamer'" (*DNB* 1, 102). The evidence is not very adequate for making this judgment; however, there can be no doubt that Bunyan was much influenced by sermons, both in the oral and written form, for they were a popular form of entertainment to which he would have adhered even before his conversion.

[21] Thomas Adams, "White Devill," in *The Workes of Thomas Adams* (London, 1629), 54.

[22] Rostenberg *Literary Publishing*, 202.

[23] Tindall, *Mechanick* Preacher, 42-67.

[24] See in Smith, *Ranter Writings*: Laurence Clarkson, *A Single Eye* (1650); Joseph Salmon, *A Rout, A Rout* (1649).

[25] Abiezer Coppe, *A Fiery Flying Roll* in Smith, *Writings*, 83.

[26] James Blanton Wharey, *A Study of the Sources for Bunyan's Allegories* (Baltimore: J. H. Furst, 1904), 136.

[27] Tindall, *Mechanick Preacher*, 200.

[28] Ibid., 193.

[29] See Psa. 74:14; Job 41:26. Bunyan alludes to the reference to Leviathan in Job with a marginal note: "Leviathan's *sturdiness*." (*TPP*, 131).

[30] All pages references to Arthur Dent, *A Plaine Man's Pathway to Heaven*, London, 1664.

[31] Lewis Bayly, *The Practice of Pietie* existed in so many printings that it is impossible to be definitive about Bayly's marginals. All page references in text are to the 30th edition, printed in 1632, which is the most complete edition in the Bruce Peel Collection.

[32] *A Commentarie of Master Doctor Martin Luther Upon the Epistle of S. Paul to the Galathians now out of Latine faithfully translated into English for the unlearned.* London: [Printed for George Miller], 1644. All references in text are to this edition, which is foliated rather than paginated.

[33] John Brown, *John Bunyan: 1628-1688: His Life, Times, and Work*, tercentenary edition. rev. Frank Mott Harrison (London: Hurlburt, 1928), 153.

[34] Spufford, *Small Books*, 258. For a full discussion of Foxe's *Acts and Monumnets* (The Book of Martyrs), see Knott, *Discourses of Martyrdom*, passim.

[35] John Foxe, *Acts and Monuments of the Christian Martyrs*, 3 vols., 8th imprint of 1583 ed., (London, 1641). All page references are to this edition and are indicated parenthetically in the text.

[36] E.g., "I came of the Race of *Japhet* whom God will perswade to dwell in the Tents of *Shem*," (*TPP*, 46) as cf. Gen 9:27, "God persuade Japheth, that he may dwel in the tentes of Shem," (*Geneva Bible*), but rather than, "God shall enlarge Japheth" (AV).

[37] Introduction, *The Geneva Bible*, facs. ed., Lloyd Berry (Madison: University of Wisconsin Press, 1969), 15.

[38] Ibid., 23. Berry's quotation is from John Eadie, *The English Bible*, vol. 2 (London, 1876).

[39] The copy of the Authorized Version with Tomson-Junius notes on which I base this discussion is a reprint of the 1642 edition, printed in London for the Company of Stationer's, 1649.

[40] "The Translatour to the Reader," *Bible*, AV (London: 1649), x.

[41] Cunningham, "Glossing and Glazing," 235.

[42] Keeble notes the *persona* in the margins, and adds that "very occasionally it is the writer, not the preacher, who addresses us" from the margins (*Literary Culture*, 149).

CHAPTER 3: SELF-CONSTRUING ARTIFICE

[1] Slights, "Edifying Margins," 687.

[2] C. S. Lewis, *Allegory of Love: A Study in Medieval Tradition* (Oxford: Oxford University Press, 1967), 58.

[3] Thomas Browne, *The Prose of Sir Thomas Browne*, ed. Norman Endicott (New York: New York University Press, 1968), 42.

[4] Jonathan Edwards, *Images or Shadows of Divine Things*, ed. Perry Miller (New Haven: Yale University Press, 1948), 44, no. 8. Edwards goes on from this passage to offer a series of aphoristic observations of such correspondences: e.g., "The serpent's charming of birds and other animals . . . and the spider's taking . . . the fly in his snare are lively representations of the Devil's catching our souls by his temptation" (45, no. 8).

[5] Earl L. Wasserman, "Nature Moralized: The Divine Analogy in the Eighteenth Century," *ELH* 30 (1953), 40.

[6] On the growing audience for books in the later seventeenth century, see Keeble, *Literary Culture*, 93-126; Spufford, *Small Books*, passim. For discussion of economic condititions encouraging increased audience and publication, see Ian Watt, *The Rise of the Novel* (Berkeley: University of California Press, 1967), 42-58.

[7] Harrison, *Bibliography*, xxvi.

[8] Edwin Honig, *Dark Conceit: The Making of Allegory* (London: Faber and Faber, 1959), 7.

[9] J. Hillis Miller, "Two Allegories," in *Allegory, Myth, and Symbol*, ed. Morton W. Bloomfield (Cambridge, Mass.: Harvard University Press, 1981), 360.

[10] George Puttenham, *The Art of English Poesie* (facs. Menston: The Scolar Press, 1968 [London: 1589], 155.

[11] Murrin, *Veil of Allegory*, adopts this trope for his work on the allegorical mode. For other discussions of allegory, see Honig, *Dark Conceit*; Northrop Frye, *Anatomy of Criticism: Four Essays* (Princeton: Princeton University Press, 1973); Angus Fletcher, *Allegory: Theory of a Symbolic Mode* (Ithica: Cornell University Press, 1964); and Maureen Quilligan, *The Language of Allegory: Defining the Genre* (Ithica: Cornell University Press, 1979).

[12] Edmund Spenser, "Letter to Sir Walter Raleigh," in *The Faerie Queene*, Bk. 1, ed. P. Bayley (London: Oxford University Press, 1966), 1-9.

[13] Frye, *Anatomy*, 90.

[14] Fletcher, *Allegory*, 305.

[15] On the ancient and medieval origins of "biblical poetics," see Ernst Robert Curtius, *European Literature and the Latin Middle Ages*, trans. Willard R. Trask (New York: Pantheon Books, 1953), 446-67; on the post-Reformation application of biblical poetics, see Lewalski, *Protestant Poetics*, ch. 2, "Biblical Genre-Theory," 77ff.

[16] G. R. Owst, *Literature and Pulpit in Medieval England* (Oxford: Blackwell Press, 1961), 485-90.

[17] Luther, *Commentary*, Fol. 218, a.v.

[18] Bunyan himself demonstrates his ability to absorb and simplify this complex allegory. See *The Doctrine of Law & Grace Unfolded; I Will Pray with the Spirit* (MW 2, ed. Richard L Greaves, Oxford: Clarendon Press, 1976), 24.

[19] Geoffrey A. Glaister, *Glaister's Glossary of the Book*, 2 ed. (Berkeley: University of California Press, 1979), 315.

[20] Paul Salzman, *English Prose Fiction, 1558-1700* (Oxford: Clarendon Press, 1985), 246.

[21] W. E. Vine, *An Expository Dictionary of New Testament Words* (Old Tappan: Revell, 1966), 208.

[22] John Milton, *Christian Doctrine* (1640-1673?) in *The Prose of John Milton*, ed. J. Max Patrick (New York: New York University Press, 1968), ch. 30.

[23] Booth discusses both the authorial voice and silence, (*Rhetoric of Fiction*, 169-205; 271-300). On metafictional techniques, see Linda Hutcheon, *Narcissistic Narrative: The Metafictional Paradox* (Waterloo: Wilfred Laurier University Press, 1980), esp. 36-56; on the relationship between conventions and beliefs, Menachem Brinker, "Verisimilitude, Conventions, and Beliefs," *New Literary History* 14 (1983), passim; on the naturalizing of conventions, Culler, *Structuralist Poetics*, 148-151.

[24] Slights, "Edifying Margins," 687.

[25] Keeble, *Literary Culture*, 148-51.

[26] Salzman, *English Prose Fiction*, 246.

[27] The great care with which Scripture was to be used when conflated, condensed, or placed into a new context is demonstrated by the severe judgment on "Clip-Promise" (HW 242-3). To "clip a promise" seems to refer to a specific misuse of Scripture, namely quoting a promise made in Scripture without observing and fulfilling its attendant conditions.

[28] Frye, *Anatomy*, 73.

[29] Spufford, *Small Books*, 47.

[30] The Lot story is also referred to in Christian's response to Charity's questioning about leaving his family behind (*TPP*, 51, passage added 2nd ed.); and in the "strange monument" whose inscription Christian and Hopeful make out to be "*Remember Lot's Wife*" (108-110, also added 2d. ed.). Both passages are glossed with marginal references to Genesis 19. The addition of these passages suggests that Bunyan may have noticed the Lot motif on a later reading of his book, and decided upon further development of it.

[31] *A Directory for the Publique Worship of God* (London: n.p., 1645), 15-16.

[32] As the Doubting-Castle episode demonstrates, the idea of suicide did present itself to Christians in spiritual despair. Hopeful encourages Christian, "[L]et us not be our own murderers" (*TPP* 116).

[33] John Bunyan, *Life and Death of Mr. Badman*, ed. James F. Forrest and Roger Sharrock (oxford: Clarendon Press, 1988 [1680]), writes that Mr. Badman, despite total im-

penitence and sure doom, dies "As quietly as a Lamb," with the marginal note repeating the chilling phrase, "He died like a lamb." Christian, on the other hand, experiences a final crisis of faith as he crosses the River, and needs to be reassured, "These troubles and distresses that you go through in these Waters, are no sign that God hath forsaken you" (*TPP* 158). For further discussion of death-anxiety in Puritan experience, see David E. Stannard, *The Puritan Way of Death: A Study in Religion, Culture, and Social Change* (New York: Oxford University Press, 1977).

CHAPTER 4: ART IN THE MARGINS

[1] I have corrected the reference. "Gal. 2.16" as given in the *TPP* (Oxford Edition) lacks the precise verbal echo from "Gal. 1.16" which I have shown.

[2] Owst, *Literature and Pulpit*, makes a convincing case for popular vernacular drama, both the morality and miracle, as springing from the medieval sermon (479 ff.). It seems, also, that by means of the sermon, the tradition of allegorical "moralities" lingered on into the late seventeenth century.

[3] A recent and comprehensive examination of the psychomachia tradition in the seventeenth century, see Arlette Zinck, "Of Arms and the Heroic Reader: The Concept of Psychomachy in Spenser, Milton, and Bunyan" (Unpublished doctoral dissertation, University of Alberta, 1993).

[4] On the structure of the emblem see Daly, *Light of the Emblem*, esp. ch. 1.

[5] The term, "emblematization" and the example are from Freeman, *English Emblem Books*, 220.

[6] Bunyan's "Picture of a very grave Person" is discussed more fully in Thomas Luxon, "Calvin and Bunyan on Word and Image: Is There a Text in Interpreter's House," *English Literary Renaissance* 18 (1988): 438-59.

[7] "Old Honest" under the tree is reminiscent of "old Adam" in the Forest of Arden (William Shakespeare, *As You Like It*, II:vii: 129-30). Tindall refers to Bunyan's imitation of Shakespeare in the hymn, "Who would true valour see" (*Mechanick Preacher*, 278). More than Bunyan's having seen *As You Like It* is the probability that both the *senex* character and the ballad were traditional and widely known.

[8] Geoffrey Chaucer, "The Book of the Duchess," in *The Works of Geoffrey Chaucer*, ed. F. N. Robinson, 2d ed. (Boston : Houghton Mifflin, 1961), line 1309.

[9] The reference should be Rev. 3.19 rather than "Rev. 3, 19" (as in *TPP*, Oxford Edition).

[10] On allegory as game, see in *Bunyan in Our Time*, ed. Robert G. Collmer (Kent, Ohio: Kent State University Press, 1989), essays by James F. Forrest, "Allegory as Sacred Sport," (93-112); and Barbara A. Johnson, "Falling into Allegory" (113-137).

[11] Iser, *Implied Reader*, 18-24; Haskin, "Burden of Interpretation," 256-78.

[12] This pun on "travel" and "travail" is also noted by Haskin, "Burden of Interpretation," 274.

[13] Hill, *Turbulent*, 323. (I presume that Hill means that it could *have been* a way of "discussing the undiscussable.")

[14] For discussion of the persecution experienced by Nonconformists see Gerald Cragg, *Puritanism in the Period of the Great Persecution, 1660-1688* (Cambridge: Cam-

bridge University Press, 1957); Greaves, *Deliver Us From Evil*; Christopher Hill, *The Experience of Defeat: Milton and Some Contemporaries* (London: Faber and Faber, 1984); William Lamont, *Puritanism and Historical Controversy*, McGill-Queen's Studies in the History of Religion 26, (Montreal: McGill-Queen's University Press, 1996).

[15] Forrest calls allegory as used by both Spenser and Bunyan, the "sacred sport in which the mind is managed through exposure to certain suggestions to which the reader is induced to respond" ("Allegory as Sacred Sport," 98). Honig sees Bunyan's "Apology" to *TPP* to be "an appeal to the fancifulness of the allegory as an imaginative sport" (*Dark Conceit*, 99). Quilligan sees allegory as rooted in the serious wordplay of the Mass, in which central images retains identity yet signify something different from themselves.

[16] Here Bunyan takes the stance Robert A. Lanham identifies as that of "the serious man" (cf. the "rhetorical man"). See Lanham, *The Motives of Eloquence: Literary Rhetoric in the Renaissance* (New Haven: Yale University Press, 1976), passim. See also Joan Webber's contrast of Bunyan's egocentric language use in *The Eloquent "I": Style and Self in Seventeenth-Century Prose* (Madison: The University of Wisconsin Press, 1968), ch. 2, in contrast to Fish's reading of Bunyan's self-abnegation (*Self-Consuming*, 224-64).

[17] Murrin sees this dual use of language as fundamental to allegory as a mode: "The allegorical poet served the truth which he had received under inspiration, and this truth exercised the primary operative control over his rhetoric. He did not really cater to his audience but tried to preserve his truth intact and communicate it to those capable of understanding it.... He had, therefore, simultaneously to reveal and not to reveal his truth, and for this double purpose he cloaked his truth in the veils of allegory. The many reacted with pleasure to his symbolic tales, and the few knew how to interpret them" (*Dark Conceit*, 168).

[18] R. Rawdon Wilson, *In Palimedes' Shadow: Explorations in Play, Game, and Narrative Theory* (Boston: Northeastern University Press, 1990), 241-242.

CHAPTER 5: READING OUT TO THE EDGES

[1] Keeble, *Literary Culture of Non-Conformity*, 148.

[2] Salzman, *English Prose Fiction*, 246.

[3] Dave Baker, notes to accompany performance, "Symphony No. 41, No. 41, K. 551 in C Major, ('Jupiter'), Edmonton Symphony Orchestra, *Signature*, December 1991, 9.

[4] Hill makes the observation that by the time *TPP* went to press in 1678, there was a slightly less hostile political climate than had existed while Bunyan was actually writing the material. "[T]here were things in *The Pilgrim's Progress* which might displease a captious censor. But by 1678 the government was being pushed on to the defensive by Whig Exclusionists, and publication was becoming easier" (*Turbulent Seditious* 198). This temporarily improved political climate for dissenters may have allowed Bunyan the liberty to reveal "*Denn" as a code word for Bedford Prison by the time the third edition was printed in 1679.

[5] Despite the efforts of Harold Golder to prove Bunyan's literary debt to Spenser (see "Bunyan's Hypocrisy," *North American Review* 233 (1926): 323-32; "Bunyan and Spenser," *PMLA* 45 (1930): 216-37), the link remains unlikely. Even Tindall can only

say, "it has been shown ... that Bunyan may or may not have read *The Faerie Queene*" (*Mechanick Reader*, 195).

[6] Alighier Dante, *The Divine Comedy*, trans. John Ciardi, (New York: W.W. Norton, 1961), Canto I.3-6.

[7] Curtius, *European Literature*, 201.

[8] Edmund Spenser, *The Faerie Queene*, ed. P. C. Bayley (London: Oxford University Press, 1966), Bk I, Canto 1.13, Stanza 13. Another interesting parallel is to Comenius (John Amos Komensky), *The Labyrinth of the World and the Paradise of the Heart* (1623), trans. and ed. Count Lutzow (1901; reprint New York: Arno Press and The New York Times, 1971) which draws on many of the same images as *The Pilgrim's Progress*. However, since there was no English version of *The Labyrinth* until 1900, and since Bunyan did not travel in the circles in which Komensky (alias Comenius) was known, Komensky's English translator, Count Lutzow is doubtless right in stating that, "[T]he idea on which both books are founded is far older than either of them" (f.n., 18).

[9] John Milton, *Paradise Regained* I:295, in *Complete Poems and Major Prose*, ed. Merritt Y. Hughes (New York: Macmillan, 1957).

[10] Benjamin Keach, *Tropologia: A Key to Open Scripture Metaphors* (London, 1682) s.v. "Den."

[11] Cragg, *Puritanism in the Period of the Great Persecution*, 94-95.

[12] Frye, *Anatomy of Criticism*, 90.

[13] On the "testimony"as discourse mode, see Swaim, *Pilgrim's Progress, Puritan's Progress*, ch. 6, "The Puritan Self as Narrative," 132-59.

[14] Owen Watkins, *The Puritan Experience* (London: Routledge and Kegan Paul, 1972), 37-39.

[15] Hill, *Turbulent Seditious*, 213.

[16] Michael McKeon, *The Origins of the English Novel, 1600-1740* (Baltimore: Johns Hopkins University Press, 1987), 302, 311.

[17] For Bunyan's description of himself at the same stage of the conversion process, see *GA*, para. 16-32.

[18] Calvin writes: "For as the aged, or those whose sight is defective ... are scarcely able to make out two consecutive words, but when aided by glasses, begin to read distinctly, so Scripture ... dissipates the darkness, and shows us the true God clearly" (Institutes, I.vi.1). See also on this, Thomas Luxon, "Calvin and Bunyan on Word and Image," *English Literary Renaissance* 18 (1988): 438-59.

[19] Fish, *Self-Consuming Artifacts*, 229.

[20] Knott, *Sword of the Spirit*, 185-86, n. 37.

[21] Although two of the "shining ones" appear at several points in the narrative, it is only after the pilgrims have crossed the River of Death that they reveal their identity, *"We are ministring Spirits, sent forth to minister for those that shall be Heirs of Salvation,"*(*TPP*, 158) adopting the definition of Heb. 1:14. The other "shining one" is identified as Jesus himself by speaking the words, "Thy sins be forgiven," (Mark 2:5), the authority to forgive sins a definitive sign of Jesus' identity and deity.

[22] Luxon discusses "passive justifcation" in *TPP* in a perceptive article, "The Pilgrim's Passive Progress," *ELH* 53 (1985), 73-98.

[23] Fletcher, *Allegory*, 109.

[24] J. I. Packer, *A Quest for Godliness: The Puritan Vision of the Christian Life* (Wheaton: Crossway Books, 1990), 153.

[25] Calvin, *Institutes* III.ii.24.

[26] Westminster Confession, Article XI.i.

[27] Martin Luther, *Lectures on Galatians* (1535), vol. 26 of *Luther's Works*, ed. Jaroslav Pelikan (St. Louis: Concordia, 1963), 4-6.

[28] By the marginal reference identifying the pilgrim's new clothes as priestly robes, Bunyan is claiming for his pilgrim the direct ordination of Christ into the "priesthood of all believers" (cf. John 15:16; 1 Pet. 2:9; Rev. 1:6), an ordination Bunyan himself claimed as having priority over ordination or license offered by church or state (see "A Relation of my Imprisonment," *GA*, 118 ff.).

[29] The scornful tone of Edward Fowler (or his deputy) in *Dirt Wip't Off* (1672) may be echoed here.

[30] *The Pilgrim's Progress*, illus. by William Blake, ed. G. B. Harrison, intro. Geoffrey Keynes (New York: Spiral Press, 1941), Plate XXII.

[31] Bunyan's concern for unjustified attacks on a Christian's reputation surfaces elsewhere. See, for example, *GA*, para. 307-11.

[32] The charge of antinomianism was levelled by Fowler (*Dirt*, 17). It has recently been repeated by Hill, who gives a whole sub-section under "Bunyan's Theology" to "Antinomianism," concluding that "Bunyan had difficulty in avoiding antinomianism; and the dilemma remained with him" (*Turbulent Seditious* 188-93). Bunyan's testiness in response to charges of antinomianism bears witness not to anxiety, as Hill avers, but to an anger at the thought that, considering the grace of God and its cost in Christ's sacrifice, anyone could ever think of abusing such love and grace by willingly choosing to sin (cf. Rom. 6:1,2). For more on Bunyan and antinomianism, see Richard L. Greaves, who places Bunyan at "the *via media* between the moderate Calvinists on the one hand and the Antinomians on the others.... [H]e refrained from the excesses of the Antinomians, and instead granted to the law ... as a rule of life—a place in the covenant of grace" (*John Bunyan*, Courtenay Studies in Reformation Theology 2 [Grand Rapids: Eerdmans, 1969], 118).

[33] Bolton, *The Wedding Garment and the Wedding Supper*, 90. The Anchor Bible commentary on the passage says re: *wedding garb*: "The scene depicted is that of the Son judging his own Kingdom. The man in question had attempted to enter that Kingdom without prior repentance. It is fruitless to discuss wehther there was a custom demanding that the giver of a wedding feast had an obligation to provide special clothing. No such custom is known to us, and ..it is probable that only clean clothes were expected" (269). The Broadman commentary mentions "[t]he conjecture that the host provided his guests with wedding garments" and suggests that while it may be correct, "it derives solely from this passage." According to the reading of this commentary, the guest without a wedding garment was exhibiting: "defiance of authority...greater even than that of the men first invited. They defied the king's authority by refusing to attend the feast. This man defied that authority in a more arrogant way, by trying to attend on his own terms (205)."

[34] James F. Forrest, "Bunyan's Ignorance and the Flatterer: A Study in the Literary Art of Damnation," *Studies in Philology* LX (January 1963), 19.

[35] Mark Twain, *The Adventures of Huckleberry Finn*, ed. E. S. Bradley, et al. (New York, 1961), 83; Rupert Bridges in Roger Sharrock, ed. *Bunyan, "The Pilgrim's Progress": A Casebook* (London: Macmillan, 1976), 108; Hill, *Turbulent, Seditious, Factious*, 227.

[36] In the listing of goods for sale at Vanity Fair, "Wives, Husbands, Children" are catalogued along with "Whores, Bauds . . . Masters, Servants, . . . Silver, Gold, Pearls, Precious Stones and what not." While this does not seem to be where critics have focused their attention, it strikes me as the most vulnerable point of Bunyan's evaluation of relative loyalties and priorities. It is important, however, to see that the title of the catalogue is "Delights of all sorts" (88). Under this rubric, "wives, husbands, children" are seen as one of the great pleasures life can afford. Furthermore, becauses it is a legitimate source of pleasure, family can operate as a competitor for the love and worship due to God alone.

[37] Keeble, "Christiana's Key: The Unity of *The Pilgrim's Progress*," in *The Pilgrim's Progress: Critical and Historical Views*. Ed. Vincent Newey (Liverpool: Liverpool University Press, 1980), 1-19, esp. 10.

[38] Ibid.

[39] In *HW*, the work of conviction is developed in the four emblematic captains (Boanerges, Conviction, Judgment, and Execution) sent by Emmanuel to bring Mansoul to repentance (*HW*, 36-47).

[40] Hill, *Turbulent, Seditious*, Factious, 213; Haskins, "Burden of Interpretation," 256-78, passim; Luxon, "Calvin and Bunyan," 459.

[41] See, for example, discussion of Jan Van Eyck's "Giavanni Arnolfini and His Wife, 1434," in M. L. D'Otrange Mastai, *Illusion in Art. Trompe l'Oeil: A History of Pictorial Illusionism* (New York: Abaris Books, 1975), 83-86.

Works Cited

I.   PRIMARY SOURCES

A.   Works of John Bunyan

All quotations in text are from the *Miscellaneous Works of John Bunyan*, Gen. Ed. Roger Sharrock. Oxford English Texts, Oxford: Clarendon Press, 1960-1991, unless otherwise indicated.

1. MISCELLANEOUS WORKS (OET)

Bunyan, John. *Some Gospel Truths Opened; A vindication of Some Gospel-Truths Opened; A Few Sighs from Hell.* Ed. T.L. Underwood assisted by Roger Sharrock. Vol. 1 of *The Miscellaneous Works of John Bunyan.* Gen. Ed. Roger Sharrock. 13 vols. Oxford: Clarendon, 1980.

_____. *The Doctrine of the Law & Grace Unfolded; I Will Pray with the Spirit.* Ed. Richard L. Greaves. Vol.2 of *MW*, 1976.

_____. *Christian Behaviour; The Holy City; The Resurrection of the Dead.* Ed. J. Sears McGee. Vol. 3 of *MW*, 1987.

_____. *The Barren Fig-Tree.* Ed. Graham Midgley. Vol. 5 of *MW.* 1986.

_____. *The Poems.* Ed. Graham Midgley. Vol. 6 of *MW*, 1980.

_____. *Instruction for the Ignorant; Light for them that sit in Darkness; Saved by Grace; Come, and Welcome to Jesus Christ.* Ed. Richard L. Greaves. Vol. 8 of *MW*, 1979.

_____. *A Treatise of the Fear of God; The Greatness of the Soul; A Holy Life.* Ed. Richard L. Greaves. Vol. 9 of *MW*, 1981.

_____. *Seasonable Counsel; A Discourse Upon the Pharisee and the Publicane.* Ed. Owen C. Watkins. Vol. 10 of *MW*, 1988.

2. NARRATIVES (0ET)

_____. *Grace Abounding to the Chief of Sinners* (1666). Ed. Roger Sharrock. Oxford: Clarendon, 1962.

_____. *The Life and Death of Mr. Badman* (1680). Ed. James F. Forrest and Roger Sharrock. Oxford: Clarendon, 1988.

_____. *The Holy War* (1682). Ed. Roger Sharrock and James F. Forrest and Roger Sharrock. Oxford: Clarendon, 1980.

_____. *The Pilgrim's Progress* (1678 and 1684). Ed. James Blanton Wharey and Roger Sharrock. Oxford: Clarendon, 1960, rpt. (with corrections) 1967.

3. OTHER EDITIONS
All works examined in earliest and later editions. The following editions are cited in text.

_____. *The Pilgrim's Progress*. Illus. William Blake. Ed. G. B. Harrison. Intro. Geoffrey Keynes. Limited Editions. New York: Spiral P, 1941.

_____. *The Works of That Eminent Servant of Christ, Mr. John Bunyan*. Comp. Charles Doe. London: 1692.

_____. *A Confession of My Faith and Reason for My Practice*. London, 1672.

_____. *A Defence of the Doctrine of Justification by Faith*. London, 1671.

_____. *Difference in Judgment about Water Baptism No Bar to Communion*. London, 1673.

_____. *Peaceable Principles and True*. London, 1673.

_____. *Solomon's Temple Spiritualis'd*. London, 1688.

B.   OTHER PRIMARY SOURCES
Adams, Thomas. *The Workes of Thomas Adams*. London, 1629.

Augustine, *De Doctrina Christiana*.

Bacon, Nathaniel, *A Relation of the Fearful Estate of Francis Spira, in the Year 1548*. London, 1665.

Bayly, Lewis. *The Practice of Pietie*. (1612?). 36th ed. Edinburgh, 1636.

Baxter, Richard.*The Saints Everlasting Rest*. First edition, London, 1649.

_____. *The Saints Everlasting Rest* (1649). 4th ed. London, 1653.

_____. *The Catechizing of Families*. London, 1683.

Bernard, Richard. *The Isle of Man*. 5th ed. London: 1628.

Bevis of Hampton. See, *Sir Bevis of Hampton*.

Bible. Authorized (King James) Version. 1611 Edition. Rpt. Nashville: Thomas Nelson, 1990. (Biblical quotations from this text unless otherwise indicated.)

_____. *Authorized Version*. With Tomson-Junius notes. London: The Company of Stationers, 1649.

_____. *The Geneva Bible* (1560). Facs. Ed. Lloyd Berry. University of Missouri Press, 1969.

Bolton, Samuel. *The Wedding Garment and the Wedding Supper*. In *The Guard of the Tree of Life: A Sacramental Discourse*. London, 1647.

Browne, Sir Thomas. *The Prose of Sir Thomas Browne*. Ed. and intro, Norman Endicott. New York: New York University Press, 1968.

Burrough, Edward. *Truth Defended, or Certain Accusations Answered Cast Upon us who are called Quakers*. London: for Thomas Simmons, 1656.

_____. *The True Faith of the Gospel of Peace Contended For*. London, 1656.

Byfield, Nicholas. *Directions for the Private Reading of Scriptures*. 4th ed. Profitably inlarged and helps presscribed to those that cannot write or read by Jo. Geree, M.A. By M. F. for P. Stephesn, 1648. STC 6383.

_____. *Directions for the Private Reading of Scriptures*. 2nd ed. E. Griffin for J. N. Butter, 1618. STC. 4214.

Calvin, John. *Institutes of the Christian Religion*. Trans. Henry Beveridge. 2 vols. Rpt. Grand Rapids: Wm. B. Eerdmans, 1975.

Chaucer, Geoffrey. "The Book of the Duchess." *The Works of Geoffrey Chaucer*. Ed. F. N. Robinson. 2nd ed.1957. Boston: Houghton Mifflin; Cambridge, Mass: The Riverside P, 1961.

Clarke, Samuel. *A Mirrour or Looking Glass for Both Saints and Sinners*. London: R. Gaywood, 1671.

Clarkson, Laurence. *A Single Eye*. (1650). In *A Collection of Ranter Writings from the 17th Century*. Ed. Nigel Smith. London: Junction Books, 1983.

Colderidge, S. T. C. *Coleridge on the Seventeenth Century*. Ed. Roberta Florence Brinkley, intro. Louis I. Bredvold. Chapel Hill: Duke University Press, 1955.

Coppe, Abiezer. *Some Sweet Sips, of some Spirituall Wine*. London, 1649. Also, in *Collection of Ranter Writings*. Ed. Nigel Smith.

_____. *A Fiery Flying Roll* and *A Second Fiery Flying Roule* (1649). In *Collection of Ranter Writings*. Ed. Nigel Smith.

Dante Alighieri, *The Divine Comedy*. Tr. John Ciardi. New York: Norton, 1961, 1977.

D'Anvers, Henry. *A Treatise of Baptism. . . And a Brief Answer to Mr. Bunyan*. London, 1673.

Dent, Arthur. *A Plaine Man's Pathway to Heaven*. London, 1664.

Dod, John and Robert Cleaver, *A Plaine and Familiar Exposition of the Ten Commandements*, London, 1604.

Dryden, John. *John Dryden: Selected Works*. 2nd ed. Ed. William Frost, San Francisco: Rinehart P, 1971.

Edwards, Jonathan. *Images or Shadows of Divine Things*. Ed. and intro. Perry Miller. New Haven: Yale University Press, 1948.

Edwards, Jonathan. *Works*. Vol. 2. Ed. John E. Smith. 7 vols. New Haven: Yale University Press, 1959.

Fowler, Edward. *Design of Christianity*. London, 1671.

_____. *Dirt Wip't Off*. London: for Richard Royston, 1672. Foxe, George. *A Journal . . . of the Life, Travels, Sufferings, Christian Experiences and Labour of Love in the Work of the Ministry of . . . George Foxe*. Vol. 1, London, 1694.

Foxe, John. *Acts and Monuments of the Christian Martyrs . . .* (Latin 1554, English 1563). 3 vols. 8th impr. of 1583 edition, with additions. London, 1641.

George on Horseback. See: Johnson, Richard. *Seven Champions of Christendom*.

Herbert, George and Henry Vaughan. *George Herbert and Henry Vaughan*. Ed. Louis Martz. Oxford Authors, Gen.Ed. Frank Kermode. Oxford: Oxford University Press, 1986.

Hobbes, Thomas. *Leviathan*. London, 1651.

Johnson, Richard. *Seven Champions of Christendom*. London, 1596, 1696.

Keach, Benjamin. *The Progress of Sin* (1684). Copy examined: 3rd ed., corrected with some additions by the author. London: for N. & M. Boddington, 1715.

_____. *The Glorious Lover* (1679). Copy examined: 3rd ed with additions. London: for G. Keith and J. Robinson, 1764.

_____. *Tropologia: A Key to Open Scripture Metaphors*. London, 1682.

_____. *War with the Devil*. London, 1684.

Komensky, John Amos (Comenius). *The Labyrinth of the World and the Paradise of the Heart* (1623). Trans. and ed. Count Lutzow, 1901. Rpt. New York: Arno Press and the New York Times, 1971.

Langland, Wm. *Piers the Plowman*. (Text B). Ed. W. W. Skeat. Early English Texts Society, original series, no.38. London: Oxford University Press (for Early English Text Society), 1869, 1972.

Luther, Martin. *A Commentary on Galathians* (1575). London: for George Miller, 1664.

_____. *Lectures on Galatians* (1535). Vol. 26, 27 of *Luther's Works.* Gen. Ed., vols. 1-30, Jaroslav Pelikan; vols. 31-55, H. T. Lehmann. 55 volumes, 1955-1986. Saint Louis: Concordia, 1963.

Milton, John. *Complete Poems and Major Prose.* Ed. Merritt Y. Hughes. New York: Macmillan, 1957.

_____. *Christian Doctrine* (1640-1673?) Summary in *The Prose of John Milton.* Ed. and intro. J. Max Patrick. Stuart Editions. New York: New York University Press and London: U of London P, 1968.

Moxon, John. *Mechanick Exercises Applied to the Art of Printing.* London, 1683.

Owen, John. *A Brief Vindication of the Doctrine of the Trinity.* London, 1669.

_____. *A Brief Vindication of the Nonconformists.* London, 1680.

_____. *Exercitations on the Book of Hebrews.* London, 1668.

_____. *Two Discourses Concerning the Holy Spirit and His Work.* London, 1693.

Penn, William. *The Sandy Foundation Shaken.* London, 1668.

Puttenham, George. *The Art of English Poesie.* London, 1589. Facs. Menston: The Scolar P, 1968.

Quarles, Francis. *Emblemes, Divine and Moral.* London, 1635.

Salmon, Joseph. *A Rout, A Rout* (1649). In *Collection of Ranter Writings.* Ed. Nigel Smith.

Sir Bevis of Hampton. London, 1639? (n.d.)

Smith, Nigel, ed. *A Collection of Ranter Writings from the 17th Century.* London: Junction Books, 1983.

Spenser, *The Faerie Queene,* Book I. P. C. Bayley, ed. London: Oxford University Press, 1966.

Westminster Directory. *A Directory for the Publique Worship of God.* London, 1645.

White, John of Corchester. *Directions for the Profitable Reading of the Scriptures.* London, ([Rich] Royston to be sold by John Long in Dorchester), 1647. STC 1776.

Wilkins, John. *Ecclesiastes: or a Discourse Concerning the Gift of Preaching.* 7th ed., London, 1693.

Wordsworth, William. *The Prelude, 1799, 1805, 1850.* ed. Jonathan Wordsworth. M. H. Abrams, Stephen Gill. A Norton Critical Edition. New York and London: Norton, 1979.

II.   SECONDARY SOURCES

Anchor Bible: Matthew. Intro., trans., and notes, W. F. Albright and
C. S. Mann. Garden City, N.Y.: Doubleday, 1971.

Appleyard, J. A., S.J. *Becoming a Reader: The Experience of Fiction
from Childhood to Adulthood.* Cambridge: Cambridge University Press,
1990.

Baker, Dave. "Symphony No. 41, K.551 in C Major ('Jupiter')."
Signature, Edmonton Symphony Orchestra, December 1991, 9.

Bennett, J. A. W. *Poetry of the Passion.* Oxford: Clarendon, 1982.

Benstock, Shari. "At the Margins of Discourse: Footnotes in the
Fictional Text." *PMLA* 98 (1983): 204-25.

Bloom, Harold. *Deconstruction and Criticism.* New York: Seabury
(Continuum Books), 1979.

Booth, Wayne C. *The Rhetoric of Fiction.* 2nd ed.: University of Chicago Press, 1983.

Brinker, Menachem. "Verisimilitude, Conventions, and Beliefs."
New Literary History 14 (1983): 253-67.

Broadman Bible Commentary: General Articles, Matthew-Mark. Volume 8. Ed. Frank Stagg. Gen.Ed. Clifton J. Allen.

12 vols. Nashville: Broadman Press, 1969.

Brooke-Rose, Christine. *A Rhetoric of the Unreal: Studies in Narrative
and Structure*, Cambridge: Cambridge University Press, 1981.

Brown, John. *John Bunyan 1628-1688: His Life, Times and Work.* Tercentenary edition, rev. Frank Mott Harrison. London: Hurlburt, 1928.

Buber, Martin. *I and Thou.* Trans. Walter Kaufmann. New York:
Scribners, 1970.

Carlton, Peter. "Bunyan: Language, Convention, Authority." *English Literary History* 51 (1984): 17-32.

Chatman, Seymour. *Story and Discourse: Narrative Structure in Fiction and Film.* Ithaca, N.Y.: Cornell University Press, 1978.

Coleman, Joyce. *Public Reading and the Reading Public in Late Medieval England and France.* Cambridge: Cambridge University Press, 1996.

Cousins, Ewert H. "Francis of Assisi: Christian Mysticism at the
Crossroads." in Katz, Steven T., ed. *Mysticism and Religious Traditions.*
Oxford: Oxford University Press, 1983, 163-90.

Cragg, Gerald. *Puritanism in the Period of the Great Persecution
(1660-1688).* Cambridge: Cambridge University Press, 1957.

Cressy, David. *Literacy and the Social Order*. Reading and Writing in Tudor and Stuart England. Cambridge: Cambridge University Press, 1980.

_____. "Levels of Illiteracy in England, 1530-1730." *Perspectives on Literacy*. Ed. Eugene Kintgen. Carbondale: Southern Illinois University Press, 1988.

Culler, Jonathan. *Structuralist Poetics: Structuralism, Linguistics, and the Study of Literature*. London: Routledge and Kegan Paul, 1975.

Cunningham, Valentine. "Glossing and Glozing: Bunyan and the Allegory." in N. H. Keeble, ed., *John Bunyan: Conventicle and Parnassus*. Oxford: Clarendon, 1988, 217-40.

Curtius, Ernst Robert. *European Literature and the Latin Middle Ages* (1948). Trans. Willard R. Trask. Bollingen Series 36. New York: Pantheon Books, 1953.

Daiches, David. "Literature and Belief." Ch. 9, *A Study of Literature for Readers and Critics* (1948). New York: Norton, 1964.

Daly, Peter. *Literature in the Light of the Emblem: Structural Parallels Between the Emblem and Literature in the Sixteenth and Seventeenth Centuries*. Toronto: University of Toronto Press, 1979.

Darnton, Robert. "Toward a History of Reading." *Princeton Alumni Weekly*, 8 April 1987: 19-24, 32.

_____. *The Corpus of Clandestine Literature in France, 1769-1789*. New York: W. W. Norton, 1995.

_____. *The Forbidden Best-Sellers of Pre-Revolutionary France*. New York: W. W. Norton, 1995.

Derrida, Jacques. *Margins of Philosophy* (1972). Trans. Alan Bass. Chicago: University of Chicago Press, 1982.

Dictionary of National Biography.

Drummond, C. Q. "Sequence and Consequence in *The Pilgrim's Progress*." Offprint. *The Gadfly*. Retford: The Brynmill Press, 1983.

Dryden, John. *The Poems of John Dryden*. Ed. Paul Hammond. 2 vols. London: Longman, 1995.

Dutton, A. Richard. "'Interesting but tough':" Reading *The Pilgrim's Progress*." *Studies in English Literature* 18 (1978): 439-456.

Eisenstein, Elizabeth. *The Printing Press as an Agent of Change: Communication and Cultural Transformation in Early Modern Europe*. 2 vols. Cambridge: Cambridge University Press, 1979.

Fish, Stanley. "Interpreting the Varorium," *Critical Inquiry* 2.3 (1976): 465-85.

_____. *Self-Consuming Artifacts: The Experience of Seventeenth-Century Literature*. Berkeley: University of California Press, 1972.

_____. *Surprised by Sin: The Reader in Paradise Lost*. London: MacMillan, 1967.

_____. "Why No One's Afraid of Wolfgang Iser," *Diacritics* 11 (1981): 2-13.

Fletcher, Angus. *Allegory: The Theory of a Symbolic Mode*. Ithaca, N.Y.: Cornell University Press, 1964.

Forrest, James F. "Allegory as Sacred Sport: Manipulation of the Reader in Spenser and Bunyan," in Robert G. Collmer, ed. *Bunyan in Our Time*. Kent: Ohio: Kent State University, 1989.

_____. "Between Presumption and Timidity": On Editing Bunyan." In *Bunyan in England and Beyond*. Edited by M. Van Os and G. J. Schutte, Vu Studies in Protestant History 1. Amsterdam: Vu University Press, 1990, 61-77.

_____. "Bunyan's Ignorance and the Flattter: A Study in the Literary Art of Damnation." *Studies in Philology*, LX (January 1963): 12-22.

_____. and Richard Greaves. *John Bunyan: A Reference Guide*. Boston: G.K. Hall, 1982.

Freeman, Rosemary. *English Emblem Books*. London: Chatto and Windus, 1948.

Frei, Hans. *The Eclipse of Biblical Narrative: A Study in Eighteenth and Nineteenth Century Hermeneutics*. New Haven and London: Yale University Press, 1974.

Frye, Northrop. *Anatomy of Criticism: Four Essays*. (1957). 3rd printing. Princeton, N.J.: Princeton University Press, 1973.

_____. *The Great Code: The Bible and Literature*. New York: Harcourt Brace Jovanovich, 1982.

Genette Gérard. *Narrative Discourse: An Essay in Method*. Translated by Jane E. Lewin, foreword by Jonathan Culler. Ithaca, N.Y.: Cornell University Press, 1980.

Glaister, Geoffrey A. *Glaister's Glossary of the Book*. Second ed., rev. Berkeley and Los Angeles: U of California P, 1960, 1979.

Golder, Harold. "Bunyan and Spenser" *PMLA* 45 (1930): 216-37.

_____. "Bunyan's Hypocrisy." *North American Review* 233 (1926): 323-32.

Graff, Gerald. "Interpretation on Tlon: A Response to Stanley Fish." *New Literary History* 17 (1985): 109-27.

Graff, Harvey J. *The Legacies of Literacy: Continuities and Contradic-tions in Western Culture and Society*. Bloomington: Indiana University Press, 1987.

Greaves, Richard. *Deliver Us From Evil: The Radical Undergound in Britain, 1660-1663*. New York: Oxford University Press, 1986.

———. *John Bunyan*. Countenay Studies in Reformation Theology 2. Grand Rapids: Eerdmans, 1969.

Haller, William. *The Rise of Purtanism*. (1938). New York: Columbia University Press, 1957.

Hannay, M. P. *Silent But for the Word: Tudor Women as Patrons, Translators, and Writers of Religious Works*. Kent, Ohio: Kent State University Press, 1985.

Harrison, Frank Mott. *Bibliography of The Works of John Bunyan*. Oxford: Oxford University Press for The Bilbiographical Society, 1932 (for 1930).

Haselkorn, A. M. and Betty S. Travitsky, *The Renaissance English-woman in Print*. Amherst: U of Massachusetts P, 1990.

Haskin, Dayton. "The Burden of Interpretation in *The Pilgrim's Progress*." *Studies in Philology* 79 (1982): 256-78.

———. "The Pilgrim's Progress in the Context of Bunyan's Dia-logue with the Radicals." *Harvard Theological Review* 77 (1984), 73-94.

Hill, Christopher. *A Turbulent, Seditious, and Factious People: John Bunyan and His Church, 1628-1688*. Oxford: Clarendon, 1988. Also published as *A Tinker and a Poor Man: John Bunyan and His Church, 1628-1688*. New York: W. W. Norton, 1990.

———. *The Experience of Defeat: Milton and Some Contemporaries*. London: Faber and Faber, 1984.

Honig, Edwin. *Dark Conceit: The Making of Allegory*. London: Faber and Faber, 1959.

Hughes, Ann. "The Pulpit Guarded." In eds. Anne Laurence, W. R. Owens and Stuart Sim, *John Bunyan and His England: 1628-1688*. London: Hambledon, 1990.

Hutcheon, Linda. *Narcissistic Narrative: The Metafictional Paradox*. Waterloo: Wilfred Laurier University Press, 1980.

Iser, Wolfgang. *The Implied Reader: Patterns of Communication in Prose Fiction from Bunyan to Beckett*. Baltimore: Johns Hopkins University Press, 1974.

———. *Prospecting: From Reader Response to Literary Anthropology*. Baltimore and London: Johns Hopkins University Press, 1989.

_____. "Talk Like Whales" (Reply to Stanley Fish). *Diacritics* 11 (1981): 82-87.

James, William. *The Varieties of Religious Experience* (1902). Intro. John E. Smith. Vol. 15 of *The Works of William James*. Eds. F. H. Burkhardt, F. Bowers, K. Skrupskelis. Cambridge, Mass.: Harvard University Press, 1985.

Jauss, Hans Robert. *Toward an Aesthetic of Reception*. Trans. Timothy Bahti. Intro. Paul de Man. Theory and History of Literature, vol. 2. Minneapolis: U of Minnesota P, 1982.

Johnson, Barbara A. "Falling Into Allegory: The 'Apology' to *The Pilgrim's Progress* and Bunyans Scriptural Methodology." In Robert G. Collmer, ed. *Bunyan in Our Time*. Kent: Kent State University Press, 1989, 113-37.

Kaufmann, U. Milo. *The Pilgrim's Progress and Traditions in Puritan Meditation*. New Haven: Yale University Press, 1966.

Keeble, N. H. "Christiana's Key: The Unity of *The Pilgrim's Progress*." In *The Pilgrim's Progress: Critical and Historical Views*. Edited by Vincent Newey. Liverpool: Liverpool University Press, 1980.

_____. ed. *John Bunyan – Conventicle and Parnassus: Tercentenary Essays*. Oxford. Clarendon, 1988.

_____. *The Literary Culture of Non-Conformity in Later Seventeenth-Century England*. Athens: University of Georgia Press, 1987.

_____. *Richard Baxter: Puritan Man of Letters*. Oxford: Clarendon, 1982.

Kintgen, Eugene R. "Reconstructing Elizabethan Reading." *Studies in English Literature 1500-1900*, 30 (1990): 1-18.

_____. *Reading in Tudor England*. Pittsburgh: University of Pittsburgh Press, 1996.

Knott, Jr., John R. *Discourses of Martyrdom in English Literature, 1563-1694*. Cambridge: Cambridge University Press, 1993.

_____. *The Sword of the Spirit: Puritan Responses to the Bible*. Chicago: University of Chicago Press, 1980.

_____. "Bunyan and the Holy Community," *Studies in Philology*. 80.2 (1983): 200-25.

Kristeva, Julia. *The Kristeva Reader*. Ed. Toril Moi. Oxford: Basil Blackwell, 1986.

Lamont, William. *Puritanism and Historical Controversy*. McGill-Queen's Studies in the History of Religion, 26. Montreal: McGill-Queen's University Press, 1996.

Labalme, P. H. *Beyond Their Sex: Learned Women of the European Past*. New York: New York University Press, 1980.

Lanham, Richard A. *The Motives of Eloquence: Literary Rhetoric in the Renaissance*. New Haven and London: Yale University Press, 1976.

Levine, Kenneth. *The Social Context of Literacy*. London and New York: Routledge and Kegan Paul, 1986.

Lewalski, Barbara. *Protestant Poetics and the Seventeenth-Century Relgious Lyric*. Princeton: Princeton University Press, 1979.

Lewis, C. S. *The Allegory of Love: A Study in Medieval Tradition* (1936). Oxford: Oxford University Press, 1967.

_____. *The Discarded Image: An Introduction to Medieval and Renaissance Literature*. Cambridge: Cambrdige University Press, 1964.

_____. *Preface to Paradise Lost*, London: Oxford University Press, 1942.

Lewis, David. *Convention: A Philosophical Study*. Cambridge: Harvard University Press, 1969.

Lipking, Lawrence. "The Marginal Gloss." *Critical Inquiry* 3 (1977), 609-55.

Lovejoy, A. O. *The Great Chain of Being: A Study of the History of an Idea*. Cambrdige, Mass: Harvard University Press, 1950.

Luthi, Max. "Goal-Orientation in Storytelling." *Folklore Today*. Festschrift for Richard M. Dorson. Eds. Linda Degh, Henry Glassie, Fleix J. Oinas. Bloomington: Indiana University, Research Center for Language and Semiotic Studies, 1976.

_____. *The Fairytale as Art Form and Portrait of Man* (1975). Trans. Jon Erickson. Bloomington: Indiana University Press, 1984.

Luxon, Thomas. "Calvin and Bunyan on Word and Image: Is There a Text in Interpreter's House." *English Literary Renaissance* 18 (1988): 438-59.

_____. "The Pilgrim's Passive Progress: Luther and Bunyan on Talking and Doing, Word and Way." *English Literary History* 53 (1985): 73-98.

Mailloux, Steven. *Interpretive Conventions: The Reader in the Study of American Fiction*. Ithaca, N.Y.: Cornell University Press, 1982.

Martz, Louis. *The Poetry of Meditation: A Study in the English Religious Literature of the Seventeenth Century*. New Haven: Yale University Press, 1954; London: Geoffrey Cumberlege, Oxford University Press, 1954.

Mastai, M. L. D'Otrange. *Illusion in Art. Trompe l'oeil: A History of Pictorial Illusionism*. New York: Abaris Books, 1975.

McKeon, Michael. *The Origins of the English Novel, 1600-1740.* Baltimore: Johns Hopkins University Press, 1987.

Miller, Arthur. *Death of a Salesman.* New York: The Viking Press, 1949. Compass Books Edition, 1958.

Miller, J. Hillis. "The Two Allegories." In Morton W. Bloomfield, ed., *Allegory, Myth, and Symbol.* Harvard English Studies 9. Cambridge, Mass.: Harvard University Press, 1981.

Mitchell, W. Fraser. *English Pulpit Oratory from Andrewes to Tillotson: A Study of its Lieterary Aspects.* London: SPCK, 1932.

Murrin, Michael. *The Veil of Allegory: Some Notes Toward a Theory of Allegorical Rhetoric in the English Renaissance.* Chicago: University of Chicago Press, 1969.

Nelson, John Oliver. *Work and Vocation: A Christian Discussion.* New York: Harper, 1954.

Newey, Vincent. *The Pilgrim's Progress: Critical and Historical Views.* Liverpool: Liverpool University Press, 1980.

Nicolson, Marjorie. *The Breaking of the Circle: Studies in the Effect of the "new Science" Upon Seventeenth-Century Poetry.* Evanston: Northwestern University Press, 1950.

Owst, G. R. *Literature and Pulpit in Medieval England.* Oxford: Blackwell, 1961.

Packer, J. I. *A Quest for Godliness: The Puritan Vision of the Christian Life.* Wheaton: Crossway Books, 1990.

Palmer, Richard E. *Hermeneutics: Interpretation Theory in Schiermacher, Dilthy, Heidegger, and Gadamer.* Northwestern University Studies in Phenomenology and Existential Philosophy. Gen. Ed. John Wild. Evanston: Northwestern University Press, 1969.

Patrides, C. A. and R. B. Waddington. *The Age of Milton: Backgrounds to Seventeenth Century Literature.* Manchester: Manchester University Press, 1980.

Pavel, Thomas G. *Fictional Worlds.* Cambridge, Mass.: Harvard University Press, 1986.

Payne, Michael. *Reading Theory: An Introduction to Lacan, Derrida, and Kristeva.* Oxford: Blackwell, 1993.

Perry, Ruth. *The Celebrated Mary Astell: An Early English Feminist.* Women in Culture and Society. Gen. ed. Catharina R. Stimpson. Chicago: University of Chicago Press, 1986.

Pollard, Alfred W. "Margins." *The Dolphin* 1 (1933): 67-80.

Prince, Gerald. *A Dictionary of Narratology.* Lincoln: University of Nebraska Press, 1987.

Quilligan, Maureen. *The Language of Allegory: Defining the Genre.* Ithaca, N.Y.: Cornell University Press, 1979.

Rabinowitz, Peter. "Truth in Fiction: A Re-Examination of Audiences." *Critical Inquiry* 4 (1977): 121-44.

Ricoeur, Paul. *A Ricoeur Reader: Reflection and Imagination.* Theory/Culture Series. Gen. Ed. Mario J. Valdes. Toronto: University of Toronto Press, 1991.

———. *Time and Narrative.* Vols. 1 and 2. Trans. K. McLaughlin and D. Pellauer. Chicago: University of Chicago Press, 1984, 1985. Volume 3. Trans. K. Blamey and D. Pellauer. Chicago: University of Chicago Press, 1988.

Riffaterre, Michael, "Intertextual Representation: On Mimesis in Interpretive Discourse," *Critical Inquiry* 11 (1984)" 141-162.

Rose, Mary Beth, *Women in the Middle Ages and the Renaissance: Literary and Historical Perspectives.* Syracuse: Syracuse University Press, 1986.

Rostenberg, Leona. *Literary, Political,Scientific, Religious and Legal Publishing, Printing and Bookselling in England, 1551-1700.* 2 vols. Preface Donald G. Wing. Burt Franklin Bibliographical and Reference Series No. 56. New York: Burt Franklin, 1965.

Salzman, Paul. *English Prose Fiction, 1558-1700.* Oxford: Clarendon, 1985.

Seelig, Sharon. "Sir Thomas Browne and Stanley Fish: A Case of Malpractice." *Prose Studies* 11.2 (1988): 72-84.

Sharrock, Roger. "Bunyan and the English Emblem Writers," *Review of English Studies* 21 (1945): 105-16.

———. Ed. *Bunyan, The Pilgrim's Progress: A Casebook.* London: Macmillan P, 1976.

———. "Bunyan Studies Today: An Evaluation." *In Bunyan in England and Beyond,* ed. M. Van. Os and G. J. Schutte. Vu Studies in Protestant History 1. Amsterdam: Vu University Press, 1990, 45-47.

———. "Evaluation of Bunyan Studies." In Van Os and Schutte, 45-57.

———. *John Bunyan* (1954). London: Macmillan, 1968.

Shaw, George Bernard. *Man and Superman.* New York: Brentano's, 1903, 1907.

Sheriff, John K. *The Fate of Meaning: Charles Peirce, Structuralism, and Literature.* Princeton: Princeton University Press, 1989.

Slights, William. "The Edifying Margins of Renaissance English Books." *Renaissance Quarterly* 42 (1989): 682-716.

_____. "'Marginall Notes That Spoile the Text': Scriptural Annotation in the English Renaissance," *Huntington Library Quarterly* 55:2 (1992): 255-78.

Smith, Nigel, ed. *A Collection of Ranter Writings from the Seventeenth Century.* London: Junction Books, 1983.

_____. *Perfection Proclaimed: Language and Literature in English Radical Religion, 1640-1660.* Oxford: Clarendon, 1989.

Spufford, Margaret. *Small Books and Pleasant Histories: Popular Fiction and Its Readership in Seventeenth-Century England.* London: Methuen, 1981.

_____. *The World of Rural Dissenters, 1520-1725.* Cambridge: Cambridge University Press, 1995.

Stannard, David E. *The Puritan Way of Death: A Study in Religion, Culture, and Social Change.* New York: Oxford University Press, 1977.

Steiner, George. *Real Presences.* Chicago: University of Chicago Press, 1989.

Stranahan, Brainerd P., "Bunyan's Special Talent: Biblical Texts as 'Events' in *Grace Abounding* and *The Pilgrim's Progress.* ELR 11 (1981), 329-43.

Sturrock, John, et al. "The Rise of Theory—A Symposium." *Times Literary Supplement* 15 July 1994, 13-14.

Suleiman, Susan R. and Inge Crosman, eds. *The Reader in the Text: Essays on Audience and Interpretation.* Princeton: Princeton University Press, 1980.

Summers, Joseph H. "Stanley Fish's Reading of Seventeenth-Century Literature." *Modern Language Quarterly* 35 (1974): 403-17.

Swaim, Kathleen M., *Pilgrim's Progress, Puritan Progress: Discourses and Contexts.* Urbana: University of Illinois Press, 1993.

Tindall, William York. *John Bunyan: Mechanick Preacher.* 1934. New York: Russell and Russell, 1964.

Tompkins, Jane P., ed. *Reader-Response Criticism: From Formalism to Post-Structuralism.* Baltimore: Johns Hopkins University Press, 1980.

Tribble, Evelyn B. *Margins and Marginality: The Printed Page in Early Modern England.* Charlottesville: University Press of Virginia, 1993.

Tuve, Rosemond. *Allegorical Imagery: Some Mediaeval Books and Their Posterity.* Princeton: Princeton University Press, 1966.

Twain, Mark. *Adventures of Huckleberry Finn.* Ed. E. S. Bradley, R. C. Beatty, and E. H. Long. New York: 1961.

Valdes, Mario J., ed. *A Ricoeur Reader: Reflection and Imagination.* Theory/Culture Series, gen. ed. Mario J. Valdes. Toronto: University of Toronto Press, 1991.

Van Os, M. and G. J. Schutte, eds., *Bunyan in England and Abroad.* Vu Studies in Protestant History 1. Papers delivered at The John Bunyan Tercentenary Symposiusm, Vrije Universiteit, Amsterdam, 1988. Amsterdam: Vu University Press, 1990.

Vine, W. E. *An Expository Dictionary of New Testament Words.* Old Tappan: Revell, 1966.

Waldock, A. J. A. *Paradise Lost and its Critics.* Cambridge: Cambridge University Press, 1947.

Ward, Graham. "To Be a Reader: John Bunyan's Struggle with the Language of Scripture in *Grace Abounding to the Chief of Sinners. Literature and Theology* 4 (1990), pp. 29-49.

Wasserman, Earl L., "Nature Moralized: The Divine Analogy in the Eighteenth Century." *English Literary History* 30 (1953): 39-77.

Watkins, Owen. *The Puritan Experience.* London: Routledge and Kegan Paul, 1972.

Waswo, Richard. *Language and Meaning in the Renaissance.* Princeton: Princeton University Press, 1987.

Watt, Ian. *The Rise of the Novel.* Berkeley: University of California Press, 1967.

Webber, Joan. *The Eloquent "I": Style and Self in Seventeenth Century Prose.* Madison: The University of Wisconsin Press, 1968.

Wharey, James Blanton, *A Study of the Sources for Bunyan's Allegories.* Baltimore: J. H. Furst , 1904.

Wilson, Katharina M. and Frank J. Warnke. *Women Writers of the Seventeenth Century.* Athens and London: University of Georgia Press, 1989.

Wilson, R. Rawdon. *In Palimedes' Shadow: Explorations in Play, Game, and Narrative Theory.* Boston: Northeastern University Press, 1990.

Woodbridge, Linda. *Women and the English Renaissance: Literature and the Nature of Woman, 1540-1620.* Urbana: University of Illinois Press, 1984.

Zinck, Arlette. "Of Arms and the Heroic Reader: The Concept of Psychomachy in Spenser, Milton, and Bunyan." Doctoral Dissertation, University of Alberta, 1993.

Subject Index

Author Index

LaVergne, TN USA
28 October 2009
162263LV00003B/33/A